SAINT-YBARS

SAINT-YBARS

MASTERS AND SLAVES IN CREOLE LOUISIANA

Alfred Mercier

Translation, Introduction and Notes

by

Elizabeth A. Julian

Éditions Tintamarre
Shreveport 2015

Mercier, Alfred, Saint-Ybars: Masters and Slaves in Creole Louisiana. Translation, Introduction and Notes by Elizabeth A. Julian, Les Éditions Tintamarre, Shreveport, 2015.

ISBN: 978-0-9857345-6-5

Library of Congress Control Number: 2015946783

Cover design by Elena W. Hibbs

Printed in the United States of America.

Les Éditions Tintamarre
Centenary College of Louisiana
2911 Centenary Blvd.
Shreveport, LA 71134
www.centenary.edu/editions

Table of Contents

Part III

Part IV

Introduction

Le jour où l'on cessera de parler le français en Louisiane, si jamais ce jour doit arriver – ce que nous ne croyons nullement – il n'y aura plus de Créoles ; le groupe original et puissant qu'ils formaient dans la grande famille nationale des États-Unis, aura disparu, comme disparaît, avec son goût et sa couleur, le vin que l'on noie dans le fleuve qui passe.[1]

Alfred Mercier

From his late teens until his death in 1894, French novelist Alfred Mercier moved between Europe and his native New Orleans at least eight times, writing articles, essays, short stories, novels, and poetry. Mercier fought publicly for all the causes he believed in—primarily, the preservation of the French language in Louisiana—but struggled to find his place in the literary world. After starting out pursuing law and then abandoning the courtroom for a literary profession, Mercier published a book of romantic poetry in 1842 and six years later wrote a drama for the Parisian democratic journal *La Réforme*. Finding it difficult to earn his living as a writer, Mercier decided to study medicine. Even as a physician, he continued to write professionally as well as personally. When he made his final move back to New Orleans in 1868, Mercier finally found the niche that would make him a prominent historical and literary figure. For the next thirty years, Mercier devoted his life to preserving French in his native state, becoming the leader of French literary efforts as founder and secretary of the *Athénée Louisianais*, a society oriented towards prolonging French language, culture, and interests with the help of its journal,

Les Comptes-rendus de l'Athenée Louisianais. Mercier insisted on writing in French, penning several novels in his native language and meticulously capturing French culture, philosophies, and peoples.[2]

However, the state that started out as a French colony and received tens of thousands of French-speaking immigrants had quickly become "Americanized" once Jefferson bought Louisiana from France in 1803. After the transfer, anglophones outnumbered francophones in fewer than forty years.[3] The disappearance of bilingual schools, the crumbling of French newspapers, and intermarriage resulted in a steep decline in French fluency, despite the fact that over two million Louisianans even today have French ancestors. Louisiana's assimilation into English-speaking America even eradicated an entire genre of literature written by French-speaking Creoles. These novels, poems, articles, and plays depict the history of a lost culture. Unfortunately, since the overwhelming majority of French Creole literature remains untranslated, the true history of francophone Louisiana remains invisible in American literature and unknown to outsiders.[4]

Canadian Pierre Le Moyne d'Iberville founded Louisiana in 1699, and his brother Jean-Baptiste Le Moyne de Bienville founded New Orleans in 1718.[5] During French colonial rule in the early to mid-eighteenth century, masses of French-speakers from France, Canada, Saint-Domingue and other French Caribbean colonies settled in Louisiana. Large populations from New France (Canada) and Louis XV's France dominated the state. By the mid-eighteenth century, 12,000 to 19,000 francophones already lived in the colony, not including slaves and indigenous people. Even in 1762, when Spain took over Louisiana, francophones continued to retain their language, culture, and even power in the government.[6]

Much of the francophone population lived along the fertile soils of the Mississippi River, employing African slaves and sometimes blacks who escaped slave revolts, such as the uprising in Saint-Domingue near the end of the eighteenth century. The constant contact between African and white francophones resulted in the emergence of a new class of people: *gens du couleur libres,* meaning "free people of color" or "Creoles of color." This group, free from birth, were of mixed heritage, generally European and African or Indian. They constituted a class between the French and Spanish colonists and the enslaved workers. As a group, they achieved moderate economic, educational, and financial success: by 1860, Louisiana's free people of color owned more property than all free people of color in the other Confederate states. They had their own society and clubs and often considered themselves superior to "darker-skinned slaves and less educated and acculturated blacks."[7]

Historically, the meaning of *Créole* has changed significantly. Generally, the word connotes a culture – traditions, identities, aesthetics – created from a hybrid of separate peoples and cultures. Scholars differ on the exact origins of the word *Créole,* but a general consensus agrees that it comes from the Portuguese *crioulo,* meaning "native to a region," and its Latin root *crear* means "to create." In Louisiana, the first Creoles were associated with the French and Spanish colonies; however, the meaning of the word shifted to include people of non-European origin and those having "mixed" or multiracial heritage.[8] In the beginning of the nineteenth century, *Créole* defined a person born in the colonies of the New World with original ancestors from France, Spain, Italy, Saint-Domingue or other islands of the West Indies. Basically, there was (and still is) no unambiguous definition for the term *Créole.*[9] Creole identification can only rely on class orientation, settlement history, and physical appearance since race and ethnicity in southern Louisiana remain flexible, intertwined terms.[10]

However, when Napoleon Bonaparte recaptured Louisiana from Spain in 1803 and immediately sold the territory to the United States, the meaning of *Créole* became more defined, perhaps a product of the state's Americanization. Due to the deep racial divide existing in the antebellum South, *Créole* could not retain its original meaning that covered diverse ethnicities, races, and skin tones. Americans felt threatened by the overwhelming immigration of slaves from the Caribbean islands as well as the constant flow of free colored refugees. In order to limit this growing population, Americans instituted restrictions against emancipation by refusing to grant equal rights to the free colored population, imposing their own biracial vision of society onto New Orleans. Thus, society created the subdivisions of *Créoles blancs* (white Creoles) and *Créoles de couleur* (Creoles of color). The division was superficial: often, *Créoles de couleur* could "pass" as whites, for many were light-skinned (as we see with Blanchette's character in *L'Habitation Saint-Ybars*).[11]

Thus, when Alfred Mercier was born in 1816, the state of Louisianan society was only a small part of the major changes that would occur throughout America and Europe in the nineteenth century. Descended from a Louisiana-born father and a Canadian mother, the Creole Mercier left his family's plantation in McDonogh (across from New Orleans) at the age of nine to enroll at the College of Louisiana (today known as Centenary College of Louisiana).[12] His years away from home in Jackson, Louisiana prepared Mercier for study at the Collège Louis-le-Grand in Paris, one of the most rigorous and prestigious schools in France where he began school at the age of fourteen. After completing his studies, he enrolled in law school. Even though Mercier was an exemplary student at Louis-le-Grand, winning multiple awards for his diligent work and even skipping a year, he disregarded his law studies and seemingly preferred attending science courses at the Sorbonne and the Collège de France and listening to lectures at the Palais de Justice by prominent (and sometimes controversial) political figures like Pierre-Antoine Berryer, Chaix-d'Est-Ange, and Odillon Barrot.[13][14]

After spending eight years in Paris, Mercier returned briefly to New Orleans before travelling to Boston to improve his English. However, Mercier dreamt of a literary career in the French capital, so he travelled back to Paris in 1842 and published his first work, a collection of poems. He travelled through all of France as well as Switzerland, Spain, Belgium, England, and Italy, where Mercier spent five months exploring, writing in his journal, and immersing himself in academic studies. Like many French romantic writers in the first half of the nineteenth century, Mercier borrowed material for his writing from Italian exoticism. In fact, during a visit to Duke Serra di Falco's gardens in Palermo, Mercier encountered a young, insane man who believed himself to be engaged to Death. Captivated by his story, Mercier recorded every detail in his journal, which eventually turned into his novel *Le Fou de Palerme (The Madman of Palermo*, 1873).[15]

Mercier also became involved in the political struggles of France, writing for a Parisian democratic newspaper called *La Réforme,* which also operated a publishing house. As a representative of the New Orleans newspaper *La Chronique,* Mercier wrote about the progress of the revolution against Louis-Philippe and planned to have his play *Auri-Fames* (*Money-Hunger*)[16] published, but *La Réforme*'s offices were burned in the course of the revolutionary struggles the very week Mercier's book was to be published. Amazingly, Mercier rewrote his novel completely from memory. After another brief journey to New Orleans and then back to Paris, Mercier temporarily abandoned literature, acknowledging the difficulty in making a living as a writer. He married Virginie Vézian in 1849 and spent six years earning his medical degree in France.[17]

Mercier and his family made two more moves between New Orleans and Paris. After brief positions with several short-lived newspapers in France, including Alexandre Dumas' *Le Dartagnan,* Mercier reluctantly returned to New Orleans for good in 1868 due to the imminent war with Prussia. In fact, Dumas predicted the Franco-Prussian War and advised Mercier to leave. Unhappy with his life and disappointed with his failed literary career in Paris, he practiced medicine to support his family but somehow couldn't entirely abandon his literary aspirations. During this period of time, Mercier composed six novels: *Hénoch Jédésias* (1869), *Le Fou de Palerme* (1873), *Lidia* (1873), *La fille du Prêtre* (*The Priest's Daughter,* 1877-78), *L'Habitation Saint-Ybars* (*Saint-Ybars Plantation,* 1881), *Johnelle* (1891), and a five-act play titled *Fortunia.*[18]

Mercier also maintained an active presence among the New Orleans newspapers, contributing more than one hundred articles, short stories, poems, and essays on an eclectic range of topics. However, when his novel *La Fille du Prêtre* was published in the *Carillon,* nearly the entire Creole population rose up against Mercier. The novel about a priest who disregards his vows and fathers an illegitimate child angered the people of New Orleans. Unfortunately, this scandal prevented Mercier's work from ever appearing in newspapers again, as he was ostracized from the literary community for being a "free thinker." His works after that were published by Mercier himself or with the help of his faithful subscribers and friends. Interestingly, Mercier changed his writing style according to the shift in audience. Now reaching a more refined and sophisticated audience, mostly composed of the intelligent, upper-class Creole population, Mercier avoided the excessive sentimentalism that had tied his previous works with literary romanticism. In his last novel, *Johnelle,* Mercier opens with a scene of a mother committing infanticide, demolishing all traces of the sentimental novel.[19]

During this time, Mercier also founded the *Athenée Louisianais,* a society that aimed to preserve the French language in Louisiana, and served as its secretary and treasurer. He became an editor and a main contributor to *Les Comptes-rendus de l'Athenée Louisianais,* the society's publication featuring Louisiana French writers whose mission was to explore scientific, literary, and artistic frontiers. Mercier himself wrote articles on topics as varied as nihilism, pugilism, and philology. *L'Athenée* grew from an initial twelve members, of whom six were physicians, to include many educated, upper-class Creoles by the end of the nineteenth century.[20]

Mercier's novels were unique and controversial for their time; unfortunately, the language barrier prevented everyone but a small francophone audience from discovering Mercier's distinctive thematic style. In *Le Fou de Palerme,* Mercier borrows from Shakespeare in a Romeo-and-Juliet tragic love story between a musician and a gypsy's illegitimate love-child. *Johnelle,* perhaps Mercier's darkest work, depicts a son's obsession with his dead sister, who was killed by his mother at birth after an earlier abortion failed her. Mercier's controversial themes are also apparent in his novel *La Fille du Prêtre,* which reveals Mercier's dislike towards the monarchy and aristocracy existing in France, especially the corruption within the Catholic Church (one has only to read the title, *The Priest's Daughter*). Mercier became increasingly concerned with the corruption of mankind, wanting his readers to reevaluate their moral and physical well-being. Most of his novels followed this "social narrative" form and focused on deep sociological and political issues.[21]

Despite the intensity of these novels, critics generally agree that Mercier's best work is reflected in *L'Habitation Saint-Ybars,* a complex novel that depicts the hierarchy of relations between blacks and whites on a sugar plantation in rural, antebellum southern Louisiana.[22] Interestingly, Mercier blends different genres together, calling his work a "récit social" but mixing in many elements of a *feuilleton*, as his novel covers much action, from suicide and an attempted rape to racial "passing" and miscegeny.[23] The story follows a French soldier named Anthony Pélasge, who seeks refuge in New Orleans from the political turmoil in Europe as a tutor for the plantation owner's children, Démon and Chant d'Oisel (Birdsong). Since Pélasge is an outsider, the reader witnesses first-hand through him the social decorum of Creoles in Louisiana, especially the relationships between slave and master, between *Créoles de couleur* and whites, and between the rich and the poor. The most striking part of *L'Habitation,* however, is Mercier's use of language. Switching back and forth from French to Creole and allowing the characters to speak their respective native tongues, Mercier uses language to reconstruct the plantation castes of southern Louisiana.[24]

The Creole language is generally believed to have developed as an initial contact language for minimal communication purposes, otherwise known as a "pidgin." These pidgins exist purely as trade languages and as a *lingua franca,* or a language that is not native to either group. However, in the case of French Creole, continued cultural contact between groups (specifically between francophones and blacks during the eighteenth-century slave trade) kept the language alive to the point where it became the mother tongue of a group of people. At the time when Mercier wrote *L'Habitation Saint-Ybars,* Creole had a degraded status in francophone society. Nineteenth-century professor and linguist J.A. Harrison claimed that the language was composed of "word-fragments" and "debris of conjugation." Since Creole sprang up almost entirely by ear, it focuses on the phonetics, or syllables as they are heard. Harrison criticizes Creole's heavy reliance on the infinitive, which he calls "the Creole's anchor of salvation."[25]

Aside from its unusual grammar, the Creole language carried social implications as well. In nineteenth-century Louisiana society, many francophones regarded Standard French as superior to French Creole. Mercier wrote an essay about Louisiana French Creole, advocating that Creole stands as a valid language, and its worth should not be diminished. Mercier portrays this hierarchy of language in *L'Habitation Saint-Ybars.* First of all, whites in Louisiana associated Creole with childhood because Creole children learned to speak solely the patois[26] before learning Standard French, normally at the age of ten or twelve. They were often cared for—and learned their first language from—Creole nannies called "mammies" who belonged to the family or were intimately associated with the family. Even Mercier himself, who was part of the Creole culture, learned to speak the Creole patois before French. In the novel, the character of Démon prefers speaking to his black nurse Mamrie in Creole. But when he comes back as a grown man after fighting the war in Europe, he addresses Mamrie in French, portraying a sense of linguistic decorum. Nevertheless Démon, like every other Louisiana-born character in the novel, retains his bilinguality, switching between Creole and French depending upon the social situation.[27]

Another reason for the French language's perceived "social superiority" lies in the use of Creole for storytelling. Harrison points out that many philologists have noted that Creole is used often in the *récit* and the *conte.*[28] "The Creole of Louisiana lends itself admirably to those *petits poèmes,* those simple little dramatic tales, compositions, improvisations which [...] recount the experiences of a story-teller, put into striking and pregnant syllabuses the memorabilia of some simple life [...]" In *L'Habitation,* Démon loves hearing Mamrie tell him stories in Creole. Similarly, when Master Saint-Ybars' two children undertake the responsibility of educating the young daughter of a slave, they make sure that they speak French, "the language of reason," rather than filling her head with "tales and legends."[29]

Mercier aimed to disprove this socially accepted view of the Creole language by juxtaposing French and Creole in his novel. He disagreed with Harrison's claim that Creole resembles French "in a fashion that suggests the relation between the *Æthiopica* of Uncle Remus and current English." As Rosenwald argues, and I concur, Mercier did not juxtapose the two languages to diminish Creole's worth. He aimed to write *exactly* as Louisianans spoke and to show how so many diverse peoples and cultures communicated, and he desired to preserve the integrity of diverse racial identities. In his use of French and Creole,

Mercier retains a huge part of the *couleur locale*[30] of nineteenth century southern Louisiana. As noted earlier, Mercier praised the way blacks formed a grammar and a way to communicate solely by hearing a foreign language. In his essay "Etude sur la langue créole," Mercier wrote, "[…] The Negro makes for himself a grammar; the words heard from the mouths of the whites are combined in his brain in such a way as to create all the parts of speech necessary for the expression of his thought." Thus, a good translation of Creole should not lessen the language's value.[31]

American literature ignores Mercier or any of his contemporaries because they chose to write in French instead of English, implying that American literature must be in English. This assumption is a false premise in itself, for one cannot praise the diverse cultures in the "melting pot" of America and expect everyone to speak the same language. Wellesley College English professor Lawrence Rosenwald best explains this incongruity:

> It seems evident that American literature ought to represent the American multilingual scene. But as we read through the classic American novels in search of such representation, what we find is in large part deceit and evasion. […] We live in an almost chaotically complex multilingual world, and the languages people speak matter to their individual identities and political communities. A novel like Mercier's, an extended experiment in letting characters actually speak the languages they must speak or choose to speak, affords us a rare opportunity for an analysis of the results.[32]

Francophone Louisiana remains today as it was in Mercier's time, an amalgamation of the different peoples inhabiting the state since the eighteenth century. Interestingly, after the Civil War, the divides between the groups blurred, and the connotation of "Creole" again shifted to what is seen in Louisiana's culture now: a mixture of African, Caribbean, American, French, and Spanish elements. The collective Creole culture remains apparent in the language, cuisine, architecture, folklore, music, and especially the literature of Louisiana. Stories like Mercier's *L'Habitation Saint-Ybars* offer a unique, first-hand glance into a fascinating piece of American history and culture. At the same time, his novel poses something new in the world of literary history and criticism and offers a complex and different view on the plantation novel, the idea of "local color" fiction, and the representation of translation and language difference.[33]

Unfortunately, almost one hundred and thirty years after its original publication, *L'Habitation Saint-Ybars* remains shut off from the English-speaking world. Mercier's usage of French and Creole marginalized his novels and hindered the dissemination of his work. Though many scholars like Alcée Fortier and Lawrence Rosenwald have stressed the desire to see the book published in English, there remains much hesitation. The great debate revolves around the greatest aspect of the novel, the realistic usage of both French and Creole. On a larger scale, no English equivalent exists to parallel the relationship between Louisiana Standard French (LSF) and Louisiana French Creole (LFC). Creole is more than a dialect of French, and retains many social and cultural implications. Rosenwald comments that translating this novel would be like translating a richly multidialectal text such as Mark Twain's *Huckleberry Finn.* The translation does not rely solely on the words themselves; the relationship between the languages and the people speaking them implicates many unspoken aspects of culture. Maintaining Mercier's writing style and his stress on the important relationship between Louisiana Standard French and Louisiana French Creole stands as a huge obstacle, for some elements are inevitably lost in translation. Dialects are associated with *place,* and portraying Mercier's characters as English speakers separates the language from its physical origin.[34]

Many scholars have pondered how literary history would look had Mercier chosen to write in English (or if his writings had been translated). Since Mercier falls into a small category of Louisiana French literature and frequently portrays a bilingual or even multilingual community, it is difficult to compare him to another American writer. In terms of subject matter, Rosenwald, as well as J.A. Harrison, George Reinecke, and Alcée Fortier, propose that Mercier would have fallen into the same category as American novelist George Washington Cable. Like Mercier, Cable depicted stories on the plantation and used the Creole patois in his works. However, Cable is criticized for his status as an outsider to the Creole community. His portrait of Creole society outraged some of his readers, especially Alcée Fortier, who claims that Cable, in his work "Creoles of Louisiana," does not distinguish between the terms *Creole, Cadian,* and *Mulatto.* "[For him,] they are synonymous terms. He chooses indifferently from these three classes the most extraordinary, the most eccentric persons, gives them the false name of typical Creole, and dashes off their portrait. He may be a novelist, but he is without a doubt a dealer in Creole caricatures."[35]

The way Cable handled Louisiana French Creole also differed from Mercier. In 1886, five years after the appearance of *L'Habitation Saint-Ybars,* Cable translated a passage of Creole into an extreme African-American vernacular English, which removed Creole's uniqueness and identity and made the language sound like a deficient version of English. Mercier admired the precision of the Creole language and regarded it as separate from standard French, for it carried its own historical and geographical importance. He makes his characters speak the languages that they would have spoken in real life and offers no footnotes to translate the Creole. Mercier was concerned with the power of language and how it helps form identities and relationships in communities, especially the Creole community. Unlike Cable, Mercier focuses more on distinctions of language and less on distinctions of dialect. This focus changes the way readers regard diverse works of literature. As Mercier was an insider to the Creole community by birth, language, and social position (at least at the time of the novel) and Cable was an outsider in all ways, Fortier publicly voiced his wish for *L'Habitation Saint-Ybars* to be translated into English, "for it is a much more correct picture of Louisiana life than is to be found in many other works better known outside of our State." Thus, the claim that Mercier is most similar to Cable disregards one extremely important aspect: Mercier's contribution to the naturalist movement in literature.[36]

Naturalism, a term that may have been first coined by French writer Emile Zola, names a literary movement that sought to replicate ordinary, daily life in opposition to the symbolism and sentimentalism used in literary romanticism. When gathering material for what would become *Le Fou de Palerme,* Mercier obviously borrowed material from Italian exoticism, as did most French romantic writers from the first half of the nineteenth century, but the elements of his story take root in a physical reality. Mercier based his novel on what naturalists would later call "human documents," the concrete details that he recorded in his journal. Interestingly, Mercier crossed paths with the famed Zola when Mercier became the manager of the Socialist newspaper *La Rue.* This newspaper printed Zola's "Une cage de bêtes féroces"[37] in August of 1867, which proves that Mercier knew Zola right at the beginning of his career. *La Rue* also published a series of scathing articles on clerical mores anonymously written by "l'abbé***,"[38] a work that heralded Mercier's novel *La Fille du Prêtre* for its anticlericalism.[39]

In order to write about elements of everyday life and represent them accurately in their works, naturalist writers often studied human beings in an objective, methodical manner. Mercier himself took a special interest in the science of linguistics and how language plays a role in social identity. One year before the publication of *L'Habitation Saint-Ybars,* he wrote an essay on the Creole patois called "Etude sur la langue creole en Louisiane" that approached the language in a scientific, sociological manner. He was extremely interested in how, during the slave trade, the blacks who arrived in Louisiana created their own language simply through hearing others speak and putting the sounds together for their own personal use: "They speak a language they have learned by instinct. Words for them are simply sounds; and each sound reaching their brains through the medium of the ear, paints there an image to which is attached a succession of ideas." His essay was his first attempt to do a scientific study of Creole, which was necessary since he was going to incorporate the language into his novels. Mercier's dedication and insistence on studying the Creole language and imitating it accurately in his works reflect the mission of literary naturalism, classifying his works as some of the earliest examples of naturalism in American literature.[40]

Regardless of scholars' arguments about where Mercier fits in the American literary canon or their theories about Mercier writing in English, one key point is missing in their arguments. Rosenwald argues that had Mercier chosen to write in English, he "surely would have attracted much attention and perhaps influenced the thought of the South and the nation."[41] He wrote this novel during an extremely pivotal time of change in American history: the social and racial effects of the Civil War and the abolition of slavery, the development of industry and mass production preceded by the huge success of Louisiana sugar plantations, and the loss of French language and francophone culture in Louisiana. But writing in English would have defeated Mercier's purpose and contradicted his vision of preserving French. As Reinecke points out, when Mercier penned his novel, the number of people speaking French was already steadily diminishing.[42] Mercier was not optimistic about the future of the French language: in fact, he soberly predicted that by the middle of the 20th century, no one in New Orleans would speak French. Despite this, he did not abandon his fierce desire to save not only the French language but francophone culture. Even though this translation stands as a contradiction to what Mercier fought for and believed in, it would be more distressing to continue to disregard such an important part of American literature, culture, and history.

Acknowledgements

There are many people whose constant help and support have helped me complete this project. I would like to thank Dr. Dana Kress, who graciously gave me this incredible opportunity. You put your trust and faith in a random graduate student who just happened to email you one day. Your guidance and wisdom has been endless, and you have showed me just how important it is to preserve the quality and originality of this piece of literature. You work to preserve American literature written in languages other than English, and I am honored to be a part of this movement.

To Dr. Jean-Marc Braem, I cannot thank you enough for all of the work you have done. When I told you about this project and asked if you would help navigate me through any rough patches, you did not hesitate to volunteer your services. All of the hours you put in to proofreading, comparing, and editing made this translation eloquent and retained the original style. You kept me motivated and focused, and this project would not have survived without you. To my readers and distinguished professors Dr. Simon Bronner and Dr. Matthew Wilson, both of you sacrificed your time to undertake this immense project and always kept me pointed in the right direction. Both of you provided a framework in which I could place the story historically and culturally, which added depth and insight to the story. I am very grateful for all of your help.

To my friend and colleague—Dr. Gary Grieve-Carlson, your keen eye for detail helped me immensely in the revision process. Thank you for graciously volunteering to look over the manuscript. To my other reviser, my friend Carli Weldon, I greatly appreciate the time and effort you spent going through the text when I got overwhelmed. Your patience and willingness kept me sane!

I would also like to thank my friend, Professor Sally Clark, who was the one who started this whole thing. When I could not think of a way to blend together the French language and American culture, you gave me the genius idea of looking into the Creole literature of Louisiana. The rest is history. Thank you for your inspiration!

Lastly but most importantly, I would like to thank my family. From my parents to aunts and uncles to cousins to siblings to friends, all of you have encouraged me to keep pursuing my goal and gave me the confidence in myself to finish the project. I am thankful to have such a large support group.

Elizabeth A. JULIAN

Saint-Ybars

Part I

Chapter 1

In Those Times

On the fifth of May in 1851, the clipper ship *Polonia,* arriving from Cádiz, Spain, entered port and quickly dropped anchor at Marigny Street. Among the descending passengers was a young man who physically looked Spanish but was indeed French. Even though he was barely twenty-three years old, he had already suffered greatly for his political opinions. Wounded and imprisoned at the barricades in Paris during the riots of June 1848, he had been deported to Africa. After having withstood the ordeals of captivity in the bloody climate of Lambessa[1] for six months, he managed to escape, and in Oran, he boarded a ship bound for Cádiz. Setting foot on Spanish soil, he had come across a former refugee whom he had met in the political circles of Ledru-Rollin in Paris in 1847.[2] Considering their friendship and the young man's naivety, the Spaniard had welcomed him warmly and had given him some advice. "Believe me," the man had told him, "don't even think about going home illegally. From now on France belongs to Louis Napoleon. He'll do with it what he wants until further notice. How long will he last? Who knows? He's a superstitious and subservient imitator of his uncle and will copy him right down to his faults. He'll persist, against common sense, in putting his trust in what his family calls 'the lucky star of the Napoleon family.' When that flickering flame of pride leads him to the same fate as his uncle, France will be done with the illusion that a monarchy can save it. Then, better times will dawn for Republican ideas. In the meantime, go to the United States. There you'll see the fruit of the governmental principles that you believe to be the most favorable to mankind's liberty and happiness. You'll observe, you'll study, and you'll think. A day will come, maybe sooner than I hope, when you'll come home with the authority that only experience can give you. This ship here is going to set sail for New Orleans, and I'm offering you a cabin. You can easily find work in Louisiana as a teacher. I have several friends in New Orleans, among them a lawyer currently employed by the editorial staff of one of the main newspapers of the city. I'll give you a letter of recommendation for him. Let's not waste time. Write a few words to your family, and then we will take care of your trunk."

The young outcast had followed his friend's advice. Standing on the deck of the *Polonia* as the sun descended upon the horizon, he thought for a while, with a sense of nostalgia, about the European soil from which he was straying and the sea that was carrying him toward an uncertain fate, perhaps an unfortunate one. Seeing the calm and confident air with which, in disembarking, he walked on the levee, no one could tell he was a foreigner. He had studied the map of the city and knew by heart the path that would take him to the offices of the *Abeille*.[3] He followed Esplanade Avenue and was about to turn left on Chartres Street when his attention was drawn to a low-lying house whose windows and doors were all wide open. The only furnishings in the two rooms opening onto Esplanade were benches lined up against the walls, occupied by male slaves in one roon and by female slaves in the other. Several people of mixed heritage with varying complexions were scattered among the blacks. On each corresponding section of the sidewalk was a narrow platform composed of three steps. On the steps, several men and women of color were standing upright, all with the strength and power of youth and seemingly blessed with good health. On the inside, a sliding door opened between the two rooms. Further on could be seen smaller, dimly-lit rooms, then beyond, a corridor opening onto a courtyard at the bottom of which were the annexes and the kitchen.

A white man, tall and robust, was coming and going from the room full of men to that of the women, glancing from time to time at the side of the street like a merchant waiting for a customer. Even though he was still young, he already had that swelling of the cheeks and violet complexion characteristic of a drunkard. It was possible that he had once been handsome. He had an intelligent but tough look. From time to time he raised his eyes religiously to the sky, as if to beg for protection, but this was more of a tic that his former functions as a protestant minister had left him rather than a reflection of his piety, for he had left the clergy five years before in order to become a slave merchant.

The young stranger slowed his step in order to see better, but he still did not understand what he was seeing. Thus, addressing a slave woman who came to meet him, he said:

"Madame, please, what is all this?"

The black woman, in hearing herself be called "Madame," let go a large and joyous laugh. Then, replying in a half-serious voice:

"Vou pa oua don, Michié?" she responded. "Cé nég pou vende."[i]

She realized he had not understood her and immediately suspected that she was dealing with a foreigner, so she responded in perfect French:

"These are slaves for sale, Monsieur."

"Ah!" said the stranger, and he did not ask anything more. There was quite a meaning contained in that simple "ah!" The slave only saw a banal expression of surprise. As for the stranger, he did not have time to analyze his feelings. His view was already fixed upon someone approaching, holding a small girl of thirteen or fourteen by the hand.

The man who came over was a Louisianan of old stock, a perfect example of Creole aristocracy. Already of considerable height, he seemed even larger due to his habit of holding his head high and tilted backwards a bit as if watching an object floating on the horizon. Thin, well-groomed, and elegantly dressed in the latest style, he walked with a casual manner that revealed, at first glance, self-esteem and a commanding presence. Seeing him, the young outsider said to himself:

"Doesn't this fellow have a proud look! The great king Assuérus,[4] in all of his glory, didn't strut more proudly."

The little girl wore an outfit that suited her extremely well, but she was so pretty and had such a remarkable appearance that the

[i] "So, you don't see what's happening, Sir? These are slaves for sale."

attention of the young man concentrated exclusively on her face. She had very fair skin and bright pink lips. Her eyes, a deep velvety black, shone with such a soft and peaceful light that a poet would have gladly compared them to a beautiful summer's night. They revealed a tender heart, a deep and contemplative soul. She seemed too serious for her age, but charming, with a candor and kindness that took shape at the corners of her graceful, small mouth as soon as she spoke.

The Louisianan entered the slave market. The merchant raised his eyes to the ceiling; sighing with satisfaction and bowing respectfully, he said:

"Monsieur Saint-Ybars, I'm happy to see you. You're lucky. I have two magnificent lots, men and women, all excellent workers, and among them several skilled craftsmen."

"Hello, Monsieur Stoval," Monsieur Saint-Ybars responded laconically without looking at the merchant, not even taking the trouble to hide the contempt he felt for him. It might appear strange and contradictory that Monsieur Saint-Ybars, who came there to buy slaves, despised anyone who made a living selling them, but this sentiment, logical or not, was nevertheless present within him.

"Yes Monsieur," Stoval resumed, "as I had the honor of telling you, all choice specimens, and excellent workers, and among them..."

"That's enough. I'm familiar with this group," said Saint-Ybars, interrupting the merchant's refrain. "These slaves belong to the estate of Widow Hawkins. The heirs are in Boston. They sent the order to sell all of them, big and small. And these are the same people who preach abolition in the name of philanthropy. Hypocrites! But, as they say, these self-appointed saints, *business is business.* I need a blacksmith to replace one of mine that I lost. You have one; his name is Fergus. Where is he?"

"Fergus, come here," said , addressing a young slave.

Fergus stepped forward. He was a strapping lad with an open and jovial expression, twenty-five years of age, built like Hercules.

"You're the blacksmith, correct?" asked Saint-Ybars.

"Oui, maite, cé moin," Fergus said. "Moin cé nég créol. Mo pa nég pacotille, moin. Pa gagnin ain forgeron dan tou la ville, ki capab forgé ain fer à choil pli vite pacé moin. Mo capab racomodé ain lessieu é tou ça qui cacé dan ain voiture. Croché, vérou, charnière, gon, piton, tou ça cé kichoge ki connin moin. Si vou achté moin, maite, vou capab di vou achté ain vaillan nég."[i]

"If I buy you," remarked Saint-Ybars good-humoredly, "I'm sure of one thing: that I'll have acquired a colossal braggart."

"Non, maite," Fergus resumed. "Mo pa vanteur, moin. Ça mo di vou cé la vérité. Vou mennin moin dan ain la forge. Va oua si mo pa fé ça mo di."[ii]

"That's exactly what I'm going to do," said Saint-Ybars. "I'm going to put you to the test."

And in turning towards Stoval:

"The price, please?" he asked.

"Eighteen-hundred piastres,[5] Monsieur," Stoval responded. "That's a good price, you must have noticed…"

"That's enough, it's enough!" interrupted Saint-Ybars. "I'm going to put him to the test and have a doctor check him. If he's the blacksmith he claims he is, and if he's in perfect condition, I'll take him."

The young Frenchman, overcome by a curiosity easily understandable for a stranger, was eagerly but discreetly observing what was happening.

As Saint-Ybars was about to leave, two men who obviously did not belong to the higher ranks of Louisiana society entered the women's holding area, where there was a slave who stood out of the crowd because of her complexion and demeanor. The young stranger, believing her to be white, seemed very surprised to see her for sale in a group of slave women. Beautiful and remarkably attractive, she knew these natural advantages could have an influence on her future. Therefore, she was confident that her new master, whoever that may be, would not treat her like just another slave. These thoughts

[i] "Yes, master, that's me. I'm a Creole slave. I'm not a cheap fieldhand. There's not a blacksmith in the city who can fit a horseshoe faster than me. I can repair an axle and anything that breaks on a carriage. Bracket, bolt, joint, hinge, hook, I know all these things. If you buy me, master, you can say that you bought a good slave."

[ii] "No, master. I'm not a braggart. What I said is the truth. Lead me to a forge and you'll see if I can't do what I say."

were evident in the gracious and impertinent manner in which she held her head. However, when she saw the two strangers who just entered watching her, whispering and nodding with lustful eyes, she lost her self-assurance. She sensed that one or the other was going to bargain for her, and the idea of belonging to a common man aroused an inexpressible horror within her. In her anguish, an opportunity for salvation arose in her mind, and she eagerly seized it. She made repeated signs to attract the attention of the young girl whom Saint-Ybars held by the hand. The girl wanted to respond to the call, but she did not dare. However, the face of the unknown woman who was begging for her wore such a desperate expression that the young girl no longer hesitated. She abandoned Saint-Ybars' hand and ran towards the pleading woman.

"How beautiful you are!" the slave said in an affectionate voice. "Vou gagnin ain ti lair si tan comifo! Vou popa riche, mo sûr. Di li achté moin. Ma linmin vou tou plin. Epi si vou té connin comme mo bonne coiffeuse é bonne couturière! Ma rangé si bien joli cheveu doré laïé! Couri vite di vou popa li achté moin."[i]

This charming child, who was the daughter of Saint-Ybars, did not need any further explanation. She understood the slave's distress and was overcome with compassion. Returning to her father and showing him the young woman, she told him:

"Papa, buy her for me. She's a good hairdresser and an excellent seamstress."

"But, young lady," responded Saint-Ybars, "we have all that at the house."

"I'm begging you," the little girl continued, "buy her for my birthday next Sunday. You'll make me so happy, dear Papa."

Saint-Ybars was very passionate. He had an ardent, unbounded affection for his daughter. What would he not do to make her happy? Could he refuse what she asked for on her birthday, the day when she appeared in the world? No, of course not. So he let his daughter take

[i] "You look like you're well-mannered! Your father's rich, I'm sure of it. Tell him to buy me. I'll be good to you. And besides, if you knew how skilled a hairdresser and dressmaker I am!... I'll arrange your golden locks perfectly! Quickly, go and tell your father to buy me."

his hand and lead him, like a large child, towards the woman who wanted him to be her master.

The young slave was named Titia. When she saw Saint-Ybars and his daughter coming, she glowed with happiness.

"My daughter would like you to be her servant," Saint-Ybars said to her. "Would you like to come with us?"

"Oh! Yes, Monsieur," she responded. "That's all I want. I was born and grew up among respectable people. I'll be right at home in a family like yours."

Saint-Ybars called Stoval and inquired about Titia's price.

The merchant, in lieu of a response, let out a long whistle, which meant in ordinary language:

"Oh! This one, Monsieur, is an expensive piece of merchandise."

Saint-Ybars gave him a sharp look and said:

"If there is one thing in the world I hate, Monsieur, it's hearing you whistle. You're not privy to my personal business. You can't know what's expensive or not to me. I'm not asking for your thoughts. I want to know the price of this woman."

"Two thousand dollars, Monsieur,"[6] responded Stoval in a more respectful tone.

An expression of irony and contempt passed like a stormy cloud over Saint-Ybars' face. He smiled bitterly then said in a restrained but biting voice:

"You Yankees take advantage of everything. In Boston, this woman would pass for white. Why wasn't she taken there and given her freedom? No, she is worth too much money for that. The philanthropy of Northerners doesn't go as far as sacrificing two thousand dollars."

"Excuse me, Monsieur, you're mistaken," remarked Stoval. "This young woman isn't part of the Hawkins estate. She belongs to a family in this area. I was asked to sell her in order to avoid a great misfortune. One of the sons of the house fell madly in love with her, and they feared that he would do something irrational. He was forced to leave the country under a sudden pretext. The family took advantage of his absence to make his lady love disappear. I believe, just between us, that she's…"

Stoval did not finish his sentence, not knowing how to express his thought without offending the delicate ears of Saint-Ybars' daughter. Besides, Saint-Ybars, who looked at him in a manner that discouraged him from pursuing his thought, said to him:

"In short, she's two thousand dollars. So be it. I'll take her. I'll return in an hour, and we will settle the two deals at the same time."

The disturbing exchange that the young stranger had just witnessed made a strong impression on him, but the scene of the sale was about to be followed by an episode that no one could have expected, a scene that was going to trouble all the bystanders, him more than anyone else.

A slave woman who was near the back door bent over in the failing light and hastily murmured several words.

A strange being that seemed to come out from beneath the earth entered, slipping and crawling. It was an old mulatto woman, a legless cripple. In order to move forward, she relied on her arms, one of which was shorter than the other, while her small legs, twisted and shriveled, stretched out alternately, scraping the floor. She was fair-skinned and had blue eyes. A *tignon*[7] worn in the traditional style hid her hair entirely and blossomed around her forehead and her temples like a wide-open fan. Her clothing consisted of a flannel jacket, a vest of blue cotton fabric with large pockets, and cotton pants reinforced by leather at all the parts that were exposed to the sun. She had an intelligent and sweet expression; despite her wrinkles and several missing front teeth, she must have had a pretty face in her youth.

Saint-Ybars' daughter was afraid; she had never seen a human deformity. Trembling and pale, she pressed herself against her father.

The old woman extended her thin arms and exclaimed in a pitiful tone:

"Monsieur Saint-Ybars, dear master, have mercy! Don't take this young woman without me. She's my daughter's daughter; she's the consolation of my old age. Her mother, who was beautiful like her, died when she was eighteen. It was I who raised her. It may seem strange to you, Monsieur, that I'm a mother, but nature is powerful, Monsieur Saint-Ybars, and this miracle proves it. Buy me as well, dear master. You'll be performing a good deed. God will bless you."

While speaking, the decrepit old woman approached the doorway, as if to block Saint-Ybars' path.

"You, here, miserable freak!" cried Stoval. "Who gave you permission to come disturb my business? Get out of here, you ugly crab. No one would pay a cent for you."

Stoval frothed with fury. He gave the poor wretch a kick that was more violent than even he could have imagined. She fell flat on her back from the stairway to the street and went rolling onto the pavement.

Stoval's furious voice had attracted several neighborhood women. They hurried to pick up the old woman.

Saint-Ybars had grown pale with rage. Knowing his hot temper, his daughter wrapped her arms around him and held him with all her strength in order to prevent him from seizing Stoval by the neck and shaking him like a wretch.

"Be calm, young lady," Saint-Ybars said. "Your father will not dirty his hand by touching this vile piece of trash."

The group of women who rushed to the aid of the disabled woman had grown. Their number gave them some courage, and, even though they were slaves, they put the merchant to shame because of his cowardly brutality.

While falling, the old woman had lost her tignon. Her white hair, suddenly appearing, increased the pity and respect that her great age inspired in all the people present.

"Monsieur Stoval," she said, "I knew you were a nasty man, but I never knew you capable of hitting a helpless cripple and laughing while seeing her fall. I know your history: at eighteen, you abandoned your parents. You stopped speaking to them. You don't know if they're living or have died in misery. After an unruly youth, you became a protestant minister, as one becomes a gambler or a politician. Since religion didn't make you any richer, you left your position to become a slave merchant. Monsieur Stoval, you'll go far. I have a feeling that at the end of the road, murder and the gallows await you."

"It's you, you old monkey," responded Stoval, hunching his shoulders, "whose insolence will bring about your hanging one of these days."

The cripple, turning towards Saint-Ybars, responded: "I am speaking to the gentleman, to the Louisianan, to the master born under the same sky as me, a humble slave. Monsieur Saint-Ybars, you, like your brothers and sisters, played with your servants when you were a child. They grew up with you, and you cared about them. I dare beg you, dear sir, buy me, Monsieur. My masters authorized me to offer myself to anyone who would buy my granddaughter. Monsieur Stoval knows it. It's out of viciousness that he pretends not to know. Monsieur, as old and as deformed as I am, I can be useful. I was raised by a good master. He was a distinguished man. He came here after the disasters in Saint Domingue[8] and was a friend of your father. You know his name, I'm sure. It was Monsieur Moreau des Jardets. He taught me to read and write. Every morning, I read him his newspaper, and I copied his letters. For thirty years, I've kept, like a relic, a small book that he treasured more than all the others. You see, Monsieur, you will find his name written in his handwriting at the bottom of the first and the last page. It was his custom, this dear and venerable man, to thus put his name at the beginning and at the end of his books."

Titia took from her grandmother's hands a small book that the old woman had just pulled from a pocket made specifically for it and handed it to Saint-Ybars. It was a small folio edition that was entitled *Pensées de Sénèque*.[9] Saint-Ybars opened it at random. His eyes came across this passage:

"This man you call your slave, are you forgetting that he is formed from the same elements as you? That he enjoys the same sky, that he breathes the same air, that he lives and dies like you? Treat your inferior as you would like to be treated by your superior. Never think of your rights over a slave without thinking of those that a master would have over you."

Saint-Ybars' stern and domineering features softened. The old mulatto woman found courage.

"Monsieur Saint-Ybars," she said, "your heart is telling you to take me with you. Listen to it."

Saint-Ybars made a gesture of consent.

"How much are you asking for her?" he said to Stoval.

"How much am I asking for her?" responded the merchant. "Pshaw! I just want to be rid of her. Take her as a *lagniape*."[10]

"By the way," remarked the infirm old woman, "Monsieur Stoval must be earning a pretty good commission on my granddaughter to be able to give me away like that."

Saint-Ybars motioned to Fergus and Titia to follow him and said to the old woman, "I'm returning home this evening at five o'clock, on the steamboat *Océola*. It's up to you to find it."

"Oh! Don't worry, Monsieur, I'll be there," responded the old woman. "The late Monsieur Moreau des Jardets had the custom of saying, when speaking of me, 'She's like justice: she arrives slowly, but eventually, she arrives.'"

Fergus laughed loudly and said to the cripple, "Ça cé kichoge ki vrai. La jistice épi vou cé comme torti dan conte. Torti-là rivé coté bite avan comper chivreil, é li marié mamzel Calinda. Mo parié va rivé coté stimbotte-là divan nouzotte. Adié jica tanto, pove vieu Lagniape. Pa faché, non, si mo hélé vou comme ça. Lagniape cé kichoge ki bon."[i]

Thus, this nickname given in jest by Fergus to the old mulatto was repeated later on Saint-Ybars' plantation. They got used to calling the legless cripple Lagniape, and this name stayed with her for good. Using the cripple's new name from now on, we'll say that Lagniape was well-taken care of by the women around her. They took her inside a neighboring house, where she was given some food.

The young stranger moved away, immersed in his thoughts. He walked without seeing or hearing anything. Finally, he stopped, and like someone waking up from a dream, said:

"Ah! Where am I? What was I supposed to do?"

He then remembered that he was in New Orleans and that he had to go to a newspaper's offices. He had overshot his goal by far. Upon the instructions of a passerby whom he questioned, he retraced his steps down Camp Street, reached Chartres Street, and finally introduced himself to the editors of the *Abeille*.

[i] "This is true. Justice and you, that's like the turtle in the story. The turtle reached the finish line before Brother deer and married Mademoiselle Calinda. I bet that you'll arrive at the steamboat before us all. Goodbye until then, poor old Lagniape. Don't get angry if I call you that. When something's *lagniape* it's always good."

"You have arrived at just the right moment," the person to whom he had just given his letter of recommendation said to him. "One of our clients from the country just sent us a request for a tutor. He's chatting in another room with one of our associates. Come, I'll introduce you."

A minute later, the young Frenchman found himself in the presence of a person whom he immediately recognized.

"Monsieur Saint-Ybars," the journalist said, "I have the honor of presenting to you Monsieur Antony Pélasge, a professor from *l'École Normale de Paris*.[11] In order to give you an idea of his abilities, I can do no better than to ask you to read the letter that was addressed to me by one of my best friends from Europe."

Saint-Ybars courteously greeted the young professor, took the letter, and read. After having read it, he greeted him again as someone pleasantly impressed. Indeed, the letter was composed in the most glowing terms for the one whom it recommended.

Saint-Ybars took Pélasge aside and said to him:

"I believe, Monsieur, that I have found the professor whom I need for the youngest of my sons. You'll find him much behind! I'll admit to you that the difficulty he experiences learning is one of my deepest heartaches. It is an inconceivable thing, Monsieur. He has a natural wit, and yet he doesn't make any progress in his studies. His current teacher has given up on him. If you manage to do better than your predecessor, I'll offer you a contract, Monsieur, that will suit you. I'll give you three months to see if you can obtain results from your student. Until then, you'll receive seventy-five dollars[12] a month. Do these conditions suit you?"

"It would be presumptuous on my part, Monsieur," responded Pélasge, "to believe right away that I will succeed where another did not obtain good results. However, what you say about your child's natural gifts entitles me to have hope. A change in teachers nearly always leads to a change of method. Often, nothing more is needed to set a child on a good path. At any rate, Monsieur, you're offering me a trial period. You preserve my autonomy in its entirety, and I thank you for that. Your offer honors me, and I accept it."

Chapter 2

Antony Pélasge and Chant d'Oisel

The day after this meeting, Pélasge woke up at five o'clock in the morning aboard the *Océola,* the most luxurious steamboat that travelled between New Orleans and Baton Rouge. When he left his cabin, the first lights of dawn were coloring the tranquil surface of the river pink. A fresh breeze from the south dispelled the bluish mist that the night had left behind on the fields of sugar cane. He went to sit in the corridor that faced the east and watched the sun rise behind the distant and somber curtain of the cypress grove. Did he remember, at this moment, his past morning walks in the countryside of his homeland? It is probable. However, he did not sigh with regret. He had accepted with good grace the place where fate had led him, and, not thinking about his future, he concentrated entirely on the present.

Antony Pélasge came from a family originally from the Cévennes. Parisian by birth, he was not Parisian by nature. He had the seriousness that religious persecution had imprinted on the spirit of his ancestors. But if he had the solemnity of a Huguenot,[1] the resemblance between him and his ancestors did not go any further. He was of an essentially philosophical nature, an introspective and strong soul. Ever since his childhood, he had shown a particular fondness for studying. At sixteen, he had brilliantly completed his studies. At nineteen, he left for *l'École Normale*[2] and reported to the Minister of Public Instruction as one of the most competent among his schoolmates. At twenty, he taught rhetoric in one of the secondary schools in Paris. Without the political troubles that threw him off track in 1848, he certainly would have ascended quickly to a career at the university. He was a man of convictions: he searched for truth in everything, and when he found it, he drew from it a strength of will that no obstacle could destroy. For him, the indefinite progress of the human mind was never in question. Consequently, he foresaw a clear future: the universal emancipation of all peoples and their communities, built on on the foundations of universal rights. Reason was his religion; science was his cult. His motto was *to know is to be free.*

Time passes quickly when travelling in an unknown country. Pélasge, hearing the breakfast bell ring, could hardly believe it was already nine o'clock. After the meal, the servants set up some table games. Saint-Ybars sat at one of them exclusively occupied by several planters he knew. Game after game ensued. Money, gold, and bills formed piles that constantly grew. Pélasge, who had never touched a card and who was not at all interested in the players' discussions, left the lounge. He came across Saint-Ybars' daughter, who was strolling with Titia. He struck up a conversation with her. Titia took advantage of this time to talk briefly with Lagniape, who was with Fergus at the front of the deck.

"So," Pélasge continued, "my future student, Mademoiselle, is your twin. What's his name?"

"He has two names, Monsieur," responded the little girl. "A real name and another name that my grandfather gave him as a joke. That's the one that's stayed with him. He's named Edmond, but you'll never hear him called anything but Démon."

"And you, Mademoiselle, allow me to ask you your name."

"You're going to laugh, Monsieur. I have two names as well. Like my godmother, my name is Amélie. But apparently when I was little, listening to singing birds made me happy, and when I was alone, I sang for entire hours gazing at the countryside and the sky. Because of this, my grandfather, who has the habit of giving nicknames, said one day, 'Well! Since she always sings like her friends, the birds, I'm calling her Chant d'Oisel.[3] That's the name of the village from which our ancestors departed to come to America.' Since then, my name

Amélie has disappeared. It's only used on special occasions. But you may, Monsieur, if you want, call me Amélie."

"No, Mademoiselle, I'll do the same as everyone else. The nickname that your grandfather gave you is charming. I'll not call you anything other than Chant d'Oisel. I'll do the same for your brother. His name for me, as for others, will be Démon… it seems that he is having a hard time learning."

"Yes, Monsieur. It's because he likes to play too much."

"Ah! Explain that to me, Mademoiselle, please."

"He's so naughty, Monsieur! He only likes violent and dangerous activities. My mother's nervous when he plays outside. To her, it always seems that someone is going to bring him back to the house with a broken arm or leg. But he's as agile as a monkey. Nothing bad ever happens to him. He's always so impatient to run outdoors that I do part of his homework for him."

"You, Mademoiselle? So you're learning Greek and Latin as well?"

"Yes, Monsieur. I asked to learn it to help my brother."

"That's very kind of you, Mademoiselle."

"Monsieur, he learns very well with me when he's calm, but he has such a boisterous nature! It's terrible."

Pélasge fell silent for a moment. He reflected on Chant d'Oisel's words: "he learns very well with me when he's calm."

"Mademoiselle," he resumed, "tell me, please, does your brother like his teacher?"

"Not too much."

"Why?"

"Because Monsieur Héhé humiliates Démon by calling him thick-headed and simple-minded."

"Monsieur Héhé's the name of his teacher?" Pélasge asked with surprise.

The young girl began to laugh, and she did so with such a kind heart that her cheerfulness spread to Pélasge as well.

"His name's another one of my grandfather's inventions," she said. "He likes to give nicknames. He wouldn't be happy without doing so. My brother's teacher has a tic, and after every three or four sentences, he laughs nervously and says 'héhé!' It's unpleasant. He always seems to be making fun of you. When refering to him, my grandfather calls him 'Monsieur Héhé.' Little by little, everyone in the house, except cousin Pulchérie, picked up the habit of saying 'Monsieur Héhé.' His real name is MacNara."

Chant d'Oisel's chatter greatly interested Pélasge. Seeing in her an intelligent and witty child, he thought that he could, with discretion, discover a great deal through questioning her.

"Your grandfather," he said, "doesn't seem to be a great admirer of Monsieur Héhé."

"Well, no. It was he who advised my father to change teachers for Démon. Besides, Monsieur Héhé has students on several plantations. He was only able to give us one hour of class per day. Grand-papa thought that it was necessary to have a permanent teacher."

"Is he very old, your grandfather?"

"Oh! I believe so. He is eighty years old."

"You seem to love him, Mademoiselle. Tell me about him."

"Grand-papa is a scientist."

"Ah!"

"Yes, Monsieur. When he was fifty years old, he handed over the entire plantation to my father in order to devote himself to his books and his instruments of physics and astronomy. He also has a chemistry laboratory. In order to have peace and quiet, he had a house built a half mile from ours. He comes often to have dinner with us; his place is always set. He travelled a lot in his younger years. During the twenty-five years that he ran the plantation, he increased his fortune considerably. He subscribes to all the important journals that are published in America and Europe."

"You have a large family, Mademoiselle?"

"I have eight brothers and six sisters. Démon and I are the last. Four of my brothers and two of my sisters are married. We all live together. Mademoiselle Pulchérie, my father's cousin, lives with us too. She and my mother manage the household together."

"I think, Mademoiselle, that you still have the same tastes that earned you your pretty name of Chant d'Oisel?"

"I still love birds, Monsieur, but not in a cage. You'll discover them everywhere on the plantation, but they never do any harm. They are as tame to me as if I were one of them."

"You're schooled in music, correct?"

"Yes, Monsieur. I'm learning piano and singing with Mademoiselle Nogolka."

"Nogolka? If I'm not mistaken, that's a Russian name."

"Yes, Monsieur. My teacher's from Moscow. She finished her classical education in France and her musical education in Italy. She taught in London. Grand-papa, who knows languages, claims that no one possesses better skills than her in French, English, Italian, and Spanish. She's also a good mathematician."

"If I can judge this based on you, Mademoiselle, your teacher is very skilled. I've never met a Parisian of your age who speaks French better than you. Not only do you speak it well, but you don't have the slightest accent."

When Pélasge left from Cádiz for Louisiana, he knew very well that he was not going into a country of savages. He had been better informed than some self-assured writer who had written, in a Sunday newspaper in Paris, that New Orleans is situated at the edge of the sea, and that each year, at the voodoo festival, they eat a small living child. However, although he knew that he was with a civilized people, he hadn't expected the refined habits of Saint-Ybars' daughter. He reflected on everything she just told him, and, as he was naturally discreet, he promised himself to keep his guard up as he entered this new environment where he would be teaching and living.

Chapter 3

The Plantation – Vieumaite

The *Océola* was several hours late. The thick fog that had covered the waters of the Mississippi the night before had forced the steamboat to slow down its pace, even to stop several times. It was two o'clock in the afternoon when Saint-Ybars, alerted by the whistle, prepared to disembark. His plantation was situated on the left bank. It was recognizable far from the dock, on which stood an elegant pavilion intended to serve as a shelter against the rain or the heat of the sun.

A carriage hitched up to two magnificent harnessed horses awaited Saint-Ybars on the river road, at the bottom of the levee. He climbed into the carriage with his daughter and Pélasge. Titia sat beside the coachman. A servant received the order to drive Fergus to meet the master blacksmith. An old slave woman, who was collecting kindling, was put in charge of showing Lagniape a shorter route. A beautiful carriage entrance connecting to the public road opened before them. The carriage entered and went down a road bordered by rows of live oaks. Surrounded by magnificent gardens, the home of the rich planter stood a half-mile away at the end of the avenue.

Saint-Ybars' residence was styled like typical houses in the Louisiana countryside. It differed from them only in its larger proportions and the distinctive layout of the roof. The roof formed a huge square, and on the first and second floor of each side, a balcony with eight columns on each side emerged. Doric columns lined the bottom while those at the top were in the Corinthian style.[1] Old Saint-

Ybars, who had it built, had not given it the angled roof so commonly seen in Louisiana. Inspired by the carefully thought-out architecture of old Spain, he had covered it with a terrace framed by a railing decorated with flower pots. Two staircases led up to this terrace, where the family often met after sunset to look at the countryside and breathe in the fresh evening air. At the front of the house, the right and the left wings opened up onto the garden, where the most beautiful native trees united with quantities of exotic plants. Behind the house, an expansive courtyard planted with magnolias led to the kitchens and ironing rooms. A six-foot-wide well occupied the center of this courtyard. Further away was the group of houses for the domestics, who were appointed exclusively to the service of the house. Behind these lodgings, a grove of orange trees fostered a delicious darkness, and then beyond stretched an immense enclosure in which stood the clinic and its outbuildings, the master's stables, the stalls for the cobblers, carpenters, and saddlers, a meeting room for the slaves, and finally, a vegetable garden.

Noticing about a hundred small white houses and a two-story house shining in the sun at the border of a sugarcane field, and further yet another group of large buildings, Pélasge thought that these were two separate villages. He referred to these two villages while speaking to Saint-Ybars, who answered with a smile that the first group of buildings consisted of the slaves' cabins and the overseer's house, and the other part was the sugar factory. He explained to Pélasge that each cabin contained two dwellings, and that the sugar factory was part of a division that contained, around the steam engine making the sugar, a saw mill, a cooperage,[2] blacksmith shops, stables, a carpenter's shop, hangers, and barns for hay and grains.

Saint-Ybars's plantation occupied, as a whole, a piece of land one-and-a-half miles wide and three miles deep. There were four hundred slaves, men and women, who worked in the fields, eighteen specialized workers, ten gardeners, twenty domestics for the service of the house, two-hundred mules, thirty horses of which twelve were thoroughbreds, a cowshed, herds of sheep and goats, several barnyards, a fishpond, four dovecotes, twenty-five hunting dogs, and an enormous mastiff that was let out only at night to guard the house.

A reasonable discipline quietly applied to all of the personnel of this domain, masters and slaves. Saint-Ybars was strict but just. Unfortunately, he was subject to outbursts of anger that were sometimes so violent that they made people doubt his sanity and the natural kindness in his heart. He was the one who suffered the most from his fits of anger, for these explosions were followed by a bitter sadness that lasted for a week. He tenderly loved his father and worshipped him, but he himself demanded that his own children, whom he knew loved him, have the greatest respect for him. Therefore, when everyone saw Saint-Ybars arriving with Chant d'Oisel, the entire family went to Saint-Ybars to greet and embrace him.

The carriage stopped under a group of palm trees whose slender trunks rose up to the level of the roof's railing.

By the manner in which everyone embraced Chant d'Oisel, Pélasge understood that she was the household favorite. She immediately inquired about Démon and learned that he had left with his bird-trap in order to catch some sparrows.

Several minutes after Saint-Ybars's return, the first dinner bell rang. Everyone left to freshen up. One of Démon's brothers led Pélasge to the bedroom designated for him. It was located at the end of the balcony on the left, facing the river.

Pélasge found the room entirely to his liking. After surveying the details with pleasure, he moved towards the balcony and scanned the entire view that spread between the house and the river. He saw two men on horseback enter the avenue he had just followed several moments before with Saint-Ybars and Chant d'Oisel. As the riders approached, he discerned an old man followed by a young slave. When they arrived, the young slave hopped to the ground with the litheness of a panther and took hold of his master's horse. The old man dismounted more nimbly than men younger than he would have done. Saint-Ybars ran up to embrace the old man, and Pélasge heard these words:

"Father, how are you today?"

"Very well, son. You too, from what I can see. And Chant d'Oisel?"

"Perfectly well. I've been spoiling her again."

"Ah! So what now?"

"I bought another servant for her."

"Well done, son. As much as we can, we ought to try to make children happy. We never know what the future holds for them. A gift given to a little girl by her father, even at the price of excessive kindness, is a small gain for her in this game of chess that we all play with life, both young and old."

"I think," continued Saint-Ybars, "that I was lucky, for Démon's sake. I found a young professor who seems to be very good."

"Good, son, that's excellent news. Démon's terribly behind! Let's hope that this new tutor will help him make up for lost time. Your Monsieur Héhé, if cousin Pulchérie doesn't mind my saying so, is, with all of his education, a tactless person who never knew..."

Pélasge did not hear the end of the sentence. The elder Saint-Ybars and his son moved away while talking and their words were lost under the balcony. When their steps resonated on the staircase that led from the first floor to the balcony upstairs, he went to meet them and greeted the old man. This sign of respect was well-received. It pleased Saint-Ybars very much and equally pleased his father.

On the plantation, Saint-Ybars' father was called "old master," or as the slaves said in a single word, "Vieumaite."[3] We will refer to him in the same manner.

Like his son, Vieumaite was tall but a bit hunched. It was not the weight of age that caused him to lean forward but possibly the habit of remaining bent over his books and papers. If need be, he stood up straight so his forehead was level with that of his son.

At first, Pélasge did not realize the extraordinary impression that Vieumaite had made on him. That impression stemmed from the fact that the two sides of the man's face did not resemble each other. Painters and sculptors, whose art compels them in turn to study all the features of the face, know very well that its two halves are never identical, but never has the painter or the sculptor seen this dissimilarity pushed as far as in the face of Saint-Ybars' father. The disparity started at the crown: on the right, his hair stood up like the mane of an angry lion. On the left, it fell in a weeping manner on his temple and forehead. The right eye, a beautiful sky blue, was open wide, and it exuded a bright but gentle light. The left eye barely showed through half-closed eyelids; a thin, cold, penetrating beam leaked from it. On the right, his lips were well-pronounced in a slight, kind smile, but on the left, they were pulled down sharply, conveying distrust. This expression of mistrust was all the more noticeable because the old man had the unusual habit of holding between his teeth, on his left side, a small twig of cypress whose weight increased the drooping of his mouth. Strangely, Vieumaite only looked at people with one side of his face, the right side if he liked and trusted the person or the left side when he had his guard up or when he did not like the person standing before him.

Slaves, as is commonly known, never let the physical or moral particularities of their masters go unnoticed. They always refer to them by a most suitable word. On Saint-Ybars' plantation, the slaves called the right half of Vieumaite's face "the sunny side" and the left half "the dark side." When they saw him coming, they would always say, depending on the circumstances, with the precision peculiar to Creole, "Coté soleil ou coté lombe apé vini."[i]

Saint-Ybars left Pélasge with his father. The old man struck up a conversation with the dark side turned toward Pélasge. It did not take long for him to realize that Démon's grandfather was testing him by allowing him to talk. Accepting the test without fear or ostentation, Pélasge rapidly skimmed through the range of human knowledge. He passed from history to philosophy to the sciences, and then, coming back to the past, he talked about poetry from its origin, citing Homer, and followed through across the ages with Virgil, Dante, Milton, Byron, Lamartine, and Hugo. He outlined, in several lines, the ancient poems of India and Judea. As he was talking, the head of the octogenarian pivoted imperceptibly. Little by little, the *side of darkness* disappeared, and the *side of the sun* appeared. Surprised by the young professor's knowledge and scholarship, Vieumaite felt joy mixed with admiration in hearing him speak simply, but with warmth and enthusiasm, about things that he himself passionately liked.

By the time the second dinner bell rang, Pélasge had completed the conquest of old Saint-Ybars.

---

[i] "The sunny side or dark side is coming."

Chapter 4

The Family Dining Room

The dining room was on the ground floor. It formed a large rectangle with the longer sides illuminated by five glass doors, the one in the middle arched and larger than the others. They opened up onto the porches that encircled the house. One of the shorter sides had three glass doors; the other had two doors separated by a fireplace. They led to the office, to the cellar, and to other rooms contributing to the service of the dining room.

When Vieumaite entered the dining room, leaning on the arm that Pélasge had offered him out of filial respect, the first course was on the table. All of the guests, standing upright, waited for the venerable head of the family. There were twenty-five places set. Vieumaite introduced the new professor to the people who had not yet met him and sat down. Next, Saint-Ybars seated himself, and then, each person took his place. Three seats were unoccupied: one was Démon's seat, and the two others were for any unexpected guests. The empty chair next to Pélasge belonged to his future student. The two sides of the long table were occupied, one by Saint-Ybars, his eldest daughter and her husband, Chant d'Oisel and Mademoiselle Nogolka, and the other by Vieumaite, one of his granddaughters and her husband, and Pélasge. Madame Saint-Ybars was seated in the middle of the row, to the right of her husband. Mademoiselle Pulchérie was beside her.

Four young slaves—a mulatto woman and three quadroons[1]—stood around the table, cognizant of their responsibilities. In one of the corners of the room, a slave with the most beautiful black skin and an intelligent appearance remained standing near a table made of solid oak. He was the overseer and also was in charge of cutting the meat.

Two small slave boys fourteen or fifteen years of age operated the two fans suspended from the ceiling above the guests.

After a sign from the overseer, the soup tureens sitting on the table were brought to him. Shortly thereafter, twenty-one dishes full of excellent soup were placed in front of the guests, and dinner commenced. Because the conversation involved issues specific to the region, Pélasge discreetly remained silent. This allowed him to become familiar with all of the faces of the family. He watched and he reflected, carefully avoiding assuming the manners of a philosopher or of an investigator.

He liked Madame Saint-Ybars. She had a look of great tenderness and of slightly sad resignation. Mademoiselle Pulchérie did not appeal to him: she seemed inflexibly proud and riddled with silly prejudices. He noticed that she gave more orders to the servants than Madame Saint-Ybars, and she spoke loudly and in an imperious tone. No one had ever asked for her hand in marriage, and it was not probable, considering her forty-five years, that she would ever be asked. She was of the same social rank as Saint-Ybars. Like everyone of this class, she was tall, yet more heavy than tall. In order to balance the enormous mass of her bosom, she felt compelled to throw back her head and shoulders, which gave her the air of a scornful and dissatisfied queen. Through her sharp and domineering manner, she had wielded much influence over Saint-Ybars. He trusted her judgment more than that of his wife. Madame Saint-Ybars, who above all things desired peace, always gave in to her terrible cousin when Mademoiselle Pulchérie, in an ordinary conversation, matched Madame Saint-Ybars' reasoning with an avalanche of words and shouts.

Mademoiselle Pulchérie had a weakness for Monsieur Héhé.

Mademoiselle Nogolka was one of the people who attracted Pélasge's attention the most. He wondered how old she might be. It was not easy to provide an answer. The teacher's hair was already almost completely white, but her face, although tired and discolored, was that of a twenty-five-year-old. She had a countenance that implied a profound concentration, something mysteriously tragic. It seemed to Pélasge that she must spend a lot of time alone with her thoughts. But in this retreat into herself, what does she think about? "Her eyes," Pélasge reflected, "have wept a lot, or have stayed awake a lot to read and write. What unexplained things happened in this woman's past? Grief, maybe, whose memory still haunts her. Who knows? Maybe the pain that she feeds on has its roots in the present."

Pélasge looked at Mademoiselle Nogolka once again.

"She must have been quite beautiful," he reflected. "She still is, yes. Her white hair does not spoil her looks at all. She looks like a young woman from the era when they powdered their hair."

Pélasge brought his eyes back to his plate and continued his inner monologue. When he looked up, Mademoiselle Nogolka's eyes were fixed upon him.

"She's watching me," he thought. "What is she thinking about me? At any rate, I'll do my best to win her respect. She seems distinguished and intelligent, and I want her to have a good impression of me."

The dinner guests were about to start eating the roast when several children, some black, the others different shades of brown, entered and lined up in a half-circle near Saint-Ybars. Born from parents who worked in the house, they were different from the children whose mothers and fathers worked in the fields. Always in contact with their masters, they were much more developed and mischievous than the small slave boys who worked in the fields.

"Ah! Here you are, you little imps," Saint-Ybars said in jest. "Are you all clean? Each of you wearing your apron?"

The small group responded in unison, "Yes, master." Each one in turn showed the backs and the palms of his hands.

Saint-Ybars himself filled several plates with the best food on the table and distributed them to the children. They went and sat down on a large oilcloth in a corner of the dining room, each one with his plate between his legs.

Vieumaite, reading Pélasge's thoughts, said to him:

"These habits surprise you. But, it's all very natural. These children were born with ours. They share their games. Each one of them has one of my grandsons for a godfather, and one of my granddaughters for a godmother. They are obedient and loving. It would be impossible not to spoil them."

"This opens a whole new perspective for me," Pélasge responded. "I'm beginning to see, between masters and slaves, endearing relations that I didn't suspect."

Pélasge, like any other human being, could only interpret the social conditions of the region by what he saw through his own eyes and through the lens of his own experience. He could not by any means approve of slavery, but, while living in Louisiana, he had to learn the reasons that could, under the roof of intelligent and good masters, mitigate an institution based on the violation of human rights.

His thoughts were interrupted by the entrance of a man who at first produced an unfavorable impression upon him. The newcomer was a thirty-year-old man with a round and chubby form, a flowery face decorated by lamb chop sideburns, and red hair that was parted in the middle like the hair of a woman. Holding his hat in his hand and a large bouquet in the other, he made five or six exaggerated waves, saying:

"Ladies and gentlemen, your very humble servant, *héhé*... Mademoiselle Pulchérie, will you do me the honor of accepting this bouquet?

"Magnificent flowers!" cried Mademoiselle Pulchérie. "You are really too nice. Oh! How charming."

And Mademoiselle Pulchérie smiled, if the unsightly distance that linked the opposing ends of her mouth could be called a smile. A silver vase was brought to her upon her request. She placed it in front of her, put the bouquet in it, and raved about its beauty and Monsieur Héhé's good taste.

Saint-Ybars stood and said to the newcomer in pointing out Pélasge:

"Monsieur MacNara, allow me to present to you Monsieur Antony Pélasge, your successor in the education of my youngest son."

"Ah! This gentleman is my replacement," MacNara said, putting his glasses on his nose and approaching Pélasge. "I am delighted to meet you, Monsieur, delighted, *héhé*. I don't doubt that you'll extract more from this unproductive land—*ager jejunus*[2]—that is entrusted to you. You see, Monsieur, much to my dismay, I confess that I don't have the patience that certain students require. I need children with swift comprehension. These children make incredible progress with me, evident in Saint-Ybars' other two sons whom I educated. Although one is only fifteen years old and the other is thirteen-and-a-half, they can translate Thucydides and Tacitus[3] open-book for you whenever you want, *héhé*."

Pélasge, who stood up, bowed respectfully as if to say that he did not have the right to keep Monsieur MacNara from praising himself.

Mademoiselle Pulchérie graciously invited Monsieur MacNara to take the place next to her. Dessert was about to be served. Monsieur MacNara liked sweets, and Mademoiselle Pulchérie knew it.

Monsieur MacNara, or, to use the nickname that the old Saint-Ybars had given him, Monsieur Héhé, was Irish by birth but had been raised in Canada by Jesuits from France. He spoke French out of preference. In addition to his classical studies, he had taken a theology course. After having taught as a professor for three years in a Catholic institution in Baltimore, he decided, due to his fading health and doctors' advice, to pursue a career in the South. For him, the climate could not be more favorable; Pélasge would never have guessed, seeing his thriving countenance, that his lungs had caused him concern several years earlier.

Monsieur Héhé had not had trouble identifying with the ideas and customs of the South. Not only did he find slavery of blacks legitimate, but he also believed that among men of the white race, some of them were born to command, others to obey. Naturally, he considered himself among the privileged born to command. Never in the world was there a happier or prouder man than him on the day when he bought an old slave at the auction block.

Guided and protected by Mademoiselle Pulchérie, Monsieur Héhé had made himself a handsome fortune. Now, comfortable in his wealth, he only accepted students who suited him. He went from plantation to plantation in an elegant carriage that Saint-Ybars had given him as a gift in exchange for giving history and literature lessons. He was talkative and a teller of anecdotes, always having something better to say than the others. Aside from telling stories, he always liked to be witty. Not only did he incessantly make up puns, he memorized all those he came across in the newspapers.

Monsieur Héhé noted that Démon hadn't yet appeared, although it was already dessert.

"Ah! For example," he added in looking sideways at Pélasge, "if my worthy colleague managed to teach punctuality to his student, I would declare him the Phoenix of professors. As for me, I was never able to get him to the table for the beginning of the meal two days in a row."

"Démon comes after the others," Chant d'Oisel said, "because he eats quickly and eats little. When he's finished, he becomes bored at the table."

"All right, Mademoiselle," resumed Monsieur Héhé. "But if your brother had the same eagerness to learn as do children destined to shine one day in the world, he'd stay at the table the whole time to listen to adult conversation. A child always gains a lot listening to an educated man who has mastered his own language. Démon doesn't know how to listen. That's unfortunate, but it's a fact. Isn't that so, Mademoiselle Pulchérie?"

"That is correct," grumbled Mademoiselle Pulchérie, "but what can one do? Monsieur Démon prefers the conversation of slaves. He's always hanging around the kitchen."

"Démon leaves the table," Chant d'Oisel pointed out, "when people talk about things that he doesn't understand. He likes to hear the slaves tell stories because nothing they say escapes him."

"If this dear girl didn't always try to make excuses for her brother," Mademoiselle Pulchérie said bitterly, "it would be quite extraordinary."

"You're right, Chant d'Oisel," Vieumaite fired back. "It's always necessary to defend those not present. I think Démon shows intelligence in listening only to what he understands. He likes the slaves' tales? That's quite natural. Who didn't like to listen to them at his age? Besides, let's make no mistake. These stories contain a subtle and delicate wickedness in addition to their dramatic interest."

Chapter 5

Démon

Vieumaite would have probably said more if it wasn't for the racket that suddenly filled the courtyard. The young slaves let out cries of joy, the dogs barked, and the roosters in the barnyard responded to each other with warning signals.

A small black boy, his eyes wide open, entered the dining room with a crash and said to Saint-Ybars:

"Cé michié Démon. Li trapé deu pap, mal é fumel."[i]

Immediately following the child, Pélasge saw a young man enter whose resemblance to Chant d'Oisel revealed to him that this was her twin. But as much as the sister's face was calm, the brother's face was animated. His eyes sparkled with joy, and his cheeks, blazing from the double effects of success and sun, were covered with dust and dripping with sweat. All of the buttons on his shirt were gone. His vest and his twill pants were torn in several places and stained with mud and grass. His wide-brimmed straw hat lined with green percale was thrown back, letting his curly chestnut hair fall on his forehead. Under his left arm, he held a bird-trap with two compartments: in the upper compartment, a stuffed sparrow was fixed in a combat stance, and in the lower compartment, two prisoners struggled hopelessly, frantic with surprise and anger.

Démon took off his hat, said hello to his father, his mother, and his grandfather, and ran to Chant d'Oisel. He set his cage on the floor,

[i] "It's Monsieur Démon. He caught two sparrows, a male and a female."

quickly wiped his face with his handkerchief, and hugged his sister. Madame Saint-Ybars beckoned him to come to her.

"What a child, my God!" she cried. "Here you are in a fine state. But you must be dying of hunger. To think that you've been gone since eight in the morning! You just refuse to stay inside the house."

"But mother!" the child responded, "I'm not some little girl who just sits inside the house."

"Ah! Yes, there you go with your same old battle cry," Madame Saint-Ybars said. "You don't want in any way to look like a little girl. Go wash up and change your clothes so your father can introduce you to your new teacher."

Démon opened his eyes wide and looked all around the table.

"Madame, by all means," Pelasge said in rising, "Let Monsieur Démon come to me as he is."

Démon, ashamed at the state that he was in, timidly approached him. Pélasge went to meet him and fondly took his hand. The child's face changed suddenly: it became sweet and thoughtful. Pélasge felt the small hand that he held squeeze his. He and Démon looked at each other and smiled. Without speaking, they each understood, in that mysterious language of mutual sympathy: "We'll be friends." This affectionate beginning was not to Monsieur Héhé's liking. He very well wanted to make a malicious remark, but not finding anything sharp enough, he contented himself with leaning back in his chair, assuming the most sarcastic expression possible. Mademoiselle Pulchérie came to his rescue. Good or bad, she always found a response, though often, instead of being witty, she was only rude.

"He," she said, looking at Pélasge, "hopes to do better than his predecessor. Hum! That's what is called having self-confidence. I'd be curious to witness his first lesson."

Pélasge bowed politely, and, in addressing Saint-Ybars, said:

"For the first lesson, if you allow me, Monsieur, I will give my student three days off. Together, we'll tour the plantation, and he'll explain its working to me."

"Start when you think it's suitable, Monsieur," Saint-Ybars responded. "From the moment I entrust you with my son, it's up to you to arrange his schedule."

"I like this first lesson very much," Vieumaite said. "If cousin Pulchérie understood Monsieur Pélasge's intention, she'd see, as I do, that his idea is excellent."

"I know someone who's happy," said Chant d'Oisel, smiling at her brother.

"Anyway," added Saint-Ybars, "Monsieur Pélasge couldn't find a better guide. If anyone can introduce him to the plantation, even down to its smallest nooks and crannies, it's Démon."

"Go get dressed," Madame Saint-Ybars said to Démon, "and come back to eat dinner."

"Yes, Mama, but first I want to show my sparrows to Mamrie."

"Ah! Yes, that's right, Mamrie before anyone," Madame Saint-Ybars retorted, looking at Pélasge. "He'd rather skip dinner than go without showing his prisoners to Mamrie."

Pélasge inquired if someone would tell him about this Mamrie who, for Démon, came before anyone.

Chapter 6

Mamrie

Mamrie was Madame Saint-Ybars' personal slave. She also served as supervisor. During meals, she stood near the kitchen and presided over the consignment of the dishes. She was a perfect example of a Creole Negress. She was born to parents who were themselves born on Saint-Ybars' plantation. Her grandfather and her grandmother, of the Bambara people from Mali,[1] were still living. They claimed to have been a king and a queen in Africa. As proof of their claims, they displayed the tribal tattoo on their faces.

Mamrie had extremely delicate skin of a brilliant black, thick hair soft to the touch, and large, faint eyes filled with goodness. But you couldn't really know her until you had seen her laugh or heard the sound of her voice. She had an infectious joviality. The way she spoke had inflections that reached the heart, revealing an affectionate, easily-moved nature. She was twenty-six years old. By the time she was thirteen, she was already a mother. Her child was four months old when Madame Saint-Ybars delivered Démon and Chant d'Oisel. Eight days after the birth of the twins, Mamrie's child was taken away by tetanus, a disease all too common in the region. She fell into such a profound grief from it that her physical being was weakened. She rapidly declined to such a point that those around her feared for her health.

A chain of unexpected events came to avert the misfortune that threatened Mamrie.

Madame Saint-Ybars had been breastfeeding her newborns for a week when she was stricken with chills followed by acute pain in both breasts. One night, despite all of her courage, she was not able to endure the dreadful torture that she felt every time she wanted to appease the hunger of her children. Mamrie was sleeping in a bedroom next to her mistress. Hearing her moan, she got up, took the twins, and sat down in a rocker to cradle them. She ended up dozing off. Her dozing put her into a posture so angled that the tip of her right breast was in contact with the lips of the little boy. Mamrie dreamt. She saw herself in the garden, sitting at the foot of a tree. Her child was not dead, and she enjoyed this blessed and sweet sensation that only a mother who nurses her child can feel. She felt a joy so profound that she woke up. Imagine her surprise in seeing, in the soft glow of the night light, a small pink mouth strongly attached to her chest! As the little girl started to cry, Mamrie gave her the other breast, which was not refused.

Madame Saint-Ybars was Mamrie's godmother.

The young slave called her mistress and said to her:

"Hé! Nénaine, ga. Vous piti apé tété moin."[i]

"So you still have milk!" inquired Madame Saint-Ybars.

"Fo croi mo gagnin ancor ain ti goutte. Mo réponne yapé tiré for."[ii]

"For sure you have it, Mamrie, because the children are no longer crying."

The satisfied twins fell asleep in the arms of the young slave woman, who herself fell asleep.

Madame Saint-Ybars, suffering from multiple abscesses, had to abandon the idea of breastfeeding her twins. Mamrie replaced her. The slave's milk came back in abundance, and her health and her cheerfulness returned. She became attached to her children. She loved them as if they had been her own. However, it was noticeable from the beginning that she had a preference for the little boy.

[i] "Hey! Nénaine, look. Your little ones are sucking at my breast." [*Nénaine* is a term of endearment.]

[ii] "I got to believe that I still have a few drops left of it. I feel like they are pulling hard."

Mamrie had always been one of the domestics most spoiled by Madame Saint-Ybars, and thus, after Mamrie starting nursing the twins, she was spoiled more than ever. She was an integral part of the family, insomuch that when speaking of the twins, everyone grew accustomed to saying *Mamrie's children.* Madame Saint-Ybars herself even said to her in the morning, "Did your children sleep well last night?"

The young woman's original name was Marie. When the twins began to speak, everyone wanted them to learn to call her *mama Marie;* but both of them, as if in an unspoken agreement, turned *mama Marie* into *Mamrie,* and this name stayed with their wet nurse.

As the twins grew up, Mamrie's preference for Démon increased. Chant d'Oisel was far from being jealous of it; she found it natural. Since she loved her brother more than anything else in the world, she thought it was fair that he held first place in Mamrie's heart.

From the day Mamrie started loving Démon, an extraordinary transformation took place within her. Men became completely irrelevant. Mamrie was pretty, with a good figure and a charming character, and when she was twelve, she had caught the attention of one of those humble residents who were called *petits blancs.*[2] He was an Alsatian, a simple, hard-working, independent, and thrifty man, gifted with a strong character and sure to make an honest fortune. He had not made a secret of his affection for Mamrie. As he was good and very gentle, she had responded to his affections. When she became a mother, he introduced himself to Saint-Ybars and offered to buy her and her child from him, his intention being to set them free. Mamrie was a first-rate slave, and she had to be expensive. The young white man had expected Saint-Ybars to request a significant amount for her, and he himself set the date on which he would bring the agreed-upon sum. Meanwhile, Démon and Chant d'Oisel were born, and Mamrie's child died. The young white man nevertheless continued with his intention to buy the young slave in order to make her his companion. But Mamrie's ideas had changed. She declared to him that nothing in the world would separate her from her babies, and she would never have another child. The Alsatian used every argument that his mind and heart could come up with to make her rethink her decision, but he did not succeed. During the ten years that passed between the birth of the twins and the arrival of Pélasge on the plantation, other men made advances towards Mamrie. She turned them all down without harshness but without hesitation. She would have felt that she was committing some sort of sacrilege if she were to give to some other person a single bit of the love that she had devoted to the babies she was nursing, especially to this dear little Démon, of whom she was more proud than Madame Saint-Ybars herself. All of her thinking and loving was concentrated exclusively on him. He became her life, the cause of all of her concerns and the object of all of her hopes. During the day, her single pleasure was to see him, to follow his movements, to hear him speak, to caress him, and to spoil him in a thousand ways. In her sleep, if she dreamt, he was always in her dreams. She was more interested in his studies than anyone. She carefully kept, in a wardrobe, his clothes and his linens as they became too small as well as the toys from his early childhood and the first book that he learned to read.

In contact with Madame Saint-Ybars and her daughters, Mamrie's intelligence had developed remarkably. Although she used Creole[3] when addressing her godmother and children, she spoke French very well, and she knew how to read and write. Since her voice had a good pitch and a lovely timbre, Mademoiselle Nogolka in her spare time had taught her to sing to a piano accompaniment. She had a sense of pitch that made her the envy of the young Saint-Ybars ladies. When they had difficulty reproducing some musical phrase from an opera, Mamrie gave them the note with the greatest ease.

On Saint-Ybars' plantation, as within the homes of many other slave owners, a certain carelessness prevailed. Everyone read, in the presence of the slaves, books in which the question of the rights of man often appeared. Left lying around here or there was a volume of Voltaire or Rousseau, a Eugène Sue novel, a poem by Lamartine or Victor Hugo, songs by Béranger, *The Némésis* by Barthélemy, and many other works that would awaken these humans who had lost their liberty through ruthless force, transformed into law.[4]

Mamrie knew as well as anyone what slavery was all about, but she was happy among her masters. This old, honest, and respected Saint-Ybars family considered her one of its own. She was attached to this house where she was born like a bird is attached to its nest in the tree. For her, her godmother was a second mother whom she loved as much as her real mother. Here on this plantation, whose limits were for her the limits of her world, lived the child who meant everything to her. Absorbed in her love for him, she never thought about the vicissitudes of life. She never wondered if a life-changing event like a death in the family might expose her suddenly to the chains of slavery. No, Mamrie thought nothing like that. She gave herself up without reservation, passionately and blindly, to her love for Démon, and she naively trusted the course of life.

If Mamrie knew how to love, she knew how to hate as well. She loathed Mademoiselle Pulchérie and Monsieur Héhé. She fell silent about the old maid because she held the blood of the family, and everything that was Saint-Ybars was sacred to Mamrie. But as for Monsieur Héhé, whom she did not forgive for having a very poor opinion of Démon's intelligence, she pointed out his absurdities with a malice that greatly amused her masters. She often said that there was more intelligence in Démon's pinkie finger that in all of Monsieur Héhé's large body, and that, as there is no animal dumber than the spider removed from its web, there was not a man more idiotic than Monsieur Héhé apart from his Greek and Latin.

Mamrie's affection for Démon had gradually endowed her with a prestige that made her, in a way, sacred in the eyes of all the plantation's personnel. Not only did they respect her as an individual, but they would not have dared to say one impolite word in front of her, any more than in the presence of Saint-Ybars' daughters. Her young mistresses liked to dress her. From their wardrobes, they chose what would suit her the best. They shared their hair ribbons with her, and she could be seen wearing necklaces and earrings that had adorned the necks and ears of Saint-Ybars' daughters.

When Démon broke the rules, Mamrie dealt with the complaints. To be scolded by her was the punishment he feared the most. Never had corporal punishment been inflicted upon Démon because striking him would have been like hitting Mamrie. Besides, one part of Mamrie's nature had stayed in a primitive state: only once had anyone seen her angry, but they had still been frightened by it. The memory of her rage lived in all of their minds, and no one, not even Démon's parents, dared strike him in her presence.

When Démon entered the kitchen with his cage, Mamrie welcomed him as if she had not seen him for a week. After being satiated with the pleasure of caressing him, she said to him, showing him a bench:

"Asteur assite là é conté moin coman to fé pou trapé pap laïé."[i]

Démon did not need to be asked twice. He described his expedition and all of its details. He expressed himself with an animation that delighted Mamrie. Crouched down opposite him, a smile on her lips, she followed all the stages of his story with growing admiration. Her face, mobile and expressive, reflected all that was happening on the face of the little boy, as if he were speaking in front of a mirror.

Démon ended his saga by accompanying his words with big gestures that terrified the birds. The male repeated his efforts to escape his prison. His head was covered in blood. Démon pushed him inside, saying with impatience:

"Resté don tranquil, bête!"[ii]

"To bon toi," Mamrie said to him. "To oté li so laliberté é to oulé li contan. Mo sré voudré oua ça to sré di, si yé té mété toi dan ain lacage comme ça."[iii]

"Mété moin dan ain lacage!" Démon exclaimed in a prideful and indignant tone. "Mo sré cacé tou, mo sré sorti é mo sré vengé moin sur moune laïé ki té emprisonnin moin."[iv]

"Ah! ouëtte, tou ça cé bon pou la parol," Mamrie replied. "Si yé té mété toi dan ain bon lacage avé bon baro en fer, to sré pa cacé arien. To sré mété toi en san, épi comme to sré oua ça pa servi ain brin, to sré courbé to laéte é to sré resté tranquil comme pap là va fé dan eune ou deu jou."[v]

---

[i] "Now sit down there and tell me what you did to catch these sparrows."

[ii] "Be quiet, beast!"

[iii] "You're a fine fellow! You took his liberty from him and you want him to be happy. I'd like to see what you would say if someone put you in a cage like that."

[iv] "Put me in a cage! I'd break everything. I'd get out and I'd get my revenge on the people who imprisoned me."

[v] "Ah! Yes, that's easy to say. If someone put you in a good cage with good

"Non!" Démon started again. "Mo sré laissé moin mouri de faim."[i]

"Ça cé ain bel réponse," Mamrie said. "To fier même! To pa ain Saint-Ybars pou arien."[ii]

The miserable sparrow, shattered from fatigue, had collapsed. His chest swelled painfully, and his black eyes sparkled with anger. His mate, taking refuge in a corner, made little mournful cries. After a moment of silence, Démon said:

"Mamrie, ga comme fumel là triste."[iii]

"Cé pa étonnan," responded the good slave woman. "Lapé pensé à so piti! Yé faim. Yapé pélé yé moman. Mé moman va pli vini. Cé lachouette ou kèke serpen ka vini é ka mangé yé."[iv]

Démon became thoughtful. While Mamrie busied herself in the kitchen, he thought about his prisoners. He stood up and left without saying anything. After several minutes, Mamrie saw him return. His bird-trap was empty.

"Eben!" she said surprisingly. "Coté to zozos?"[v]

A deceitful shame prevented Démon from saying what became of them. He responded in an uncomforting voice:

"Yé chapé."[vi]

"Yé chapé?" Mamrie resumed in shaking her head. "To menti! Mo parié to rende yé la liberté."[vii]

"Eben! Cé vrai," Démon confessed. "Cé vou faute. Ça vou di moin su fumel là é so piti té fé moin la peine."[viii]

---

iron bars, you'd break nothing. You'd spill your own blood, and then you'd see it was no use and you'd bow down your head and you'd stay calm like this sparrow here will do in a day or two."

[i] "No! I'd let myself die of hunger."

[ii] "That's a good answer. You're pride personified! You aren't a Saint-Ybars for nothing!"

[iii] "Mamrie, look at how sad the female is."

[iv] "That's not surprising. She's thinking about her babies! They're hungry. They're calling their mama. But their mama's not going to come anymore. An owl or snake will come instead and will eat them."

[v] "Well! Where're your birds?"

[vi] "They got away."

[vii] "They got away? You're lying! I bet that you set them free."

[viii] "Ok! It's true. It's your fault. What you told me about the female bird and

Mamrie's eyes filled with tears. She reached out to Démon, smiled broadly at him, and said:

"Vini icite, céléra! Vini mo mangé toi tou cru."[i]

She devoured him with caresses, and turning towards the cook and several cleaning ladies, said:

"Ça cé mo tresor. Ça cé kichoge ki vo plice pacé tou dilor dan moune."[ii]

"Vou rézon, Mamrie," the cook remarked. "Can michié Démon va gran, la fé ain bon maite pou nouzotte."[iii]

"Cé bon tou ça," Mamrie said to Démon, "mé to faim, vini mangé."[iv]

She made him dinner but he ate little. His sacrifice had cost him a tremendous effort, and he was still feeling a little sad. After he had finished, Mamrie made him go up to his room. She helped him bathe, and when she had given his hair one last brush stroke, she said admiringly:

"Asteur to propre é bel comme ain rayon soleil. Couri en bas coté to nouvo maite d'école."[v]

Dessert was coming to an end when Démon entered the dining room. Saint-Ybars, not wanting to scold him at the start of his relationship with his new tutor, ordered a servant to serve him his dinner.

"There's no need," Démon said. "Mamrie fed me."

A servant offered him dessert. He refused and went to sit next to Pélasge, which surprised everyone present, because, as Chant d'Oisel had observed, he normally left the table once his hunger was satisfied. Mademoiselle Pulchérie looked down her nose at him. Monsieur Héhé blushed.

During the silence and calm, a pensive, melancholy expression that took over Démon's face caught Pélasge's attention. He wondered

her babies upset me."

i "Come here, you naughty boy! Come here so I can eat you up!"

ii "He's my precious. He's worth more than all of the gold in the world."

iii "You're right, Mamrie. When Monsieur Démon grows up, he'll make a good master for all of us."

iv "All of that's good, but you're hungry. Come eat."

v "Now you are clean and as handsome as a ray of sunshine. Go downstairs where your new schoolmaster is."

if it was a simple change of mood or an indication of an aching soul. He knew from experience that a thirteen-year-old boy could already harbor real grief. He would discover, after several weeks staying on the plantation, the cause of the sad expression that showed on his student's face:

Saint-Ybars had stopped loving his wife. She had realized it long before. She had never criticized him for it, and she had not complained to anyone. As always, with Saint-Ybars, everything ended passionately. His conjugal indifference had quickly become antipathy on his part. Then, his antipathy became repulsion, which he showed with bitter words or deprecations that made Madame Saint-Ybars look ridiculous and lessened the respect that the servants had for her. Sometimes, under the vainest pretext, Saint-Ybars' anger towards his miserable wife exploded with a suddenness that was like the crash of a thunderbolt. Then, everyone trembled around him. No one dared make the slightest remark to him. Even Vieumaite himself refrained from intervening. Judging his son's bad temper an irreparable malady, he had come to terms with it. As soon as he suspected an approaching storm, he moved away and went to find peace among his books.

Of all of Madame Saint-Ybars' children, Démon was the one who loved his mother the most, though maybe he loved Mamrie more. Saint-Ybars' behavior towards his wife was, for the child, a source of hidden pain and the cause of thoughts too complicated for his age. When he saw a male slave, emboldened by the model of his father, lack respect for his mother, he felt like stabbing him. But he was ashamed of his father. He pretended not to see these acts of cruelty. He swallowed his pain alone; he even kept it from Mamrie.

Only Pélasge would guess the secret that prevented Démon's young soul from developing a happy and healthy temperament. On the very first day Pélasge noticed his student's melancholy expression at the end of the meal.

Chapter 7

Man Sophie and Her Two Small Daughters

The dinner guests rose from the table to have their coffee and their excellent Havana cigars on the second-floor balcony, where they could enjoy a fresh breeze from the river.

Pélasge did not like to rest after eating. He suggested to Démon that they go for a walk together.

After having visited the garden, whose size and beauty reminded the young professor of dazzling villas in Italy, they headed towards the savannah. The dying glow of the sunset turned the countryside crimson. The sugar cane, already knee-high, trembled in the increasing wind and reflected the dying light of day. The slaves were returning from work, some of them on foot and in groups, others in carts pulled by four mules. They were happy: the week was finished, and they enjoyed imagining the pleasures of Sunday. The women's singing and the men's roars of laughter gently came across the distance to the ears of Pélasge and Démon. They were just entering a path that crossed a field of sugar cane when a human form blurred into the red background of the horizon. As the advancing form expanded and was more clearly outlined in the dying light, Pélasge soon recognized that it was a female slave who seemed to be carrying two small children clutched to each side of her chest. When he and Démon were not more than twenty steps from the woman, she stopped. Her face expressed concern. Pélasge was then able to distinguish the objects that she carried in her arms: they were two large dolls.

"It is Man Sophie," Démon said. "She is crazy, Monsieur, but not malicious. She believes that those dolls are her daughters. She gave each one a name."

Addressing the woman, Démon raised his voice and said:

"Man Sophie, pa peur. Michié là pa lé fé vou di mal."[i]

The Negress confidently approached.

"Get her to talk a little," Pélasge said, "so I can get to know her."

"Yes, Monsieur," Démon responded. Looking at the mad woman, he asked:

"Man Sophie, vou piti filles bien!"[ii]

"Merci bon dgié, michié Démon," the Negress responded. "Jordi yé bien, mé lote lanouitte yé té empéché moin droumi. Emma té toucé tou plin, é Caroline té gagnin colic ki té fé li soufri martir."[iii]

"Coté vapé couri comme ça, Man Sophie?"[iv]

"Mapé couri coté vieu madame é coté vou seurs. Mo besoin zétoffe neuve pou abillé mo piti filles. Fo oucitte mo maitresses donne moin ruban, cofair mo oulé fé Emma é Caroline bel tou plin dimin, sitan bel tou moune a admiré yé. Dimin, vou connin, cé ain gran jou, cé jou niversaire vou nessance é kenne mamzel Chant-d'Oisel. Fo mo fé vou honair, à vou é à vou jumel."[v]

"Anon. Bon voyage, man Sophie. Bonne santé pou vou é vou piti."[vi]

"Merci, michié Démon. Bon dgié béni vou."[vii]

---

[i] "Man Sophie, don't be scared. This gentleman isn't going to hurt you."

[ii] "Your daughters are doing well?"

[iii] "Thank you. God is good, Monsieur Démon. Today they're well, but last night they kept me from sleeping; Emma coughed a lot, and Caroline had stomach pains that made her suffer in agony."

[iv] "So where are you going, Man Sophie?"

[v] "I'm going to see the old mistress and your sisters. I need new fabric to dress my little daughters. I also need my mistresses to give me some ribbon so I can make Emma and Caroline all beautiful for tomorrow, so beautiful that everyone will admire them. Tomorrow, you know, is a big day. It's your birthday as well as Chant d'Oisel's. I've got to honor you and your twin."

[vi] "We're going. Have a nice trip, Man Sophie. You and your children take care."

[vii] "Thank you, Monsieur Démon. May God bless you."

The mad woman left cradling her dolls and singing the old romance of Saint-Domingue:

Lisett' to kité la plaine,
Mo perdi bonhair à moué;
Ziés à moué semblé fontaine,
Dépi mo pa miré toué.
Jour là can mo coupé canne.
Mo chongé zamour à moué;
Lanouitt' can mo dan cabane,
Dan droumi mo tchombo toué."[1]

Démon translated his conversation with Sophie for Pélasge as well as the verse she sang. There was a silence. Pélasge mused in silence.

"This woman," he said to himself, "lives wholly awake in a dream. Sometimes she's happy in this dream; sometimes she suffers. And all of us who possess the ability to reason, don't we also live in a dream? When man, at the end of his days, looks back at his past, what becomes of his desires, his loves, his hopes, his despair, his ambitions, his hatred? Everything fades like the fleeting images that live in dreams. Oh! Yes, truly, life is a dream. Let's not give it any more importance than it deserves."

Chapter 8

The Camp

It was night when Pélasge and his young guide arrived at the camp. It was one of those beautiful clear and mild nights when the Louisiana sky rivaled the splendor of the Egyptian heavens. The starry sky opened up like a great book written in silver, crimson, topaz, and sapphire-colored letters. Taking advantage of it, Pélasge gave his student an idea of the divisions of the sky and its movements. He taught him to recognize several major constellations.

The slaves had lit fires in front of their huts to cook their supper and drive away the mosquitoes. Pélasge and Démon followed this long line of fluttering and crackling flames. Slave boys, dressed in nightshirts, amused themselves by jumping over these fires. Everyone respectfully greeted the two visitors. Démon, proud of his new mentor, introduced him to the slaves by calling each head of the family by his name. Many of them addressed the teacher and the pupil with clever compliments.

Arriving at the end of the camp, the two friends caught sight of a small fire distant from the others. They heard sounds from a musical instrument that Pélasge did not recognize.

"That's old man Ima," Démon said, "who's playing the *banza*[1] in front of his hut."

"Who is he?" Pélasge asked.

"He's an old slave from Africa," Démon responded, "the first one my grandfather bought. He doesn't work anymore, and that's been the case for a long time. He has his share of food like the others and a hut for him alone. During the day, he makes big brooms out of palm tree leaves, like you might have seen at the market in New Orleans. He sells them to the steamboats that come down the river and keeps the money for himself. He has a garden and a poultry-yard, he's fattening a pig, and he harvests his own tobacco. During the evening, he plays his instrument, and he sings as he gazes into the sky. He spends almost the entire night doing this. He knows the stars very well, so well that he can tell what time it is just by looking at them."

"What is a *banza*?"

"It's a kind of guitar with four strings. Pa Ima makes his himself. He takes a large gourd and cleans it out. On top of it, he stretches snakeskin: that is his soundboard. He makes his handle out of cypress wood because it is a very close-grained wood which resists warping. He makes his strings out of horsehairs. He has a very good ear: he remembers all the tunes that he hears. He comes to the house from time to time, and Mademoiselle Nogolka and Chant d'Oisel play the piano and sing for him. Standing upright and leaning on a tall wooden stick, he listens, and you can tell that he is happy. Returning to his hut, he replays what he heard on his *banza*. He combines all of that, in his head, with motifs and variations of his making. When he plays, he really goes! He's like a man in a dream who gets lost in music."

Pélasge, surprised and pleased by the boy's speech, warmly patted Démon on the shoulder and said:

"My young friend, what you know, you know well, and you explain it perfectly. I'm sure that you'll make progress with me."

They approached. The old slave, his eyes raised towards the stars, his aged but still-flexible fingers fluttering about the strings of his *banza*, was immersed in the beatitudes of his musical rapture.

"He doesn't see us," Pélasge said. "Let's not disturb him. Another time, during the day, we'll come back. We'll get him to talk, and you'll serve as an interpreter for me."

They went back down the pathway to the house, talking the whole way. While passing through the camp again, Pélasge noticed several men who were cleaning rifles and pistols. Since he seemed surprised to see firearms in the hands of slaves, Démon explained to him that they had borrowed them from their masters.

"In the early morning," he added, "they'll begin firing to celebrate my birthday and Chant d'Oisel's. You'll be awakened by a real racket. You'll see!"

The day had been very busy for Pélasge. He had seen a lot, heard a lot, and learned a lot in a few hours. Back in his bedroom and finding himself alone, he mulled over the people and the things that had attracted his attention the most.

"In short," he said as he was about to fall asleep, "here I am taking a new road in my life. How long will I be here? Six years? Ten? Fifteen? What a silly and futile question! The future keeps its secrets, and it is crazy to want to put time into ordered sections. Life is like a journey of exploration where every first step leads to the unknown. Let it go! Sweet sleep, my best friend, come: bury my fears and hopes in oblivion. Fear? Hope? They are capricious shadows; one is as uncertain as the other. The famous quote by Francois I[2] about women can be applied to both: 'Crazy is he who trusts her.'"

On this last thought, he fell into a profound sleep.

Chapter 9

Man Miramis and Monsieur Salvador

The night passed peacefully. Its silence was interrupted only two or three times by the purring of steamboats travelling up or down the river. Pélasge, already accustomed to the noise of these powerful machines, slept without interruption. When he opened his eyes, the gunshots that Démon had told him about resounded as if the plantation were being invaded by assailants. But he was more interested in a human voice, hoarse and rumbling, that came from the courtyard. It gave orders in an angry, menacing tone. Each time the voice thundered, the increased shuffling of a broom could be heard.

When Pélasge exited his bedroom, his student was waiting for him in the hallway.

"Come on," Démon said. "Mamrie will give us a cup of coffee with water, and if you want, we will go visit the Indians' quarters while we wait for lunch."

"With great pleasure," Pélasge responded, "but first, tell me who is that old woman who's giving orders so loudly?"

"That is Man Sémiramis," Démon responded. "She's the one who trains the young slaves. She doesn't play around, I guarantee you! The Negresses are afraid of her like the devil. She makes them start the day by sweeping the courtyard and the corridors downstairs. The domestics young and old obey her instantly, like soldiers obey their captain. They call her Man Miramis for short. She is almost as old as my grandfather. When my father's away, she runs the house.

She doesn't know how to read or write. To count, she uses kernels of corn that she always carries with her in a small sack. She spreads them out on a table, and after having added or subtracted, according to the occasion, she tells the domestic who does the shopping, 'You must bring me back *this* much change.' You have to be really clever to cheat her out of money. She's been free since her youth, but she never thought of leaving our family. She's looked after all of my grandfather's and father's children, except for Chant d'Oisel and me."

"From what you say," Pelasge remarked, "this Sémiramis must be an important person."

"She's very smart," Démon continued. "She gives good advice in hard times. She's loud, as you see. All the same, everyone here respects her tremendously. Only my grandfather's allowed to joke with her. He said to her one day, 'Miramis, you were born to command, but you missed your destiny. You should've been born in Saint-Domingue. Toussaint Louverture[1] would've taken you for his wife.' She told him, 'You're joking. But if I'd been his wife, I promise you the whites would never have taken him prisoner.'"

Vieumaite's words, said in a joking tone and now quoted by his grandson in the same manner, had a foundation of truth. Miramis was born to command, if there is such a thing as people born to command others. She certainly had all of the instincts of those who rise to absolute power. She divided humanity into two parts, the one consisting of a herd doomed by nature to obedience and servitude, the other forming a small group gifted with superior minds and purposely set up to lead the herd. Obviously, Monsieur Héhé held the same belief, only Miramis did not share the high opinion that Monsieur Héhé had of himself. He allocated himself a place among the masters, and she classified him as part of the herd.

While making their way through the courtyard, Démon told Pélasge that he must not forget to wish Miramis a good day. The first thing that anyone approaching her saw was her large nostrils. She held her head haughtily, her face turned towards the sky as if she belonged to a divine race. Her hair was wrapped in a red and yellow madras[2] that she wore like a crown. By way of scepter, she brandished a cudgel, that terrible club made of twisted cow skin, painted and varnished, sold by the barrel to retailers in the South by Northern philanthropists.

According to reputation, Miramis had not been bad-looking in her youth, despite her large nostrils. Now, with her gauntness and her wrinkles, she could pass for the queen of witches. In spite of her old age, she had a stunning vivacity. Her eyes were open and bright like those of an owl. She responded politely but laconically to Pélasge's greeting. She looked him up and down. Sure of the judgment she formed of him from first glance, she nodded her head approvingly and said to Démon:

"Well done! That's the school teacher you need and not that pompous, dried-up Monsieur Héhé. If you don't advance in your studies with this gentleman, you don't have any excuse."

And turning herself towards Pélasge, she added:

"Take good care of this child, Monsieur. You'll make something distinguished of him. There's never been anyone stupid in the Saint-Ybars family."

She briskly made an about-face to the right, and shouting at two young black girls who looked at Pélasge furtively, she bellowed:

"Hé là-bas! Ça vapé gardé comme ça? Cé vou louvrage ki fo gardé, ou sinon baleine cila a di kichoge à vou do, oui!"[i]

Miramis had only one child. She was already free when her son came into the world. As she liked grandiloquent names, she had given him the name Salvador. He was a strong, handsome man, this Salvador. He was a little older than Saint-Ybars. Although his complexion was that of a mulatto, he had the physical characteristics of a white man, and by one of those curious effects that result from the mixing of various bloods, he had silky hair and a smooth beard. Who was his father? Miramis had never told anyone, but people had always gossiped that he very much resembled the old Saint-Ybars, as seen from his good side, the *side of the sun*. What is certain is that Vieumaite had spoiled Salvador a lot during his childhood and had taken special care of his education. Salvador was the master carpenter of the plantation. When people talked to him, they called him *Monsieur*. He

[i] "Hey, over there! What are you looking at? It's your work that you should be looking at, or else my *baleine*[3] will say something on your back, yes it will!"

was an excellent man, peaceful and obliging. Gifted with Herculean strength, he was inclined by his natural good will to protect the weak. More than once, he had put himself between his mother and the slave whom she wanted to punish. He loved children, and he devoted his spare time to making them toys. No one treated animals with more gentleness than him.

Although Salvador thought very differently from his mother concerning the relations between masters and slaves, he had a great love and the deepest respect for her.

Saint-Ybars and Salvador had a complex relationship. In front of others, each man accepted the position that social conventions assigned to him. In privacy, they talked to each other with an affectionate familiarity. Salvador knew who his father was, and Saint-Ybars knew it as well. But both being discreet, they loved each other like brothers, without ever saying that they were so. Salvador had one of those affections for Saint-Ybars that would endure any sacrifice. He had always been the confidant of his brother's sorrows, and Salvador appreciated more than anyone the good at the bottom of his brother's imperious and stormy nature. Wise and always his own master, he sincerely pitied Saint-Ybars when he saw him in the grips of some passion that made him unhappy. He suffered over it and did everything he could to reestablish calm in this angry soul.

Miramis liked the Saint-Ybars family more out of pride than affection, almost like a duchess who is attached to her title. Her passion for commanding had stifled the emotional capabilities within her. She loved only one being in the world, and that was Salvador. But to be fair to her, she had for him the kind of affection that could only be recognized in the most devoted mothers.

Chapter 10

The Indians – The Old Sachem

After having drunk Mamrie's excellent coffee, Pélasge and his student set off for the Indian camp. Looking at the sunset from the balcony after dinner the day before, Pelasge had noticed a mass of dark greenery that stood out from afar against the immense sheet of sugarcane, similar to an island in the middle of a lake. Démon had explained to him what this hill was, and they decided that they would go see it.

The land that Saint-Ybars' paternal grandfather, who emigrated from Canada to Louisiana, had bought in 1749 was then only a barren piece of land whose center was occupied by a grove of ancient live oaks. The remaining members of a local tribe had had their meetings under the branches of these venerable trees. The newcomer was a man with a generous heart. He respected the Indians, who saw him as a trustworthy friend, and so they did not move away. The eldest son of the white man, having become the master of the plantation upon the death of his father, imitated his father's conduct towards the natives. Saint-Ybars, in turn, treated the descendants of the tribe hospitably. But as the white race and the black race grew in number around this expanse of oaks, the number of natives had diminished. When Saint-Ybars' grandfather arrived, there were eighty warriors; currently, the tribe consisted of fifteen individuals, one of whom was at the end of his life.

When Saint-Ybars' grandfather had come to speak with the chief or sachem of the tribe in order to offer his friendship, they had welcomed him in the shade of the oak that stood in the middle of the grove. When this took place, the tree was already gigantic. In its grandeur, it resembled a patriarch surrounded by his sons and grandsons. As long as one could remember, it had served as a meeting place for different tribes to discuss matters of war or peace. It was known as *le sachem de la plaine*.[1] The whites who settled in Louisiana became accustomed to simply calling it the *sachem,* and from the turn of the century, when anyone said this word on the Saint-Ybars plantation, it was understood that he was not only referencing the chief of the natives but the huge ancient tree as well.

When Démon and Pélasge approached, the men of the tribe, seated in a circle at the edge of the grove, were having their morning meal. It consisted simply of gumbo. Each one, in turn, plunged a wooden spoon into the pot that held the nourishing soup, raised it to his mouth, and then passed it to his neighbor.

The women, seated away from the men, were waiting until the men had finished. Among them was a mixed-race woman. She had a white complexion that was slowly turning greenish, bulging cheekbones, and a strongly-shaped jaw. Her eyes and her hair, with their light shade, resembled someone of European ancestry. Devoured by fever, she coughed almost constantly. It was easy to see that she did not have long to live.

When the Indians saw Démon and his friend arrive, they did not utter a word. Pélasge noticed the dazed, bored look on the men's faces and the sad, gentle look of the women. Thinking that he saw there, in their eyes, the last remnants of the land's natural owners, he was filled with pity. There was not the slightest doubt of their imminent extinction: of the fifteen individuals who made up the tribe, there was only one child.

"How do they provide for their sustenance?" he asked Démon.

"The women," Démon responded, "go to the plantations to sell sassafras to make gumbo, plantain leaves to scent laundry, palm tree roots as a polish, and small baskets that they braid themselves. They do all the hard work. The men do nothing. Whiskey is killing them."

"What are those mounds of earth over there, under that half-dead oak tree?" the young professor asked.

"That's the Indian cemetery," his student responded.

Pélasge counted the graves. There were twenty-five of them.

"There are more dead than living," he murmured.

Pélasge had stopped. He thought about the human races that had disappeared one after the other and whose remains had been discovered in different layers of dirt. He spoke about it to his student, and Démon listened with the greatest eagerness.

"Do you want to continue our walk?" Pélasge asked.

"Yes, Monsieur. Let's go see the sachem."

Vieumaite had uprooted all the smaller trees that hindered the sachem's growth or prevented the air from circulating freely between its branches. With a plow pulled by his four most handsome horses, he himself had drawn a line isolating the large majestic tree. From then on it acquired a sacred nature. Its peaceful shadow sheltered a tomb that had recently received the remains of Vieumaite's parents. A row of beautiful cypress trees native to Provence had been planted in the circular hollow. They had grown vigorously and had not taken long to establish an impassable barrier against animals. A gate formed an entrance on the west side of the nearly-black oak. An old retired slave was assigned to guard this holy place, and the key to the gate was entrusted to him. Once a week, he removed the dried branches and dead leaves that fell from the sachem. He lived in a small hut that could be seen from the clearing shaded by banana trees and orange trees.

The sachem's upper roots, bulging and winding, snaked along the ground like two enormous tentacles. The trunk stood like a tower. From a height of forty yards, five branches radiated from the trunk, each one larger than the trunk of an ordinary oak tree. As they grew, each one bent under its own weight and extended far to brush the ground with its tips. The other branches arose more or less at an angle, subdivided into branches and twigs, giving the impression of a colossal dome.

The sachem's old caretaker, hearing a call and recognizing the voice of his young master, left his hut and came to open the gate.

The men had to push aside the foliage in order to reach the arch of the old sachem. The weak light that penetrated the vast rotunda formed by the tree's canopy was pale and soft like the light of the moon when its roundness is veiled by autumn fogs. Since the air outside was calm, not one leaf swayed; there was not the slightest rustle in the branches. Tufts of Spanish moss hung here and there like long veils of mourning; their gloomy stillness increased the melancholy of the solitude and intensified the silence.

A severe and solemn sadness suddenly came over Pélasge. His vigorous mind ordinarily rejected all superstitious fright, but suddenly he seemed to see in this lonely place a connection to unfortunate events in his own future, and he experienced an anticipatory, irrefutable pang of sorrow. He slowly moved forward, walking with the lightest steps as if he were afraid of disturbing the silence that reigned around him. The tomb of white marble in which Vieumaite's mother and father rested rose in the shadow of the sprawling branches towards the east. The façade of the tomb was facing Pélasge as he approached. He respectfully removed his hat and stopped several steps from the sepulcher. His dark premonition no longer troubled him. His usual serenity returned as he cast an eye over all the surroundings and said in a soft voice:

"How quiet! It's as if I've been transported beyond worldly limits to a place where movement and noise no longer exist."

"Don't you like the peace and quiet?" Démon asked.

"I like it very much," responded Pélasge.

"I wondered," continued Démon, "because there are people who don't like it. My father and my brothers don't like to come here, especially my father. He says that the stillness and silence are too much like emptiness and nothingness. Oh well! As for me, Monsieur, I like coming here. I'd only ask one thing of those who live longer than me, and that is that when I die, they lay my body in the earth shaded by the old sachem."

These words from the mouth of a young man, who on this very day ended his thirteenth year, shocked Pélasge. After a moment of thought, he asked:

"What you just told me, would you have said it to Monsieur Héhé as well?"

"Oh! Never," the child replied sharply. "Not to him, not to anybody."

"Then you trust me, my young friend?"

"Yes, Monsieur, totally."

"You're right," Pélasge said, affectionately placing his hands on Demon's shoulder. "I have a feeling that we'll be good friends."

The distant sounds of a bell barely reached them in the stillness beneath the sachem.

"It's time to go back," Démon said. "Did you hear the first chime of the bell for lunch?"

"Yes, let's go."

They went past the Indian camp again. The women were in their huts made of branches and foliage. They were sewing. The men, intoxicated from whiskey and tobacco, were lying on the grass, their faces exposed to the sun and covered with flies.

Chapter 11

Monsieur le Duc de Lauzun[1]

At dinner, Pélasge became acquainted with someone new. A young quadroon, meticulously dressed and with a hairstyle like Monsieur Héhé's, served Saint-Ybars and only him. He had a casual, insolent manner. It had been said that he served the master of the house through sheer smugness. Since his childhood, he had shown such a shameless character that Vieumaite had nicknamed him Monsieur le Duc de Lauzun. This name stayed with him, and he was proud of it. Since he bore the name of the famous courtier, he believed himself to be equally important. During Monsieur le Duc de Lauzun's childhood, Saint-Ybars had spoiled him just as much as his own sons, and now, the master still had a forbearance for him that Mademoiselle Pulchérie described as "deplorable." Although a slave, Monsieur le Duc de Lauzun had his own bedroom, a small library, and a rifle. Astonishingly, he had a slave, or at least a servant—a young man named Windsor whose brutish appearance hid the mind of a courtier and who declared himself to be Monsieur Duc de Lauzun's valet. Windsor followed Lauzun's every step and benefitted from the favors that the master of the house bestowed upon the Duc.

The privileges that Monsieur de Lauzun enjoyed resulted from the fact that he (as is commonly said in Louisiana) owed his existence to Saint-Ybars' eldest son, which in plain language meant that this insolent rascal was the offspring of a slave and the eldest son of the family.

Pélasge's first impression of Monsieur le Duc de Lauzun was not flattering to his Excellency. Pélasge saw something deceitful and cruel in his eyes.

Saint-Ybars

Part II

Chapter 12

A Simple Change in Method

In the sixteen months that had passed since the young professor Antony Pélasge settled into the Saint-Ybars plantation, Démon had made surprising progress. His desire to learn had become a passion within him: all he thought about was his books. Everywhere he went, he mentally repeated everything he learned for fear of forgetting it. Sometimes, extreme measures were necessary to moderate his newfound obsession; if too overtaxed, his mental activity might ultimately be harmful to his health.

Except for Vieumaite, Chant d'Oisel, and Mamrie, everyone on the plantation was surprised to see this change in Démon. As for Monsieur Héhé, he was stunned.

However, Pélasge used fairly simple means to obtain these results. In the mornings, he had his student work on projects that required manual labor. At Pélasge's request, Saint-Ybars provided him with a small piece of land that was a short distance away from Vieumaite's hermitage. Every day, Pélasge went there with Démon. A squad of small slave boys walked behind them, some of them carrying carpentry tools, the others gardening tools. Pélasge, with a hammer or a spade in his hand, set a good example. These little workers established a farm that was given the name of *Bonnejoie*.[1] From it, they sold products to the steamboats.

By applying the principles of arithmetic and geometry to the building of the farm and the farming process itself under the direction of his tutor, Démon became an arithmetician and a geometrician without experiencing those tortures of the mind that theoretical instruction inflicts upon its victims. He learned to appreciate the material benefits of work by seeing his profit being used to support him and the small slaves who helped him.

After a good meal and a walk, sometimes on foot and sometimes on horseback, class started. Démon, having spent his excess energy on the useful work of the farm, was now calm and enjoyed a powerful sense of physical well-being. He plunged with delight into his beloved studies. Chant d'Oisel was there, facing him, happy with his progress and proud to see him charge ahead of her.

Everyone admired the young professor, but no one as much as Mademoiselle Nogolka. Little by little, she confused her admiration with a feeling that she believed to be friendship but was actually much more than that. Consumed by the need to see Pélasge and to hear his voice, whose sound alone made her heart quicken gently, she suffered when he was away. She became worried and was sad. Life to her was oppressive and dreary. One time, she surprised herself by being jealous of Chant d'Oisel, but that discovery was confusing to her. She believed herself to be jealous of friendship, as often seen with people of her gender. Nevertheless, she regretted her impulsive resentment. She, a twenty-six year old woman, wanted what a little girl had—what a child had—because Monsieur Pélasge looked at her with kindness. That was unpardonable! That was being more childish than her student.

But Chant d'Oisel, despite what Mademoiselle Nogolka said of her, was no longer a child. She had entered her fifteenth year, and fifteen years for a precocious nature like hers was like sixteen years for other young ladies. She grew up: the shape of her body already announced her young womanhood. Her tendency to blush quickly revealed that she had a sense of the changes that had happened within her.

Although Nogolka was the victim of her own heart, she listened to the voice of instinct that advised her to carefully hide from all eyes the affection that she felt for Pélasge. She was loved by a man she did not love, someone who loved her with furor, loved with all the fierceness of a criminal passion. That was the cause of the sadness that

Pélasge had noticed on her face the first time that he saw her. If the man who was consumed with love for her, a love she rejected, came to suspect that Pélasge was more fortunate than he, God only knew what would happen! A storm would certainly strike, and it would leave a catastrophe in its wake.

As for Mamrie, she could not control her joy in seeing Démon justify, with so much brilliance, the opinion that she had always had of his intelligence. She composed a lament in Creole to bemoan Monsieur Héhé's defeat, and she sang it to the tune of *Malbrouck s'en va-t-en guerre*[2]. All of the young domestics knew the song by heart, and they never failed, when Mademoiselle Pulchérie's protégé passed by, to fire off a verse toward him.

Lagniape provided more service than anyone could have ever expected for a poor, unfortunate being like her. Little by little, Madame Saint-Ybars, her daughters, and her daughters-in-law became used to looking at the legless cripple without the terror and dreadful pity that they had felt in the beginning. These ladies admitted this in privacy. Because Lagniape spoke easily and wittily, she was a history book for her mistresses, one from which they pulled information about the origins of the notable families of the state, about the ways and gallant adventures of past times, and about the adoption of children born in secrecy. Everyone would heartily laugh when the horrid old woman would reveal the family secrets of certain racial bigots whose own skin had grown whiter from generation to generation.

Chapter 13

Li Mouri[i]

But what had become of Titia, Lagniape's granddaughter? She was no longer seen on the Saint-Ybars plantation. When Saint-Ybars bought her, Stoval, the slave trader, had intimated that she was pregnant. Indeed, she was. When she felt her child move for the first time two months after her arrival on the plantation, she went to find Lagniape and told her while weeping that she was the most miserable of women to think that she would bring a little being fated for slavery into the world.

"My child," the old woman responded, "if you're willing to listen to me and do as I tell you, your child won't be a slave."

Titia wiped her eyes and listened. The events, as they unfold, will reveal the advice that Lagniape gave her.

This is what occurred in June: every day, an Indian woman[1] belonging to the tribe camped in proximity to the sachem would bring a basket of blackberries she gathered in the woods to Saint-Ybars' plantation. These berries, mixed with milk and sugar, were a treat for Chant d'Oisel and her sisters. The squaw who sold them spoke a slang composed of Indian and Creole, and since Lagniape was the person who understood her the best, they frequently spoke. One afternoon when they were alone in the courtyard, while the masters were eating dinner, the Indian said in a low voice:

"Li mouri."

[i] She died.

"Ah! Métisse là mouri," murmured Lagniape.[i]

"Oui," the squaw added, looking at the sun. "Li en ba là."[ii]

"Ouzot enterré li dijà?"[iii]

"Oui."

"Alor ouzot apé parti?"[iv]

"Oui."

"Can?"[v]

The Indian cast a defiant eye all around her. Sure that no one saw her, she raised her eyes towards the mountaintop and said:

"Can lune là."[vi]

"Cé bon."[vii]

Lagniape slipped a small sack filled with picaillons[2] into the Indian's hand.

Not surprisingly, this meeting was the first of many.

The squaw stood up, put the empty basket on her back, and said goodbye in a single word:

"Bonjou."[viii]

"Yes, goodbye," murmured Lagniape, talking to herself. "Goodbye until next spring."

Hardly had the woman walked away when Titia crossed the courtyard. Passing by Lagniape, she let her handkerchief fall and bent down to pick it up.

"It's tonight," Lagniape whispered.

"Ah!"

"Yes, at one in the morning."

"Good!"

Titia stood up straight and continued on her way.

Each year in June, the Indians on Saint-Ybars' plantation migrated, only to come back in the autumn. This time, they had

[i] Ah! The half-breed is dead."

[ii] Yes. She's down below, there."

[iii] "Have you already buried her?"

[iv] "So you're getting ready to leave?"

[v] "When?"

[vi] "When the moon is there."

[vii] "Good."

[viii] "Good day."

delayed their departure several days due to a dying tribe member: a mixed-blooded woman. Once she was dead, they had resolved to leave, taking advantage of the coolness of the night. By sunset, the preparations for voyage were finished; the baskets were filled to the top and well-put together. At midnight, the men were still sleeping. The women, seated in a circle in front of the huts, spoke in low voices. They saw a human form cautiously leave from the sugar cane field and approach, snaking in and out of the grass like a serpent. It was Titia. They led her into a hut, where they took off her clothes and made her put on those of the mixed-blooded woman. The women undid her hair and styled it like that of an Indian woman. When the moment of departure arrived, she was told to take the mixed-blooded woman's basket. The men left the camp first. The women followed them within half the distance of a rifle shot, marching in a row, each one bent by the heavy load held in place by a strap wrapped around her forehead. Titia was placed in the middle. The only child of the tribe was carried by the woman who was last in the line. Astride her mother's neck, it slept, its little head resting on hers. The swaying of the march rocked the baby in its sleep. Its pretty copper-colored face shimmered in the light of the moon.

The caravan headed towards the river without a single word interrupting the silence of the night. Arriving at the path that ran alongside the levee, the group turned to the left and marched side-by-side with *le Père des Eaux*,[3] whose curves they intended to follow all the way to New Orleans. From there, after a short stop, they would go to Lake Pontchartrain to board one of the wooden boats that made the journey to Bonfouca, Louisiana. From the landing on the northeast shore, they had more than a league to walk before they met the friendly tribe of the Choctaws,[4] who waited for them at the Bayou Lacombe.[5]

Chapter 14

The Twentieth and Twenty-First of September

The very next day, a Donaldsonville newspaper announced Titia's disappearance. The notice appeared in a box in the upper corner. Readers saw, on the left, an etching depicting a woman in a running position, carrying on her shoulder a travelling bag at the end of a wooden stick. The description of the fugitive was given in great detail. Fifty dollars was promised to whoever brought her back to the Saint-Ybars plantation.

Two people were sadder than anyone else about Titia's escape but for very different reasons. Chant d'Oisel felt the bitter and disheartening grief that stems from ingratitude. Since she could not appreciate the maternal devotion of her slave, she believed that Titia lacked loyalty. For Monsieur le Duc de Lauzun, the beautiful young woman's actions were a horrible wound inflicted upon his self-esteem. In love with her since the day of her appearance on Saint-Ybars's plantation, he had not stopped pursuing her with his propositions and declarations of love. Believing himself to be the most handsome and the most charming of men for having seduced a few young slave women, he did not doubt his eventual triumph. In his presumptuousness, he had set the day and the hour of his conquest, but now, Titia had disappeared on the very date that he had designated for his victory. What a shock for Monsieur le Duc!

The notice published by the Donaldsonville newspaper was reproduced in the newspapers of the surrounding parishes and even in New Orleans. The trackers responsible for hunting down fugitive slaves found their search had come up cold this time. Titia remained untraceable. They concluded that she had succeeded in reaching some free city in the West or in the North.

Soon, however, people ceased talking about Titia. It was September. The heat that had been less oppressive than usual in the summer threatened to take its revenge in autumn. The temperature had risen steadily since the beginning of the month. On the twentieth of September, it was unbearable. The day was not typical, made up alternatively of a stifling, dead calmness and gusts of wind that rose from the ground in different directions, suddenly spiralling and sweeping up whorls of dust. The people forced to go out in it felt like they were breathing not air but hot ash. Even inside the houses, the heat weighed down upon everyone's chest, and a tickling, burning sensation tormented everyone's skin. Everyone was impatient and irritated.

After sunset, a tinge of dark red metallic brightness pervaded the sky and remained until the evening. Clouds of a blackish-gray, some small, some enormous, all with jagged edges, started to pass by slowly at nightfall, some of them separated from the others by varying intervals like huge strips of cloth ripped up by the wind. They were not very high and were headed towards the northwest.

Around eleven o'clock, the wind stopped blowing, the clouds stopped moving, and the stars sparkled.

Pélasge was spending the evening with Vieumaite. They were in the observatory.

"The sky seems to be clearing," Pélasge said.

"Don't trust this calm," the old man responded. "The heat is still rising, the barometer is very low, and look how the compass is shaking with small, convulsive jerks. Look how the stars in the southeast part of the sky are twinkling more brightly than anywhere else! I always thought, along with a few astronomers, that the flickering of starlight is connected to fluctuations in our atmosphere. If I'm right, the atmosphere over there is being pounded by violent gusts of wind. I believe we'll have a hurricane tonight or tomorrow morning."

At one o'clock in the morning, the weather was still calm and the sky serene. Pélasge was about to return to the house. Vieumaite wanted him to take his shotgun.

"There's no point, but thank you," Pélasge said. "I never go out armed."

"Yes, I noticed that," Vieumaite responded. "You're wrong. It's always good to take precautions. Just between us, I think you're a bit fatalistic."

"That's not it," Pélasge continued, "It's just that I don't have any sense of danger. Believe me, I don't take any pride in this. It's just something I lack, that's all."

"I understand," replied Vieumaite. "Certain people lack specific elements of human nature. Like me, for example, there are several passions, gambling for instance, that I've never cared for in the slightest. It's not the same for my son. All of the passions that could disturb a man seem to gather inside his mind. Fortunately, his education has taught him to control them. Only his anger remains uncontrollable. Come on, listen to my wise advice: take my shotgun so you won't find yourself at the mercy of one of those large bears we sometimes encounter crossing these vast sugarcane fields. The right barrel is loaded with a shell, the left with buckshot."

"Since I'm eager to please you," Pélasge responded, "I cannot refuse any longer."

He took the shotgun.

"Here's some extra precaution," the old man said, presenting him with a few cartridges. "You might miss."

Pélasge smiled at this excess of foresight and left without a definite route in mind. He strolled leisurely, as he was in no hurry. He did not have the slightest urge to sleep. Chance made him pass by the sachem's enclosure. He stopped for an instant to look at the cypresses that rose up, black and motionless in the light of the stars and the imposing dome of the old oak tree. At times, the whole mass grew darker. After a few minutes, it reappeared from its obscurity and seemed to grow larger. This effect was due to the clouds that had once more begun their journey above the savannah. The alternating darkness and light inspired him to approach the gate of the enclosure to see the play of shadow and light under the dome of the tree through the wire netting. He enjoyed the spectacle for a few minutes, his arm resting on the gate, when he realized that the portal gave way under the weight of his body. He pushed it, and it opened without resistance. He thought that the caretaker had forgotten to close it.

"Well," he said to himself, "since I have the chance, let's go see the sachem in *cette obscure clarté qui tombe des étoiles*,[1] as Corneille says, that towering oak of French poetry."

Chapter 15

Under the Sachem

Pélasge had just moved aside the branches to enter the arch of the tree when the night turned pitch-black. Large black clouds covered the entire sky. He moved forward, groping in the dark. Gradually, a faint light reminiscent of the glow of dusk descended from the branches and spread throughout the vast rotunda. Pélasge took advantage of it. He wanted to go around the enclosure, passing behind the tomb. As he approached, he saw the pediment and the columns of the entablature take form. He stooped down to pass under the end of a branch that blocked him from the path. But he stood up right away, as if he had suddenly changed his mind. He silently hid in the leaves so that he could look out without being seen. He had just realized that he was not alone under the old sachem. From what he was able to make out in the shadows, a woman was approaching. He was sure of his guess when the unknown person stopped in front of the tomb. She was dressed in a white gown. Her face vaguely took shape under a white veil that fell on her shoulders and ended just below her waistline. Standing in front of the sepulcher, she seemed as motionless as it was.

Pélasge wondered who this women was and what she was doing in such a place at such a late hour. Why had she come to this mausoleum?

Pélasge listened more carefully. He heard footsteps. The woman turned. Someone was approaching. At that moment, the darkness returned. Pélasge could no longer see anything, but he could hear the conversation between a man and the woman.

The man's voice—"You should be grateful I came."

The woman's voice—"Thank you for that."

The man's voice—"Why here rather than somewhere else?"

The woman's voice—"I want you to promise me something. If you promise it in front of this tomb, you'll respect it."

The man's voice—"That's typical of you. You're like no one else. All right then, speak."

The woman's voice—"Give me your word to no longer bother me. If you can't, let me leave."

The man's voice—"What, no longer speak to you? Take away from me the hope that I'll finally convince you? ...No, never."

The woman's voice—"Well then, Monsieur, accept my resignation."

The man's voice—"And yet you've got the courage to break my heart. I'm so miserable! At my age, I feel for the first time—yes, the first time—the strongest, sweetest passion that fills my soul, and to realize that the person to whom this passion is directed has no pity for me! No, no, you can't be cruel enough to leave me. Remember my last offer? Think about it. Think about your future. Later, whatever happens, if you accept my offer, you'll have a guaranteed position."

The woman's voice—"That's enough, Monsieur! That's too much of an insult. *I* should be telling *you*, 'Think about it. Your honor's at stake." But no, I won't speak to you about that since you said your dignity's an affair that only concerns you. But me, Monsieur, if I accepted your offer—let's call it what it is—I'd be your whore, for money...ah! Monsieur, don't start this again. You're responsible for the worst pain in my life. Just think about it! It'd be lies on top of betrayal. For me, it'd be the worst kind of betrayal towards your wife, who's always been so good to me."

The man's voice—"Don't talk to me about my wife unless you want to infuriate me. She's ruined my life. She's my life's curse because if it wasn't for her, I'd be able to marry you."

The woman's voice—"If you no longer love the mother of your children, at least respect her. As for your daughter, Monsieur, you can't keep me from talking about her. Would you like me to reduce myself—me, her protector, her second mother—to putting on a mask of hypocrisy when I speak to her about the virtues that honor her gender? No, a poison would leak from my eyes, from my voice, from my touch, and it would tarnish her youth."

The man's voice—"Stay, then. Your presence is as necessary to my life as the air I breathe. I agree to no longer speak of my love for you. I'll take an oath on it, but I at least want my sacrifice to have its reward. I want to seal our agreement with a kiss, one that will condemn me to despair."

The woman's voice—"No, never! Let's terminate our contract. Let me leave."

There was a moment of silence. The glimmering light reappeared under the oak tree and revealed objects as through a thick veil. The two people whom Pélasge vaguely caught a glimpse of seemed like ghosts rather than human beings. But there was no need to see them more clearly. The voices he heard were familiar to him. They were the voices of Saint-Ybars and Nogolka.

Saint-Ybars stepped forward. Nogolka moved back.

"No, that's impossible," Saint-Ybars said in a trembling voice. "You can't leave. It'd be the death of me."

"I will leave," Nogolka responded firmly. "If necessary, I'll invoke the protection of the law."

"Well," Saint-Ybars continued, "the kiss I asked for, let me have it as a memory, as a consolation for the little time I have left to live."

"No, Monsieur," Nogolka responded, trembling. "Don't come any further! You're repulsive."

Nogolka could not back up any more. Her back was against the tomb. Saint-Ybars still pushed forward, his eyes blazing. The rest of his features took on the sinister expression of murder.

"Well, woman I love as much as I hate," he said, grinding his teeth, "since you don't want to give me anything, I'll take everything."

He threw himself onto Nogolka like a ferocious beast.

"Monsieur, ah! Monsieur," she cried, struggling, "This is sacrilegious! You're desecrating the tomb of your ancestors. If your father were here, he'd kill you."

Indignation gives strength. Nogolka, her arms bruised and her hair disheveled, managed to free herself. She pushed Saint-Ybars away violently and returned to the tomb. She felt drained. Seeing Saint-Ybars coming at her again, she froze with terror and and felt the shame of her approaching dishonor.. In despair, she slammed her two hands on the marble, shouting like a mad woman:

"Oh sacred dead, come help me!"

Pélasge thought it was time to intervene.

"Noble woman!" he said to himself. "She defended herself well, but she's in dire straits."

He opened his mouth to hurl these two words at Saint-Ybars: "Stop there!" But an unforeseen incident froze the words in his throat.

Nogolka was still hitting the tomb when a strange cry, a kind of high-pitched and sobbing moan, descended from the canopy above the mausoleum.

Several seconds of profound silence followed. Then, the entire area under the sachem changed in rapid succession from darkness to light and from light to darkness. The echoes of distant thunder died, swallowed up by the branches of the old tree.

Nogolka was neither superstitious nor inclined to believe in supernatural events, but never having heard an owl's cry, she did not know to whom she should attribute the voice that responded so adequately to hers. In any case, she saw in it a sign of escape. Her confidence returned: a look of sublime pride replaced the imprint of terror on her face.

The owl's cry was nothing new for Saint-Ybars, but he was superstitious like many people whose passions are stronger than reason. The mournful voice of the nocturnal bird had on him the same effect that the clock has on the condemned when it announces the moment of his execution. His strength abandoned him, and shame and contempt seized him. He thought of his children. Then, changing over abruptly from amazement to despair, he said:

"Since you absolutely want to leave, leave. But know this: five minutes after you leave my house, a gunshot will be heard in my bedroom. Someone will rush up to my room and find a corpse lying on the floor. Goodbye."

"What you say is abominable, Monsieur," Nogolka exclaimed. "It's torture, immoral, barbaric, and cowardly."

Saint-Ybars heard only half of what she said. He was rushing towards the exit.

The night became silent again. The rumbles of thunder in the distance were so muffled that they did not disturb the restored calmness under the sachem. However, the flashes of lightning became more frequent and flooded a large part of the sky. Nogolka, lost in her thoughts, did not hear the thunder or see the lightning. She began to speak aloud, as if she was addressing people present in front of her. "My dear parents," she said, "after spending your small fortune to educate me, you told me, 'Go into the world now. You have everything necessary to earn an honest living,' You were far from suspecting the dangers and the heartaches that you were sending me to face. You thought you did your best, dear father, dear beloved mother. I'm not criticizing you. God bless you."

After uttering these words, she headed towards the gate without even thinking about fixing her hair. Pelasge followed her cautiously. He picked up her veil, torn in the struggle, and put it under his jacket.

Nogolka took the wide path that went across the sugarcane fields. She returned to the house through the back courtyard. The guard dog (his name was Cerberus), having smelled her from afar, went to meet her and happily put his muzzle on her dangling hand to attract her attention. She responded to him with several caresses and went inside.

When Pélasge saw the light in Nogolka's bedroom, he retraced his steps in order to take the path that led to the river. Many tree trunks, removed to make the path, lay on the bank. He sat upon one of them, as close as possible to the water and breathed in the fresh air. In the distance, sparks of lightning wound through a black background. The center of the storm seemed to be moving toward the east. Up until then, it had not threatened to pass over the Saint-Ybars plantation.

Chapter 16

A Mother Gives Up Her Child

Around four o'clock in the morning, Pélasge, tired of thinking, stood up to return to his room and attempt to sleep. He thought that the chapter of surprises and emotions was finished for the rest of the night. Perhaps he was wrong.

He took the path the wagons travelled. This route followed the avenue of oak trees, the gardens, the house, and the courtyards, passed fairly closely behind the camp, and disappeared in the forest of cypresses. A fence ran along each side, almost entirely hidden by honeysuckle and jasmine bushes. Between the path and the fence, there was a ditch on either side. Since it had not rained for a long time, the ditches were dry.

Pelasge approached the house. His intention was to pass through the courtyard of magnolias as Nogolka had done. Before he returned, he wanted to consult the weather one last time. He stopped at the edge of the ditch on the left and looked at the sky. He noticed that the clouds that had raced northward the day before had been coming back towards the south, and that the highest ones were starting to swirl. At this last sign, he determined that a storm was brewing above the plantation. His attention was brought back to the ground by the sound of branches being moved. Was this some dishonest slave looking to steal something? Was it a savage animal? Having doubts, he stepped over the ditch, crouched down behind the fence to hide himself better, and cocked his rifle. A woman peeked out slowly from the foliage. The unknown woman looked and listened. Not seeing anyone or hearing anything, she went down the ditch and crossed the path, bent over like someone carrying an object that she wanted to hide. She made her way through a passage in the opposing hedge and disappeared.

"Obviously," Pelasge thought, "this is a night full of adventure."

He wanted to follow the nocturnal prowler without wasting any time, so he went through the same hedge that she had. But looking around in all directions did no good. He did not see anyone.

"If she goes around the side of the house," he thought, "I'll know because of Cerberus. If she's headed towards the servants' houses or towards the camp, she'll run into me."

While he was walking towards the rear of the courtyard, the strange woman was headed in the opposite direction. She only had a few more steps before she reached the house. She stopped. Two lights appeared in the darkness of the staircase that led from the lower balcony to the top one. They burned brightly like two iron marbles made red hot by a fire. She became fearful and tried to retreat. It was too late. In two leaps, Cerberus descended in front of her, stood straight, put his enormous paws on her chest, and bared his enormous fangs.

At first, the unfortunate woman stood there, petrified. But revived by maternal love (for it was her child that she clenched against her breast), she regained her presence of mind and said in the most natural voice possible:

"Cerberus, come on! Cerberus, what're you doing? Would you bite me, Cerberus, your friend?"

Cerberus growled more softly. The woman felt confident. She gently freed her right hand and patted the head of the terrible dog, still repeating his name. Cerberus quieted all of a sudden. Then, after having smelled the woman's neck, he got back down on four paws. However, the hair on his back was still standing on end. His muzzle approached the knees of the unknown woman several times. Then, his tail started to wag. In order to finish his examination, he passed behind the woman and sniffed her legs. Nothing more was necessary. He recognized her. In his joy, he began to run in big circles, stirring up a cloud of dust. The woman called his name in a low voice, and putting her index finger to her lips, she repeated "Shh!" several times. Cerberus pricked up his ears in a meaningful way. The woman uncovered the face of the sleeping infant.

"You see how beautiful my baby is," she said. "Cerberus, sniff her."

The dog's large nose grazed the cheek, the neck, the hands and the feet of the tiny infant.

"Now, come," the woman added. "Quietly! Quietly!"

The dog imitated the one who spoke to him; he walked stealthily. She climbed the stairs, stopping every two or three steps in order to listen. All was calm. Not one leaf rustled. It looked like the woman glided rather than walked along the balcony upstairs. When she reached the middle door, she took off her cover, folded it in four, put it down on the floor, and put the infant on it. She was shaking all over. She had counted on a dark night, and the flashes of lightning had become so frequent that the balcony was lit almost as if it were day. But having already started, the woman had to follow through. She undid her dress, and leaning on her knees and hands, she approached the closed lips of her infant with her breast, which was full of milk. Then she woke the infant, who opened its eyes, smiled, and took hold of her breast. Satisfied, it fell asleep again. The mother was crying. She was leaving her child, maybe for good.

Cerberus, intrigued, seemed to be asking for an explanation of what he was seeing.

"My dear Cerberus," the unknown woman whispered, "you are surprised to see me leave alone. It's for the good of my baby. Be a good guard! Don't let anyone approach except Chant d'Oisel. Do you hear me, Cerberus? Only Chant d'Oisel. Chant d'Oisel."

Cerberus lay down at the child's feet. The mother went back down the stairs. In less than five minutes, she had disappeared into the sugarcane fields…

When Pélasge returned to his bedroom, his clock was striking five o'clock.

Chapter 17

Blanchette

The day struggled to break through. A thick layer of clouds covered the whole sky. However, a small, bright spot opened up from the east. Saint-Ybars' house was suddenly lit up by the sun. When the infant left on the balcony woke up, the first object that came into her view was a cardinal resting on the handrail of the balcony. The bird was preening its brilliant feathers in the sun. For the child, this was such a beautiful and captivating spectacle that she began to wave around her arms and legs with such abandon that by the time she was done, her garments had gone flying to the left and right. All that was left on her was her undershirt. The bird, not at all frightened by this commotion, began to whistle. Oh! The infant's joy then became true delight. Joining her voice to that of the bird, she offered up her own song.

Mamrie was in Madame Saint-Ybars' bedroom. She was helping her get dressed.

"Nénaine," she said, "cé drol. Vou pa tendé comme ain piti capé babiller?"[i]

"Yes," the mistress responded, "that's definitely the babbling of a small child."

Mamrie left the room. Madame Saint-Ybars heard a cry of surprise.

I "Godmother, that's odd. Don't you hear something that sounds like a baby babbling?"

"Nénaine! Nénaine!" Mamrie shouted. "Vini oua ki joli piti fie."[i]

Madame Saint-Ybars rushed up the stairs. The cardinal flew away. The baby's eyes, wanting to follow him in his flight, instead met the gazes of Madame Saint-Ybars and Mamrie.

"Li tro joli!" exclaimed Mamrie. "Ga comme li gai, comme lapé ri."[ii]

"You're right," Madame Saint-Ybars said. "She's got such a happy look! Look how she's holding out her arms to us. Pick her up."

Up until then, Cerberus had not moved. When he saw Mamrie bend down to pick up the child, he got up and snarled.

"Ki ci ça?" Mamrie said, speaking to Cerberus. "Dabor ki permette toi entré dan la mézon? Cofair tapé grognin? Èceque to oulé empéché moin pranne piti cila?"[iii]

Cerberus growled louder and bared his teeth.

"Mamrie, be careful," Madame Saint-Ybars said. "He's really angry. Let me try."

Madame Saint-Ybars took her turn and bent down, but Cerberus, putting his front paws over the infant, growled louder and rolled his large yellow eyes.

"What's all this about?" Madame Saint-Ybars said. "Mamrie, go tell Monsieur Saint-Ybars."

In a few minutes, Saint-Ybars, his sons, his daughters, his sons-in-law, his daughters-in-law, and several servants were on the balcony. Cerberus walked around the infant in a threatening way. He responded to Saint-Ybars' threats and orders with a furious bark.

Nogolka had woken up later than usual. While leaving her bedroom, she heard Démon call for Chant d'Oisel, telling her to come see something extraordinary. Chant d'Oisel hurried. As soon as Cerberus saw her, he stopped, looked at her then looked at the baby, and whimpered affectionately. Chant d'Oisel picked up the child. Everyone was utterly puzzled by Cerberus' strange behavior. As far as he was concerned, his mission was finished. He calmly walked down the courtyard path.

---

[i] "Godmother, godmother! Come see such a pretty little girl."

[ii] "She's too lovely! Look at how happy she is, how she smiles."

[iii] "What's this? First, who let you come inside the house? Why are you growling? Why don't you want me to pick up the baby?"

Never did a little girl who was given a beautiful doll show more joy than Chant d'Oisel. She smiled at the baby, caressed her cheeks with her tiny hands and pressed her lips to the baby's.

Vieumaite arrived in the middle of the sound and fury that was swirling around the child. Someone explained to him what had caused the racket. At first, he looked at the child with his dreadful, wary side, but in less than a minute, his face turned.

"She is rosy-cheeked!" he said. "She is *blanchette*![i] Yes, Mademoiselle, you are such a pale little thing. I predict that you'll conquer many hearts with your lily-white complexion."

"Grandfather," said Chant d'Oisel, "you found her real name. We'll call her Blanchette."

"Blanchette's fine," Vieumaite responded.

It had been four hours since Mademoiselle Blanchette had been nursed. She suddenly began to make a sad and weepy face. At this moment, one of Saint-Ybars' daughters-in-law was breastfeeding a fat little boy. She gave him to Mamrie and put Blanchette in his place. Blanchette drank her fill. When she finished, she smiled so graciously that several voices said at the same time:

"She's so sweet!"

The young woman who had just given Blanchette her milk looked at her husband and said:

"I feel like adopting her."

"If that's want you want, my beloved, let's adopt her."

"I'll be her godmother," Chant d'Oisel exclaimed, clapping her hands.

"And I her godfather," said Démon.

There was only one person in the house who did not know what was happening, and that was Pélasge. He was sleeping. The lunch bell awakened him. He was at first a bit disoriented seeing himself fully dressed. Sleep had snuck up on him while he was sitting in his chair. Not liking to be late, he hastened to plunge his face into a bowl of fresh water and to fix his hair. He descended the front balcony. At the

[i] Untranslatable. Vieumaite is commenting on the baby's milky-white complexion. "Blanche" means white, and the suffix "-ette" refers to something little and dear, like a baby.

bottom, he met Vieumaite, whom Madame Saint-Ybars had invited for lunch. Unfortunately, important business had called the old man to a plantation some nine miles away, so he excused himself for not being able to stay. His neighbors were waiting for him, and he had given his word. He needed to pack his travel bag since he was to be gone for three days. Madame Saint-Ybars was saddened by his departure. She had noticed that her husband looked more somber and sullen than ever, and she hoped that the presence of his father would stifle his son's bad temper. Raising her eyes to the sky and sighing, she went back inside.

Vieumaite told Pélasge about the morning's events in a few words. In return, Pelasge informed the old gentleman about the woman he had seen on the wagon road.

"I believe I have the key to the mystery," Vieumaite said. "I know that a family of *petits blancs*,[i] six miles from here, took money for giving shelter to a young woman from New Orleans who was compromised by a stranger who ran away. You probably saw her or some woman who works for her. Oh well, what does it matter? Someone gave us a child; we're keeping it. You're going to see she's a charming little girl. Goodbye. I don't have too much time. The weather's still very menacing."

While talking, Vieumaite, with the help of a young slave who always accompanied him, mounted the horse and settled into the saddle.

"I see that you're prepared," Pelasge said, putting his hand on a coat fastened behind the saddle.

"It's very old," Vieumaite responded, "but it's still useful. You wouldn't believe how attached I am to it. We've seen many countries together, endured more than one storm, camped outside in Italy, Spain, Greece, Asia Minor…"

Vieumaite's horse was chomping at the bit. The storm's approach made him nervous.

"Let's go!" Vieumaite said, jabbing his spur into the horse's flank.

The ebullient animal whinnied with joy and took off with the speed of an arrow.

[i] See page 28.

Chapter 18

The Hurricane

By eight o'clock, the sun had completely vanished. The light was dull and gloomy. No birds crisscrossed the sky, and not a single insect shrieked in the grass or trees. In the dismal silence, only the little green frogs called and responded to each other with their reedy voices, happy to feel the storm approaching. The tops of the tallest trees had begun to tremble, and a rain as delicate as steam floated in the air rather than falling.

A second ring of the bell called the family into the dining room. The beginning of the meal was silent. Saint-Ybars thwarted all conversation with his sullen and menacing grimace: he resembled the hurricane that was now advancing rapidly.

Madame Saint-Ybars, worried and uneasy, served the food poorly, and her husband was quick to criticize her clumsiness in bitter and sarcastic terms. Nogolka ate half-heartedly. Monsieur de Lauzun, attentive to Monsieur Saint-Ybars' merest signal, served him with an intensifying, conspicuous gallantry, for as much as Monsieur de Lauzun was impertinent towards Saint-Ybars' wife, he feared his master. As mean as he was cowardly, Monsieur de Lauzun secretly rejoiced at the scene that he saw coming. Lagniape remained near the arched door in the middle, which opened onto the courtyard.

Madame Saint-Ybars, while passing a plateful of *court-bouillon*,[1] dropped a bit on the tablecloth. Her husband made fun of her in a tone that was hard at first, then became progressively rude and even offensive. She turned to leave, but changing her mind, she silently crept back to her seat. Her daughters and daughters-in-law blushed, and the men looked at one another, upset but indecisive. Chant d'Oisel was weeping. Démon choked back his tears.

Madame Saint-Ybars' resignation, instead of calming her husband like she hoped, unleashed his fury. He called her a name so insulting that she hid her face in her hands. All of the guests except Mademoiselle Pulchérie stopped eating. There were several seconds of frightening silence that were only interrupted by consistent *whacks* coming from the courtyard. A slave was chopping wood for the kitchen.

Suddenly Démon, his fists tight, face ablaze, pounded on the table and cried out:

"That's enough! No more! It's unfair."

Everyone looked at each other and then at Saint-Ybars. They all felt the same anxiety.

Saint-Ybars fixed his eyes upon Démon and said to him in an icy tone:

"Enough of what, Monsieur?"

"Stop insulting my mother," the young boy responded.

"Leave the table!" Saint-Ybars shouted, towering over Démon.

"Démon, my child, obey him," Madame Saint-Ybars said pleadingly.

"I'll obey, mother."

Saint-Ybars, pointing towards one of the windowed doors that opened onto the courtyard, said to Démon:

"On your knees, there!"

"Me, get on my knees?! On my knees because I'm defending my mother! I'd rather die."

"We shall see, won't we?" Saint-Ybars said with a cruel snicker.

And turning towards Monsieur de Lauzun:

"Go get me my *baleine*."

A horrid shudder passed through everyone.

Monsieur de Lauzun, a smile on his lips, left like a bolt of lightning and came back the same way.

Saint-Ybars took the *baleine* and repeated:

"On your knees!"

"No," the child responded proudly. "I'll kneel before God alone."

Saint-Ybars walked towards his son. Anger made him hideous. Pélasge was both afraid and sorry for him.

"For the last time," he roared, "on your knees."

Démon was terribly pale but determined. Raising his head, he responded:

"No!"

The menacing *baleine* whistled through the air and lashed him twice between his head and shoulder. He took it well. The pain filled his eyes with tears, but not a single one fell.

"Will you get on your knees now?" his father demanded in a ferocious voice that sounded more beastly than human.

"Never!" Démon responded.

Pélasge stood up, putting himself between father and son, and said:

"Please, Monsieur, calm down. What you're doing is horrible. There are other more dignified ways for you to punish your son."

"Ah! You think you can give lessons to me as well," cried Saint-Ybars with a quivering laugh.

And intentionally using the term that a Louisianan would use to send dogs away, he added:

"Get out!"

Pélasge felt insulted, but he contained himself.

"Get out, I'm warning you!" Saint-Ybars shouted, shaking his *baleine*. "Or you'll feel the lash across your face."

Nogolka raced to put herself between the two enemies. Pélasge pushed her aside gently.

"No, Monsieur," he said, "you will not do that. You know very well that if you were to lose your temper to such an extent, one of us would have to leave this world."

"A threat! A duel!" Saint-Ybars said. "Would you by any chance be trying to intimidate me, Monsieur Schoolmaster? Intimidate me, who in my previous duels heard the pistol's bullet whistle through the air four times as they grazed my body!"

"Stop bragging, Monsieur," Pélasge retorted. "As for me, during the four days that I fought on the barricades in Paris, I can't count the bullets that whistled by my ears. There were too many. I took note only of the ones that penetrated my flesh."

"Well! Your flesh will receive one more, bravest of the brave," Saint-Ybars said.

He drew a circle in the air with his weapon, but Nogolka, more swift than the weapon, threw herself onto Pélasge in order to protect his body. It was she who received the blow on her head and on the nape of her neck. Her comb shattered in several pieces. Her hair, stained with blood, covered her shoulders and back. Pélasge tried unsuccessfully to make her turn loose, but her secret love for him gave her arms, which were wrapped around him, a superhuman force.

Saint-Ybars, holding Démon responsible for the bloodshed, came at him again like a tiger on its unsuspecting prey. But Chant d'Oisel, emboldened by Nogolka's example, ran to her father without his seeing her, snatched the weapon from him, and fled to the front balcony. Saint-Ybars seized Démon by the collar of his shirt, and threatening him with his fist, he repeated the order for him to get on his knees. A firm *no* raised Saint-Ybars' anger to its paroxysm. His wrath became stark raving madness. He battered the miserable child several times about the face. At that very moment, the storm foreseen by Vieumaite arrived. A terrible gust of wind shook the entire house. The doors and the windows trembled violently: upstairs, downstairs, and everywhere, broken panes fell like a hailstorm of glass. Crashes of lightning coming from three different sources in the sky surrounded the house in an infernal circle.

Lagniape crawled to the balcony on the side of the courtyard. There, stretching her uneven arms towards Mamrie, she cried:

"Help, Mamrie! Yapé tué vou piti."[i]

"Tué mo piti!" Mamrie cried out. "Ki céléra qui osé fé ça?"[ii]

At that moment, Mamrie was wearing only her shirt and a petticoat. She was barefoot. She ran to the slave who was cutting wood, took his axe, and rushed into the dining room.

"Ki apé tué mo piti?"[iii] she said, raising her axe.

---

[i] "Someone is about to kill your child."

[ii] "Kill my child! Who's the villain who would dare do this?"

[iii] "Who's killing my little boy?"

Then, she scanned the room with a quick glance. As soon as she saw Démon being shaken by his father against a door, she bounded towards Saint-Ybars:

"Largué mo piti," she said. "Si vou pa largué li, aussi vrai que yé pélé moin Mamrie, ma fende vou la tête!"[i]

Saint-Ybars threw a look of contempt her way and turned around to strike his son. Démon, struggling to avoid another blow, bashed his forehead into one of the doors violently flung open by the wind. A shard of glass wounded him between his eyebrows, and blood spurted out.

Madame Saint-Ybars let out a scream. She threw herself in front of Mamrie. But Mamrie saw her coming. Realizing she would not have a second chance to stop Saint-Ybars, she suddenly changed tactics, took three steps sideways, widened her stance, and hurled her axe at Saint-Ybars' head. The crowd let out a frightened cry. Only Monsieur de Lauzun did not make a sound. He was as pale as a dying man, as he was about to faint. The axe's sharp edge passed like a bolt of lightning in front of Saint-Ybars' eyes and lodged in a magnolia tree in the courtyard.

Dumbfounded, his mouth gaping, Saint-Ybars looked at Mamrie. Everyone wondered what he was going to do. His left arm was as tense as a rod of iron, and his clenched fingers still held Démon's shirt. Madame Saint-Ybars, with great presence of mind, took advantage of this pause. Like many mothers, she always carried a pair of scissors hanging from her belt. She cut Démon's shirt between his neck and his father's fist.

"Run!" she said quietly.

Démon vanished. His father turned around, and his face changed. He resembled a man awakening from a horrible dream. Finally, he regained his calm, collected his thoughts, and ordered Monsieur de Lauzun to call Sémiramis. The terrible old woman rushed to the house with her inseparable *baleine*. Her son Salvador, informed of what just happened, followed her, looking upset.

"Alà moin!" Sémiramis said.[ii]

---

[i] "Let go of my child. If you don't let him go, as sure as my name is Mamrie, I'll split your head open."

[ii] "I'm coming!"

"Put this slave in the stocks," Saint-Ybars said, pointing to Mamrie.

Sémiramis grabbed Mamrie by the arm:

"To marché drette, or else...."[i] she said in a hoarse voice, waving her *baleine.*

"Vou pa besoin serré moin comme ça," Mamrie remarked. "Ma marché san ça, mo pa envie parti couri marron. Mo connin ça mo mérité. La mor pa fé moin peur."[ii]

One of the dovecotes in the courtyard, solidly built out of bricks, contained a room that served as a prison for recalcitrant slaves. A block of oak with three holes was bolted to the floor. It was made up of two parts, one lying on top of the other, the top part movable on a hinge. Sémiramis, having lifted the top part of the block, ordered Mamrie to sit on the floor, extend her legs, and put them down on the half circle on the bottom half of the block. That being done, Sémiramis put down the top half and clamped it down on the other half by means of a padlock that she closed with two turns.

"Asteur," she said, "to gagnin tou plin tan pou zonglé, jisca jour là yé pende toi."[iii] Mamrie did not respond. Sémiramis shut the door, leaving the prisoner alone with her own thoughts.

---

[i] "Walk straight ahead."

[ii] "You don't need to grip me like that. I'll go without force. I'm not the kind to run away. I know what I deserve. Death doesn't frighten me."

[iii] "Now, you'll have plenty of time to think, until the day you hang."

Chapter 19

The Escape

Nogolka led Pélasge outside. Madame Saint-Ybars, her daughters, their husbands, and her daughters-in-law left the dining room. Only Mademoiselle Pulchérie stayed with Saint-Ybars.

"Come on, cousin," she said. "Sit back down at the table. What's the matter with you? Why are you making such a fuss over a disobedient child and an insolent slave? You don't lack the means to bring them back to their senses."

Saint-Ybars went back to his seat but did not eat. Mademoiselle Pulchérie finished her meal without being able to extract one word from her cousin. She left the room, shrugging her shoulders. The domestics disappeared without a sound, like ghosts. It was raining in torrents. Thunder roared constantly for fifty-five minutes. The clouds finally started to disappear; some of them disappeared entirely, while the still-powerful wind violently chased others before it. Although the doors and the windows had been closed, the house trembled, and the prolonged, plaintive howling of the hurricane infiltrated the darkened residence through every crack and keyhole. Saint-Ybars listened to the storm's sinister voice. It seemed to him, at moments, that it uttered threats and prophecies of misfortune.

Nogolka led Pélasge upstairs to the front balcony, the furthest place possible from Saint-Ybars, and took shelter with him behind a column. Her long white hair, stained with blood, whipped around in the wind and scattered in the air like the foam of a wave breaking against a rock. Fearing that Pélasge would leave her, she still held onto his neck and his hand.

During all of this physical and moral clamor, even in the midst of Saint-Ybars' anger and the hurricane's fury, Nogolka had felt a moment of happiness. She had protected the one she loved; she had clutched him against her chest, her face had touched his, and she had mingled her breath with his.—Oh, human heart, what strange secrets you hide in your depths!—Nogolka had felt, for the first time, that a few elusive seconds could bring profound emotion, a delicious rapture to a pure and loving soul like hers. She had not felt Saint-Ybars' blow. She did not know that she was wounded and her blood was flowing. She was happy. She did not yet wonder if the altercation between Pélasge and Saint-Ybars would have consequences. No, she did not think of it. She watched the hurricane and smiled.

The wind, at first blowing in a straight line, had flattened all of the fences. Afterwards, it began to swirl in whirlwinds, causing the leaves on the avenue's oaks to flutter in all directions like the mane of a furious lion. It produced a wailing sound punctuated by cracking noises. Enormous branches fell, tearing off and dragging down other limbs. The avenue was strewn with debris as if someone had made a line of defense to block the way.

All night long, the river had carried along trees ripped from its shores. Since early morning, the overseer had dispatched twenty-five men to grab the wood as it floated down the river. They were occupied with this when the hurricane's arrival forced them to take shelter under the wharf's hangar.

Nogolka, growing calmer, finally relaxed her grip on Pélasge. They started to exchange thoughts about the dreadful scene that had taken place and about Mamrie's likely fate. Suddenly, Pélasge stopped in the middle of a sentence. Despite the noise of the trees, he seemed to hear clamoring in the distance. Nogolka listened as well. They clearly heard cries and caught sight of several slaves coming from the river, running and giving distress signals as they ran. Salvador, who was talking to his mother on the balcony below, went to meet the slaves to find out what happened. They told him that Démon had taken the small skiff to cross the river and was caught unaware by the gusts of wind and the unpredictable current. All he could do now was fight against the large waves closing in on him from every side, threatening to engulf him.

Hearing the slaves' cries, Saint-Ybars threw open the door. Salvador broke the awful news to him.

"My child is lost, and I'm the cause of it," Saint-Ybars cried out in despair. "God's punishing me."

"Come on, now, Saint-Ybars," Salvador said. "Let go of this ill-fated idea of a God taking vengeance upon an innocent boy for his father's misconduct. Come on, let's be men. Let's hurry and go rescue your son."

"You're right, Salvador. Have someone saddle Castor and Pollux."[1]

Castor and Pollux were the two best horses on the plantation. They were readied instantly. Saint-Ybars and Salvador followed the wagon path beside the river; a bit behind them, a tilbury[2] carried Pélasge and Sémiramis.

Madame Saint-Ybars had a widowed sister whose plantation was located on the other side of the river. This woman had always shown a great affection towards the Saint-Ybars children, especially towards Chant d'Oisel and Démon. Démon, in his desperation and humiliation, had decided to escape his father's house for good and to seek refuge with his aunt. He had jumped into a frail one-man skiff, and without worrying about the storm, he had set off into open water.

Since the rain had stopped, the slaves in charge of gathering the drifting wood returned to the levee, but it was impossible to resume their work. The wind still blew viciously. The river, rising like an inland sea, erupted in enormous and rapid waves. Its shores were fringed with a froth that blew across the the levee top. Under the triple momentum of the wind, the waves, and the eddies, the undercurrents clashed and became entangled with one another. The drifting wood bounced around like pieces of a broken raft, some dragged by the main current, some turning back against the current, and some pivoting like horizontal wheels.

The slaves looked fearfully at Démon's skiff, expecting any minute to see him sink.

As young as Démon was and despite his impetuous nature, he kept his composure. Alone, confronted by danger on all sides, he faced it with a reasoned and energetic determination. He was not thinking about death. He had just been whipped like a slave. He was humiliated and dishonored, and he had fled to hide his shame. He only had one idea in mind: to put this great river between him and his father's plantation.

The slaves winced at the sound of Saint-Ybars' voice.

"Slackers!" their master cried out. "You're standing there like logs. You aren't helping my son!"

And he gave the order for four of them to go out in a small boat. To them, this task foreshadowed an inevitable death. Their master, they said to themselves, did not have the right to demand this from them. They ran away.

"Let's not waste time," Salvador said. "We can go without those cowards."

They climbed into a skiff with two oars. Saint-Ybars seized the helm, and Salvador rowed.

The clouds had returned. They passed over in tightly-packed groups. Despite their dense mass, they were rapidly rolling towards the north. The air was warm, the day somber, the water a dirty yellow.

Sweat streamed down Salvador's face. His shirt was glued to his body.

"Saint-Ybars," he said, "cut off my shirt. It's holding me back."

With a few movements of his pocketknife, Saint-Ybars cut Salvador free so he could row more vigorously. He was fighting against a riptide that threatened to propel them even further from Démon.

The sun, completely veiled until then, passed between two clusters of clouds and fell directly on Salvador's bronzed chest. Light in the midst of a storm: that means hope. Saint-Ybars felt his heart jump for joy.

"Have courage, Salvador," he cried out. "It's working! We're getting closer. Salvador, we have to save my son, or else I won't be returning to the house. The river will take away my lifeless body as well."

"We'll save him," Salvador responded with a calm confidence.

Unfortunately, the small boat was hindered by the driftwood. To avoid it, Saint-Ybars was forced to navigate to the left.

An entire sycamore tree floating down the river suddenly appeared before Démon. Saint-Ybars saw the danger and trembled. The tree was the tallest and broadest of its kind he had ever seen. Not only did the sycamore roll upon itself, but it also made a seesaw movement that made its branches and roots alternately rise and fall.

Saint-Ybars pointed out the danger to Salvador.

The two dinghies were nearly aligned. However, Démon's was a bit upstream.

The sycamore's trunk was approaching slowly but with dreadful power. The roots and branches were turning from side to side, half in the air and half in the water, like two large hydraulic wheels.

Measuring with a glimpse the distance that separated him from Démon, Salvador said to Saint-Ybars:

"Tell him to steer towards us."

"Démon, my son," Saint-Ybars shouted, "move towards us! Come here!"

Démon heard, but he shook his head and paddled desperately.

Saint-Ybars shouted again.

"Leave me alone," the boy responded. "Leave me alone. I'm trying to get away."

The sycamore arrived, majestic in its mass, ruthless in its force. Its roots came out of the water on Demon's side and rose in the air like mammoth, menacing claws.

The slaves, drawn by nervous curiosity stirred up by the sight of danger, were grouped upon the shore and watched the scene. Pointing out a rowboat moored at the quay, Pélasge ran and urged them to go with him to help the two dinghies. They remained immobile.

Sémiramis stormed up onto the levee. Hearing Pélasge's futile pleas, she fell upon the slaves like lightning. Before they had time to recognize her, she grabbed one by the collar, and hitting him over and over with her terrible *baleine*, she pushed him towards the rowboat.

"Canaille! Capon sans pareil! Ma fé vouzot marché, moin,"[i] she shouted.

A young slave whom she was rushing towards held out his arms to ward off the blows.

[i] "Scoundrel! Coward like no other! I'll make you move…!"

"Man Miramis," he said, trembling and alarmed, "pa taille moin! Ma obéi."[i]

"Ta obéi encor mieu avé ça."[ii] The old woman lashed back with a blow that made him howl with pain.

The young slave jumped into the rowboat.

Four other slaves hurried to catch up with the first two.

Sémiramis got into the boat. Pélasge took the helm.

In a few seconds, six oars plunged into the water, and the small craft took off. Each time the bow pushed through a wave, a shower of foam sprayed the slaves. Then, Semiramis's imperious and hoarse voice yelled:

"Hardi là! Ramin, ramin for!"[iii]

For the old woman, it was a matter of first saving her son, then Saint-Ybars, the head of an important family, and then his son. From time to time, she stood up to see better. Salvador recognized her. The courage and devotion of his elderly mother warmed his heart, and he redoubled his efforts to row with even more energy. Saint-Ybars was delighted when he saw they were drawing near. All Démon needed to do was let himself drift. They drew nearer, and all three boats seemed to have escaped the sycamore tree. But Démon, in his despair and chagrin, did not want them to catch him. He would have preferred to hide his shame at the bottom of the Mississippi. Seeing it would only take a few more strokes of the oar to get out of the central current, he increased his efforts as well. Suddenly, a huge wave lifted his skiff like a feather, yet when it crashed, the skiff continued to rise in the air. He was entangled in the sycamore's roots.

Démon did not lose his presence of mind. If he stayed in the skiff, either the small boat would drag him under the water, or he would be hurled up at the height of eight or nine yards into the air and risk breaking a limb. He abandoned the small craft, straddled one of the limbs of the root, and held fast to the tip. There he waited. The sycamore's rotating movement came to a halt, but the seesaw movement continued. Démon was alternately raised into the air then plunged into the water. When Salvador finally freed himself from the main current, the riptide propelled him towards Démon.

[i] "Man Miramis, do not beat me! I'll obey."

[ii] "You'll obey better yet with this."

[iii] "Row, row hard!"

The tree started to turn again. Démon's skiff fell with a crash as he was thrust into the air like a wisp of straw stuck to a wheel.

Saint-Ybars was quaking with fear.

"Démon, my son, my dear child," he shouted, "I beg you, jump into the water! Swim to us!"

The child said nothing! The sycamore was still rolling.

Saint-Ybars kneeled down on the edge of the dinghy and clasping his hands together, said:

"Démon! Démon! I'm on my knees, begging you!"

The child relented. The words had touched his heart. He crouched down, bent his knees, thrust himself forward, and slid into the surface of the water. He was sturdy and swam well.

At the moment when Démon threw himself into the water, the sound of Sémiramis' voice reached Saint-Ybars and Salvador. She was still urging on the rowers, but they no longer needed her words. The moment of fear had passed. One of them started to sing a slave song. His workmates responded in chorus. These men, until that moment fainthearted, were now proud to be fighting danger. In their exalted contempt of death, they showed great valor.

Just three waves separated Démon from his father's rowboat when he was suddenly stopped by a force that pushed him back and tugged at him from below. His movements slowed and he began to spin. Saint-Ybars shouted:

"He's in a whirlpool!"

It only took the father two seconds to take off his frock coat and boots and fling himself into the water. The eddy that trapped Démon was carrying him towards the central current. Saint-Ybars, raised up by a wave, saw his son turn like a top and disappear. He dived in. Salvador stopped rowing. He no longer used his oars except to hold steady in a good position. He felt a moment of terrible panic: he looked everywhere and saw only the turbulent water rising and falling. Suddenly, he heard someone calling. He turned around and saw Saint-Ybars holding Démon with one hand and swimming with the other.

In bringing his son back from the abyss, the father had exhausted his own strength.

"Salvador," he cried, "save my son. Give my blessings to my family."

"Démon, dear child," he added in a weak voice as he hugged his son, "forgive your father. We're going to leave each other."

"Father," Démon responded, "a son doesn't need to forgive. He loves his father, and he forgets. I want to die with you."

"Démon, listen to me," Saint-Ybars gasped. "Think of your mother, your brothers, your sisters."

He was unable to say any more. He broke down, choking on his words. He seized Démon with his hands and lifted his arms in order to hold him above the water. He kicked with his feet to hold their place so Salvador would have the time to reach them.

At the sound of Saint-Ybars' cry, Salvador threw himself into the river. He swam like a seal. Démon, released by his father, barely had enough strength to keep himself above the surface. Salvador grabbed him in time and carried him piggyback. No sooner was this done when they heard a violent crash. A large wave in front of them parted, foaming, and the rowboat leaped up to meet them.

Salvador, still keeping his composure, shouted:

"Everyone stay in the boat."

He grabbed the edge of the boat with his iron fist and said to Démon:

"Can you get into the boat by yourself?"

"Yes."

"Get in."

Demon climbed in.

"Now," Salvador added, "do you see him?"

Saint-Ybars had tried his best to come back up to the surface. His hands and forearms waved above the water. His movements were less like a swimmer and more like someone dying.

"Hurrah!" shouted one slave. "Alà li. Là, là!"[i]

"I see," Salvador said. "Follow me."

Before Salvador had covered half the distance that separated him from Saint-Ybars, the main current seized the master and quickly swept him aside. Salvador followed him into the powerful eddy. He

[i] "There he is. There, there!"

slashed through the water with such vigor and flew with such speed that the others no longer doubted Saint-Ybars' rescue. Sémiramis looked at her son with pride. They no longer saw anything but Saint-Ybars' hands. Eventually, they disappeared. Salvador dived down.

Sémiramis gave the order to two of the rowers to bring in their oars and hold them upright on their bench. She told the others to drift gently. She trusted her son. She was well-acquainted with his strength and composure. But even the strength of the sturdiest man could run out. The water's intensity remained tireless and inexorable. There was a moment of cruel suspense which seemed very long to the aged mother. She did not let any of this show: she knew how to control herself.

A gleam of sunlight illuminated the water between the rowboat and the river's left bank. Sémiramis saw her son's chest pop up in the light. Beside Salvador's bronze face appeared the pale face of Saint-Ybars.

Sémiramis climbed down, saying:

"Alà yé!"[i]

And speaking to Pélasge:

"Mister Pélasge," she added, "you see the glimmer of light over there?"

"Yes, Man Miramis."

"There they are. Let's hurry."

All the rowers understood the necessity of not losing a single second. The rowboat pushed forward like a flying seagull skimming the tide. It entered blazing into the luminous area. It was just in time; Salvador's strength was abandoning him. At Sémiramis's command, one slave grabbed him and another grabbed Saint-Ybars. Salvador took a moment to catch his breath. Then he climbed into the rowboat. Saint-Ybars, unconscious, was lying on his back. Démon, believing him dead, leaned over him, crying, and covered his face with kisses. Pélasge gave his oar to Salvador so that he could take care of Saint-Ybars. He put his hand on the chest of the drowned man and said:

"His heart's still beating. Have courage, Démon! We'll bring your father back to life. Stop crying. Help me."

[i] "There they are!"

Pélasge knew what to do in the case of drowning. He immediately started to go to work while recommending nevertheless that they get back to shore as quickly as possible.

Sémiramis raised her harsh, imperious voice.

"Zot tendé?" she said to the rowers. "Cé pa tan pou zonglé, non! Ramin, ramin, ramin! Can nou rivé, chakenne a gagnin ain bon cou ouiski."[i]

All of Saint-Ybars' family and several strangers were waiting on the wharf. When they saw Pélasge wave his handkerchief in a sign of triumph, they responded with shouts of joy.

Just as the rowboat reached land, the sycamore disappeared in the distance.

[i] "Do you understand? This is no time to dream! Row, row row! When we arrive, each of you'll have a good swig of whiskey."

Chapter 20

Repentance and Reconciliation

When Saint-Ybars came to his senses, he was inside the wharf's pavilion, his family surrounding him. The hurricane had passed. All was calm; only the usual lapping of the water under the wharf could be heard. Among those present was the plantation doctor, who recommended that Saint-Ybars not speak and made him take a spoonful of Madeira wine every ten minutes.

Eight slaves awaited the doctor's orders. Since Saint-Ybars had been ordered to be still, two beams were slid under the litter and four slaves carried him. The four others followed to relieve their comrades. The whole family accompanied the stretcher on foot, silent and rapt in prayer. Démon, his wounds dressed by the doctor, wore an eye patch and held his mother's hand. Beside him walked Chant d'Oisel. He had a solemn and thoughtful look, and she appeared exhausted. Her eyes still bore the trace of her tears.

At some distance behind the procession of relatives, Nogolka and Pélasge walked together, he calm and thoughtful as always, she terribly sad.

Since the main avenue was obstructed by debris, they took the road the wagons travelled. When they arrived, Pélasge asked Nogolka in a low voice what she thought of the awful day that was coming to an end.

"I have very dark premonitions," she responded. "Misfortune's come into this house today, and I don't think it's going to leave."

In the evening, Saint-Ybars summoned Pélasge and told him in his family's presence:

"I was told, Monsieur, about everything you did to save us, my son and me. I thank you from the bottom of my heart. I immensely regret having offended you this morning. Do me the honor, I beg you, and please accept my apologies."

Pélasge shook the hand Saint-Ybars held out to him and responded:

"All is forgotten, Monsieur."

Chapter 21

Mamrie's Punishment

Two days later, starting at six o'clock in the morning, the overseer, Mademoiselle Pulchérie, and Sémiramis were deliberating with Saint-Ybars about what to do about Mamrie. Saint-Ybars leaned towards leniency. The overseer was of the opposite opinion. For some time, he claimed, a certain insubordinate spirit had been observed among the slaves. He had found, near the camp, one of those brochures abolitionist emissaries were secretly circulating around the plantations, and the slaves were always able to find someone to read these inflammatory documents to them. It was necessary to make an example. Since Mamrie was a prized slave, she was not to be handed over to the justice of the criminal courts. It was better to impose a harsh punishment on her in front of the other slaves.

Mademoiselle Pulchérie shared the overseer's opinion.

When it was Sémiramis's turn to speak, she said:

"Neither clemency nor half-measures. You're either the master or you're not. When you're the master, you must be respected at all costs. There aren't two ways to *reign*. Those who are born to obey must tremble in the presence of their masters. Mamrie raised her hand to her master. She deserves death. Hang her."

The overseer's opinion prevailed.

The pretentious Duc de Lauzun was eavesdropping. He was proud to be the first to announce to the household that Mamrie would be flogged in front of all the slaves at noon in the courtyard of magnolia trees.

Whipping Mamrie! Upon hearing the news, every heart stopped. Chant d'Oisel burst out sobbing. Démon grew pale and remained silent. Madame Saint-Ybars, her sons, her daughters, her sons-in-law, and her daughters-in-law went to beg Saint-Ybars to have mercy on his two youngest children's nurse or at least to limit the punishment to a lengthy imprisonment. Unfortunately, the general idea that it was absolutely necessary to make an impression on the minds of the slaves by an exemplary punishment had so deeply penetrated Saint-Ybars' mind that he would not abandon his determination. He was inexorable. Then a gloomy silence spread throughout the entire house, punctuated only by the footsteps of the domestics who came and went. The lunch bell rang in vain. Only Madame Saint-Ybars, obeying her duty as mistress of the house, went downstairs. She, her husband, and Mademoiselle Pulchérie sat down at the large table that was recently so animated and so merry but now was empty and silent. Saint-Ybars was bitterly mortified. Every unoccupied place was a disapproving voice.

Monsieur Héhé entered, skipping along.

"What's this I hear?" he said. "Is what Monsieur de Lauzun told me true? Mamrie is to be flogged?"

"That's right," Mademoiselle Pulchérie responded.

"Well done, Mademoiselle. She'll pay once and for all. She was becoming unbearably insolent."

At noon, the magnolia courtyard resembled a public place of execution. The slaves, men, women, and children were lined up like soldiers. The overseer, his rifle on his shoulder, walked back and forth in front of them.

A ladder leaning on the trunk of a magnolia tree was securely set by a rope. Mamrie was to be attached to this ladder, flat on her stomach and naked from her feet to her waist. The order was twenty-five lashes with the whip. The man chosen for this job was Jim, a slave known for his strength and skill. Standing at the foot of the ladder, his whip tucked into a shoulder strap, he held a bundle of cords with one hand and nonchalantly scratched his head with the other.

Saint-Ybars, Mademoiselle Pulchérie, Sémiramis, Monsieur de Lauzun, and Monsieur Héhé chatted in the dining room.

Saint-Ybars' sons and sons-in-law had all left the house. The ladies closed the windows and doors and gathered in the room most distant from the courtyard. Chant d'Oisel, distressed and outraged, knelt on the floor, hid her head, and sobbed in the lap of her mother, who was also silently crying.

Where was Démon? No one had seen him for an hour.

Pélasge was in his bedroom. Standing in front of his worktable, he fixed his eyes on Nogolka's veil, but it was not she who occupied his thoughts. He mechanically looked at the veil and thought of Mamrie. He still wondered if there was a way to save her.

Everyone in the courtyard awaited the victim. It was Sémiramis who led her outside.

A door on the ground floor flew open. Everyone believed it was Saint-Ybars coming to give the signal to begin. Instead, Démon appeared. He stepped forward and said in a low voice:

"Jim, remember what I'm telling you. I'll be on the balcony upstairs. If you dare strike Mamrie even once with your whip, you're a dead man."

Démon went back into the house, leaving the slave in a terrible state of agitation. Then the arched door of the dining room opened and Saint-Ybars, Mademoiselle Pulchérie, Monsieur Héhé, and Monsieur le Duc de Lauzun appeared. Sémiramis arrived shortly afterwards, holding Mamrie by her arm. Mamrie knew nothing of the punishment that had been decided for her. She believed up until then that she would be handed over to the legal system and pay for her crime on the scaffold. At the sight of the ladder and the whip, she understood everything. She let out a blood-curdling scream. Joining her hands, she said to Saint-Ybars in a sweet voice and reproachful tone:

"Ah! Maite, vou pa juste. Mo mérité la mor, é vapé désonoré moin. Non, maite, pa fé ça. Pa fé taillé moin comme ça divan tou moune comme ain voleuse. Vou riche, maite. Ain nesclave de moin ça pa fé arien pou vou. Fleuve pa loin. Comandé moin, ma parti couri néyé moin laddan tou suite."[i]

Saint-Ybars remained solemn, unyielding.

[i] "Ah! Master, you're not fair. I deserve death, and you're going to dishonor me. No, master, don't do that. Don't have me whipped in front of everyone like a common thief. You're rich, master. One slave is nothing to you. The river isn't far. Order me, and I'll go drown myself immediately."

"Anon, assé jacacé comme ça,"[i] Sémiramis said, pushing Mamrie towards the ladder.

Jim raised his eyes towards the balcony. Between a column and a curtain, in the darkness of a crevice, he saw the gleam of a double-barreled shotgun. He did not budge.

"Ebin! To paralizé don," Sémiramis shouted to him. "Ça ta pé attanne pou comancé to louvrage?"[ii]

Jim rolled his large white eyes and looked discreetly in the direction of the balcony. He saw the two barrels take aim. They seemed as large as smokestacks on a steamboat. He moved towards Saint-Ybars, trembling the whole way, and said:

"Maite, mo pa capab fé kichoge comme ça. Mo ain nomme tro comifo pou taillé Mamrie."[iii]

A furious Saint-Ybars made frightening threats, but they created less of an effect than Démon's shotgun.

The overseer ran up, leaned his shotgun against a tree, took Jim's whip, and barked:

"Just wait. I'm going to teach you how to obey."

But Jim did not wait. He broke away, running for his life. Then the overseer, replacing him, grabbed Mamrie in order to tie her down. At the same time, a high-pitched grating noise was heard. One of the curtains on the balcony parted, scraping along the curtain rod. Everyone looked in that direction. Démon was poised like a hunter taking aim with his rifle.

Saint-Ybars' furious roars echoed all the way to the room where the ladies had taken refuge.

Madame Saint-Ybars understood immediately that something unusual was happening. She ran out onto the balcony. Two of her daughters followed her. They arrived just in time to hear Démon shouting to the overseer:

"Stop, fool! Or else I'll kill you like I would've killed Jim."

Madame Saint-Ybars and her daughters threw themselves on Démon to grab his weapon from him. He defended himself doggedly.

[i] "Let's go. You've rattled on enough like that."

[ii] "I see, you seem to be paralyzed! What are you waiting for?"

[iii] "Master, I'm not capable of doing something like this; I'm too good a man to whip Mamrie."

The trigger got caught in Madame Saint-Ybars' dress. Two shots went off, but fortunately, the bullets passed between Demon's two sisters and sank into the wall. The three women grabbed him and led him away, despite his screams.

At the sound of the gunshot, Pélasge rushed onto the balcony. There, he saw Nogolka.

The overseer had caught up with Jim and brought him back. Now, no longer worried, he leisurely prepared to tie Mamrie down.

Pélasge walked up to Nogolka and said, pointing to Saint-Ybars:

"Please, Mademoiselle, won't you make one last effort to spare Mamrie the pain and shame of torture? Spare Saint-Ybars from a never-ending remorse that will poison his future? Everyone here will praise you, me more than anyone else. Save Mamrie. You have absolute power over this madman."

"Me, absolute power?" Nogolka asked, surprised and worried.

"Yes, absolute power!" Pélasge repeated.

And lowering his voice:

"I was under the sachem," he continued. "I was going to rescue you, but the owl interrupted me."

Nogolka blushed then grew pale and she stumbled. Pélasge took hold of her arm and hand to support her.

"Come on, be brave!" he said. "Throw yourself at the feet of this madman. Save Mamrie. Do it for the family. Do it for me."

This *for me* made the teacher tremble. Her heart raced, her cheeks regained their color, and her eyes blazed with an extraordinary love. She squeezed Pélasge's hand, and with a determined stride, she walked down into the courtyard. Saint-Ybars, seeing her approach, lost his composure. Nogolka's contained emotions made her more beautiful than ever. She walked up, and with nothing to lose but her dignity, she knelt down in front of him.

"Have mercy on Mamrie, Monsieur," she said. "You'll become greater in everyone's respect and affection. They'll say, 'He has a noble heart. He had pity on an unfortunate slave led astray by her love for the child whom she nurtured with her own milk.' Monsieur, I beg you, pardon her for my sake."

A sense of justice awakened in Saint-Ybars. He greatly needed the pardon as well. He thought he read in Nogolka's eyes that she would forgive him if he pardoned Mamrie.

The silence in the courtyard was frightening. Mamrie stood on the next-to-last rung of the ladder, covering her face with one hand and leaning on one of the posts with the other. Jim uncoiled his ropes.

Mamrie turned at the sound of Nogolka's voice. She climbed down the ladder and ran towards Saint-Ybars as he was helping Nogolka stand up.

Jim stepped forward to retrieve Mamrie. Noticing the look Saint-Ybars threw his way, he stopped.

"What are you doing there?" Saint-Ybars demanded.

The unfortunate slave stammered several excuses. Saint-Ybars cut him off, saying to him in a booming voice:

"Go away!"

Jim quickly fled. Saint-Ybars said to Nogolka:

"Mademoiselle, take her away. I'll pardon her for you."

"Thank you, Monsieur, thank you a thousand times," Nogolka responded.

Mamrie, in turn, wanted to thank Saint-Ybars, but she had hardly uttered a word before she began to sob. Nogolka led Mamrie away.

Saint-Ybars, in a booming voice, called Monsieur de Lauzun. The would-be duke rushed to him, his knees knocking like a frightened spaniel.

"My rifle and my bag," Saint-Ybars ordered.

Monsieur le Duc left and returned with astonishing speed.

Saint-Ybars, his rifle on his shoulder, crossed the courtyard, heading towards the woods. The slaves stepped aside respectfully as he passed.

Pélasge went back into the house, shouting, "Saved!"

Démon and Chant d'Oisel raced to throw themselves into Mamrie's arms. They led her into their mother's bedroom. There, she was comforted and rewarded with caresses.

Pélasge went down into the courtyard the moment the overseer was ordering the slaves back to work. He ran into Sémiramis. She shook her omnipresent whip and looked unhappy.

"Monsieur," she said, "whites no longer know how to rule. They're getting weaker. In ten years, there won't be any more slaves."

"So much the better," Pélasge responded.

Sémiramis looked at him with an expression of pity and walked away without adding a word.

Saint-Ybars

Part III

Chapter 22

After the Storm

Calm returned to the Saint-Ybars plantation, but while the damage produced by the hurricane was quickly repaired, the moral storm that had disrupted the peace in the family left a deep mark, especially on Démon. He was sad and taciturn. He no longer studied with the same fervor, and he became more and more indifferent to everything. Pélasge tried in vain to rekindle his interest, but to all of his exhortations his student responded, "I've been disgraced. I want to leave."

Pélasge, alarmed by Démon's growing melancholy, spoke at length with Vieumaite about it. "Believe me, Monsieur," he said, summing up, "let's not wait any longer to send Démon away. It's unwise to keep him here, where everything reminds him of those traumatic events. The longer Démon stays, the more his pain will worsen. There will come a moment when he'll give up on life itself. Then, we'd lose everything."

"You're right," Vieumaite responded. "The tragedy of September twenty-first profoundly scarred Démon and left a sadness in his soul that only distance and time can ease. He must leave as soon as possible. I'll speak to his father about it."

Two weeks after this discussion, Démon boarded a clipper in New Orleans that was leaving for Le Havre, in Normandy. He was going to finish his studies in Paris. He bid his father and Pélasge farewell from the deck the moment the anchor was raised.

With Démon away, everyone saw just how large a space he had occupied in the household. His absence left an enormous emptiness. Everyone except Mademoiselle Pulchérie found the house to be as sad as if it were draped in mourning.

Démon's departure left Nogolka full of anxiety. She thought, and rightly so, that it would not be long before Pélasge left the plantation. He would certainly not wait for someone to make him feel that his presence was no longer necessary. He was too proud for that. With him gone, what was going to become of her? She hardly slept. The little sleep that she had was troubled by bad dreams. She was absent-minded and confused dates and days. She was disorganized in her lessons with Chant d'Oisel and unhappy with herself.

Saint-Ybars believed he had redeemed himself in Nogolka's eyes by granting Mamrie's pardon. He began to hope again. But Nogolka maintained such an icy demeanor in his presence that he was forced to admit that he was pursuing a fantasy. He felt that after having been so hateful he had become an object of ridicule. Then his pride rebelled. He decided to put an end to the situation that tortured his heart and wounded his self-esteem, but he resolved to do it like a gentleman. He went to find his father and confess everything to him. Even though a man might reach maturity, he is always a child to his father. Saint-Ybars' trust in his father, his regret, his pain, and his tears moved Vieumaite. The old man scolded his son gently, pitied him, and embraced him.

"You're doing the right thing," he told him, "by giving Mademoiselle Nogolka back her freedom, for us as well as for her. We need to put an end to this before people find out about it and someone gets hurt even more. Since you so desire, I'll take responsibility for dismissing Mademoiselle Nogolka and giving her a sum of money as if it came from me. That's the only way, you say, to make her accept the remuneration she's owed. So be it. It's very hard for me—I'm not going to hide it from you—to lie even if it's justified. Don't forget that in doing this, I'm giving you and your family the greatest proof of affection you could ask of me. Go tell Mademoiselle Nogolka that I want to speak with her."

In the afternoon, a carriage came to a halt in front of Vieumaite's house, and Nogolka stepped out of it. Vieumaite welcomed her in the sitting room.

"Mademoiselle," he said, "I don't need to tell you how much I respect you and admire you. You know that very well, don't you? And I must tell you that my respect and affection for you have grown since I know everything now. My poor son confessed it all. Have pity on him, but don't hate him. He knows it's wrong to deprive you of your freedom. Reclaim it, Mademoiselle. So you want to leave—that's fair and necessary, and I support you completely. The loss will be great for Chant d'Oisel. Fortunately, Monsieur Pélasge can replace you for the literary portion. As for music, we'll ask our friends from New Orleans to help us find someone who possesses the art as expertly as you and knows how to teach it with as much skill.

"You've always shown me a genuine, filial affection. As for me, I insist on giving you proof of my sincerity. Take this purse. It contains a token of our appreciation. It's not so much remuneration as a richly-deserved reward for your five years of devoted and intelligent service. Go and return to your parents. Be happy, and think of me from time to time."

Nogolka wanted to thank Vieumaite, but he interrupted her with a benevolent gesture and kissed her forehead in a fatherly way. She was left aghast. The prospect of Pélasge's departure had made her suffer so much, and it was she who was leaving! Trembling all over, she climbed into the carriage. While descending the avenue of oak trees, she felt so overwhelmed that she told the coachman she wanted to get out and walk the rest of the way. In the garden, she decided to sit down on the bench where she often sat when she wanted to be alone to collect her thoughts. Through the brush, she saw the bench occupied by two people. She spotted Pélasge and Chant d'Oisel. They were leaning towards each other, their heads touching. Pélasge held her small hand, and Chant d'Oisel did not attempt to pull back. The shock Nogolka received left her reeling. She moved away, tottering like a fatally-wounded animal. She went to hide her pain in her bedroom, where she stayed locked up for several hours.

Chapter 23

Nogolka's Departure

The few days that Nogolka had yet to spend on the Saint-Ybars plantation were the most difficult days of her teaching career. It was she who was seemingly resigning, and everyone interpreted her behavior unfavorably. They accused her of having secretly looked for a better position. Mademoiselle Pulchérie harshly reproached her for being deceitful and ungrateful. On the day of her departure, she only saw cold, almost scornful faces all around her. Only Chant d'Oisel remained the same until the end. She had an inkling about the cause of Nogolka's departure and was perhaps even sure of it, but decency and filial respect demanded the greatest discretion.

Vieumaite and Chant d'Oisel took Nogolka to the boat that was transporting her to Cincinnati. Judging by the way Chant d'Oisel embraced her at the moment of farewell and by the few words she uttered, even a person less perceptive than Nogolka could sense that Chant d'Oisel did not cast any blame on her. They exchanged one last look, one last handshake in which there was clearly a protest against the necessity that was separating them.

One thing hurt Nogolka most of all: not seeing Pélasge before she left. Not to be loved by him was without doubt a great tragedy, but no one is master of his own heart. She could not blame him for loving Chant d'Oisel. But that he was indifferent to the point of not being there to bid her farewell was something she could not understand. She preferred to believe that some serious reason prevented him from coming. But what could that reason be? She could not think of any.

Did Pélasge know Nogolka loved him? It is possible that he was still unaware of it, like everyone else on the plantation. Nogolka was naturally reserved. In addition, she had always had a strong reason for hiding her secret: the fear of arousing Saint-Ybars' jealousy. It did not matter. It is hard to believe that a man as observant and shrewd as Pélasge suspected nothing.

When the ship left, Nogolka withdrew to her cabin, where, in an attempt to fight her sadness, she began to unpack and repack her trunk. There were few travelers. They were all on the upper decks, so the lounge was deserted. Nogolka thought that she could leave her door open without any problem. The shadow of a human form appeared on the clothes she was putting away, and when she raised her head she saw Pélasge standing in the doorway. What did she feel at that moment? What words could she ever say that could express her joy? Tears glistened within her eyes. She was trembling; breathing became difficult.

Pelasge spoke first.

"You would've refused," he said, "to let me come with you on the first leg of your journey, so I acted without your permission."

"Thank you, ah! Thank you a thousand times, Monsieur Pélasge. If only you knew how good you make me feel! Your presence makes up for the injustice of the others. Come sit down by me. I'm going very far away, and this might be the last time we talk. I want to tell you everything. What I'm doing now is very hard, but it's for your good. Monsieur Pélasge, I love you. I've loved you since the day you arrived on the plantation. But you—how unfortunate for me!—you love Mademoiselle Saint-Ybars. Oh! Don't try to deny it out of pity for me. I know you love Chant d'Oisel. You love her in good faith, honestly and with all the confidence of a young man who knows his own worth. But she, are you so sure that she loves you as you deserve to be loved? You're the only gentleman she's ever known. But when her father spends the winter with her in New Orleans and leads her into a world where she'll see many young men from good families, who can assure you that she'll remain faithful to the memory of the humble country professor? I'm hurting you by saying this. Forgive me. Be very careful, Monsieur Pélasge! You're in a place where I lived for five years, an environment where many kinds of prejudices reign despotically. Do you believe that Chant d'Oisel has enough strength of character to overcome the opposition of her entire family, no matter how strong her feelings are for you?

"Vieumaite is the only person whom you can count on, but don't forget that when you ask Mademoiselle Saint-Ybars to marry you, what he thinks will be crushed by the coalition of the others. Anyway, be cautious and patient. Don't rush. Maybe time, which always leads to changes, will work for you. I'll write you. You'll write back to me, won't you? No one cares more about you than I do."

"We don't have to part as if we'll never see each other again," Pélasge responded. "Sooner or later, I'll return to Europe. In this age of steamboats and railroads, communications are too easy and too frequent for friends to say farewell forever. Let's hope and just say goodbye for now!"

The boat stopped. Pélasge and Nogolka kissed.

"One last word," Nogolka said, squeezing his hands. "I had two moments of happiness in my life, and I owe them both to you. I was happy the day I shielded you from Monsieur Saint-Ybars. I just had the second by kissing you. Now, if death should come, I'll receive it without protest while thinking of you."

"And," Pélasge responded, "whatever may come, happy or sad, I'll faithfully keep your memory and always be your devoted friend, whether near or far."

Chapter 24

Calm Returns

Several months after Démon's and Nogolka's departures, the Saint-Ybars plantation had resumed its usual pace. Who would have believed it? It was a small creature, white and rosy, a child who brought joy back to the heart of this family that not long ago had been so troubled and sad. Blanchette, through her gentle nature, had won everyone's good graces. Everone wanted to be a recipient of her affection. Saint-Ybars, who never did things halfway, played the role of the jealous father with true passion. He wanted Blanchette's first kiss in the morning and her first thought to be for him. The little slave girl who took care of her had been ordered, as soon as she saw Blanchette open her eyes, to tell her, "Let's go see Papa Saint-Ybars."

Something happened that no one was expecting: Blanchette brought about a sort of reconciliation between the master and mistress of the house. As soon as Madame Saint-Ybars witnessed her husband's fondness for Blanchette, she concentrated on making the child love him, and Saint-Ybars was much obliged to her for that.

Chant d'Oisel took her role as little mother to Blanchette very seriously. She cleaned her clothes, minded her toiletries, and took her on walks. At meals, Blanchette was seated next to her godmother, who taught her how to eat correctly. Chant d'Oisel came up with fine educational projects for Blanchette. Monsieur Pélasge would be her French, geography, and history professor, and her godmother would teach her English and music.

Everything seemed to be going well. They had heard from Démon several times. He was in Paris, staying with a friend of Pélasge's family named Adolphe Garnier,[1] a gentle, open-minded man, humble as well as knowledgeable, a philosophy professor at Sorbonne. At first, Démon's persistent sadness had troubled the professor. He had wondered if he should not decline the responsibility of being in charge of his studies. This young boy was disgusted with everything and was tired of life. He was good-hearted and polite, no doubt about that, but suffered from a debilitating taciturnity. He was struggling with his conscience, but his health was failing more and more. Fortunately, Démon eventually felt the healthy influence of his new environment. He grew fond of Monsieur and Madame Garnier, and his presence eased the grief that the loss of their only son had left. They became accustomed to seeing him less as a lodger and more like a member of the family. Démon's enthusiasm for studying returned, and his health improved. He attended classes at the Saint-Louis academy as a day student, and during the evening, he worked under Monsieur Garnier's supervision. In the summer, they made a journey to the regions surrounding Paris every Sunday, and in winter, they went to the theatre or to a concert performance. Démon was happy. His letters to his family revealed his spiritual serenity. Always affectionate, they were sometimes cheerful. But he opened his heart particularly to Pélasge and Mamrie. Time did not diminish the affection he had for them in any way. He wrote to Mamrie in Creole, and she responded to him in the same manner. Mamrie's letters earned the admiration of Monsieur and Madame Garnier, who showed them to friends of the family, and Démon translated them. Monsieur Garnier had several of them published in a journal of philology with notes about the Creole language by Pélasge. Mamrie became a subject of study for a number of scholars, and that made her laugh wholeheartedly.

Chapter 25

How Monsieur de Lauzun Took Possession of a Secret

In one of her letters to Démon, Mamrie told him about Titia's return. Early one morning, an Indian man and woman from the small tribe camped near the sachem had asked to speak with Saint-Ybars. The man said that he knew where the young girl who escaped was and that if Saint-Ybars promised to pardon her, she would agree to come back. Saint-Ybars gave his word. Then the woman asked for and received some clothing for Titia. Two weeks later, the runaway returned. Monsieur de Lauzun thought she was more beautiful than ever. He voiced his compliment to her in pompous language imitating Monsieur le vicomte d'Arlincourt,[1] his favorite author in terms of style.

Titia resumed her functions as Chant d'Oisel's chambermaid. In addition, she replaced the slave girl who acted as companion to Blanchette.

Monsieur de Lauzun started to harass Titia again with his declarations. His effusions of affection unsuccessful, he offered her jewelry. It was refused with contempt. His pride hurt, Monsieur le Duc from then on considered his passion for Titia a matter of honor, a campaign against a beguiling slave who thought herself superior because of the lightness of her skin.

"Ah! She doesn't want to be pursued with tenderness," he said to himself. "Fine! I'll take her by terror."

Once the idea was implanted in his head, he waited for an opportunity.

Monsieur le Duc not only eavesdropped, but he looked through keyholes. He picked up every scrap of paper with writing on it. Crouching in dark corners, he watched like a cat. He kept a notebook in which he took note of everything, omitting nothing, not even the most trivial incident. The young ladies of the house, had they read this journal, would have been amazed and alarmed to see how many minute details the evil little man knew about them and the others.

In one of his raids, Monsieur de Lauzun stooped in front of Chant d'Oisel's bedroom and peered through the keyhole. Titia was alone with Blanchette. Kneeling down in front of a daybed on which the little girl was seated, Titia devoured her with kisses. Monsieur de Lauzun had never seen a child showered with such passionate kisses. He immediately locked himself in his bedroom to record the event in his notebook. He had a formidable ability: when he discovered a clue, he never let go of it. He pursued it and its possible implications with a tireless tenacity. If he had been employed by the secret police in a large city, he would not have taken long to win the highest regards of his superiors.

Titia and Lagniape did not mistrust him enough. Lagniape called him a shameless little boot-licker. She should have called him the *wicked and dangerous little boot-licker*. He had noticed signs of complicity between them. He eventually realized that every ten days, Lagniape left as soon as dawn broke. She followed the pathway the wagons travelled and patiently crawled all the way to the levee. There, she would wait at the foot of a tree for the arrival of the *Belle Ida*, the steamboat that served the coast and came down to New Orleans. The cook on board, whom Lagniape knew, approached her cautiously and either received a letter or gave one to her, depending on whether the ship was sailing up the coast or down. When Monsieur de Lauzun had documented this double event, there was only one thought in his mind—unveiling the secret behind this correspondence. "When you're master of a secret, you're always powerful," he told himself. And in order to reach his goal, he used a method that was as diabolical as it was ingenious. He waited for Lagniape at a spot on the pathway where he was sure that her cries would not be heard. Hidden behind the hedge, he slipped a blowpipe into an opening in the foliage level with Lagniape's face.

He had loaded it with powder composed of a mixture of various peppers. He saw the old woman coming from afar. She was following the path at the top of the levy, coming in his direction. When she was within reach, he blew the powder into her eyes. Lagniape cried out in pain and called for help. In the middle of her wailings, Monsieur de Lauzun calmly climbed down the levy where she had fallen, snuck up from behind, and stole a letter from her pocket.

Chapter 26

A Villainous Plot

Lagniape lay there for over an hour moaning and calling for help before she was discovered by several slaves going to collect wood on the levee. Driven to despair, she thought she was blinded for life. Fortunately, with constant care she was to avoid this misfortune but was going to have to follow treatment for several weeks to regain full vision.

The letter was from Titia. She had written to the young master from whom she had been separated when she was sold. She still loved him. Judging by her words, he had never abandoned the idea of buying her back. He was working and saving up for that. Titia's letter revealed many things. Monsieur de Lauzun retreated to his bedroom to read it. When he finished, he looked at himself in the mirror, smiled, and said:

"Lauzun, you're a clever man. Titia's yours!"

However, a serious problem stood in the way of his triumph—how to profit from Titia's secrets without betraying the abominable plot by which his Excellency had stolen them. But minor technicalities, however great they were, never discouraged Monsieur de Lauzun. During the course of his readings, he had discovered one of La Rochefoucauld's maxims[1] and made it a personal rule. It was the one where the author affirms that nothing is impossible to those willing to try different means to achieve a goal. Monsieur de Lauzun thus delved into his mind, and as he did not have the slightest qualm over the moral nature of the means, he found a solution.

Chant d'Oisel routinely sent Blanchette for a walk with Titia in the morning and at sunset. Titia pushed the small carriage, which the child sat in when she was tired of walking. Most often, Titia followed the long avenue of oak trees. Monsieur de Lauzun never neglected to meet her on these walks. As he no longer spoke to Titia of his love, she believed him to be cured and easily allowed him to push the tiny carriage.

The moment to deliver the decisive blow finally presented itself.

Monsieur de Lauzun skillfully lured Titia to the bank of the river. As a game, he placed Blanchette in a canoe that he began to push and pull back to the shore using the rope to which the canoe was attached. The rocking motion amused Blanchette very much. She laughed and constantly repeated, "Again." As for Titia, she kept repeating, "Lauzun, be careful."

"Calm down," Monsieur de Lauzun responded. "There isn't the slightest danger."

Little by little, he unwound the cord until it had gone past the spot where he had almost entirely severed it the day before. Then, pulling up, he broke it off. He cried out in surprise and said in an alarmed voice:

"The rope broke!"

Titia looked and trembled. The current carried the canoe away in a very slow but continuous movement. Terrified, she was about to call for help when Monsieur de Lauzun made her hush by saying to her coldly:

"That's useless. We're too far from everyone. No one will hear you. I'm the only one who can save Blanchette."

"So save her!" Titia exclaimed.

"Hell!" Monsieur de Lauzun continued, "she's already pretty far out. It might be too late."

Blanchette put her little hands on the side of the canoe and bent over in order to look at the water, whose whirling noise aroused her curiosity.

"She's going to fall," Titia said, pushing Monsieur de Lauzun, "help her, quickly."

"You're ordering me to put myself at risk of drowning," Monsieur de Lauzun protested, "as if you held the power of life or death over me."

"No," Titia resumed, getting down on her knees, her eyes filling with tears. "I'm not ordering. I'm begging."

Monsieur de Lauzun fixed his burning eyes on the young woman and said:

"Titia! Blanchette's your daughter. Admit it, and I'll save her. Otherwise….look! See how far she's drifting away."

The poor woman joined her hands in supplication.

"Lauzun," she said, "save my child!"

"Ah! Ah! I knew all along that she was your daughter. I'll save her on one condition—that you be mine. Do you understand? Mine from this evening on. What's your decision—yes or no? Look at how far away the canoe is. There's not a second to lose."

"Lauzun, save my daughter," Titia said in despair. "I'll do whatever you want."

"You'll be mine?"

"Yes."

Monsieur de Lauzun had come prepared. He was lightly clothed and wore slippers. He threw himself into the water and reached the small craft in twenty strokes. He climbed into it and came back paddling, faking great effort.

Titia held Blanchette against her bosom, bursting into tears.

"Titia," Monsieur de Lauzun said, "you know where my bedroom is. I'll expect you tonight at eleven o'clock."

Titia looked down in shame as Monsieur de Lauzun walked away. He had hidden a bundle in the rows of sugar cane. He changed clothing and returned as calmly as if he were on his way back from an ordinary walk.

Chapter 27

How to Escape Dishonor?

Proud as a general who had won a great victory and as patient as a creditor sure of being paid, Monsieur le Duc waited, smoking cigarettes and reading *Les Amours du chevalier de Faublas*.[1] Eleven o'clock rang out. At each stroke of the bell, his body quivered with an erotic tremor. The exhilaration of gratifying conceit rose up to his brain, and he thought himself equal to the greatest of men.

However, Titia did not come. Half past eleven sounded, then midnight, without the rustling of a gown coming to put an end to Monsieur de Lauzun's furious impatience. Suddenly, changing his mind, his mood changed from anger to a fresh upsurge of pride and hope.

"A simple case of prudery," he told himself. "She's playing the role of the woman who doesn't dare come because she's ashamed. The never-ending play-acting of women, so what! Well, since she's not coming to me, I'll just go to her."

Monsieur le Duc reached Titia's bedroom as stealthily as a wolf. He was surprised and filled with spite when, reaching into Titia's bed, he realized it was empty. He left, his heart clenched by a fierce rage, thinking that Titia had once again run away with her child. The disappointment and anger kept him awake until three in the morning. He fell asleep promising himself to get his revenge as soon as the occasion presented itself.

The rest of the night passed peacefully. With the return of the day, everything in the house resumed its ordinary pace. Chant d'Oisel had someone call for Titia several times. No one knew where to find her, and the servants had looked for her all over the plantation.

The disappearance of the young slave became the subject of every conversation. The idea that she had escaped yet once again naturally came to everyone's mind.

Everyone finished lunch. Monsieur de Lauzun was still sleeping despite the murmurs in the courtyard.

A young slave girl whom Madame Saint-Ybars had sent to retrieve water from the well returned to the house, crying out in terror. They tried to question her, but her wails prevented her from answering. Her whole body shook convulsively. It was as if she was dancing on burning coals. Her screams drew everyone to Madame Saint-Ybars' bedroom. Her eyes were bulging out of her head, her teeth chattering like a rattle.

Sémiramis ran upstairs.

"Atanne," she said, "ma fé li parlé, moin."[i]

And moving towards the slave, she shook her whip and said:

"Acé grouillé comme ça, é to pé to ladjeule."[ii]

The young girl stopped and grew silent.

The terrible old woman fixed her large, bright, and harsh eyes upon her and said:

"Ça to té gagnin pou crié comme si moune tapé corché toi?"[iii]

"Titia…"

"Titia, what?"

"Li néyé."[iv]

"Ça to di? Parlé clair, ou sinon…"[v]

"Oui, man Miramis, ma parlé bien clair. Ça mo di cé vrai. Titia néyé dans pi. So ziés ton gran ouvert, lapé gardé on ciel."[vi]

Everyone ran to the well. What the young slave had said was only too true. Titia, her arms crossed over her chest and her head

[i] "Wait, I'll make her talk."

[ii] "That's enough of jumping around like that, you shut your mouth."

[iii] "What happened that's making you shout as if someone was hurting you?"

[iv] "She drowned herself."

[v] "What'd you say? Speak clearly, or else…"

[vi] "Yes, Man Miramis, I'll speak clearly. What I'm saying is true. Titia's drowned in the well. Her eyes are wide open, looking up at the sky."

half out of the water, her eyes open and fixed towards the sky, was lying on her back, rigid as a statue.

The chaotic uproar from the courtyard put an end to Monsieur de Lauzun's long slumber. The distraught voices and the crowd of people around the water well aroused his curiosity. He hastily got dressed and was about to walk out when he noticed a playing card that someone had slid under the door. It was an ace of spades upon which something had been written. He picked it up and read:

"You are responsible for my death. Respect the innocence of my little girl's secret, or else suffer my curse!"

Monsieur de Lauzun immediately recognized Titia's handwriting and hid the card in his wallet. He walked out, trembling. An uncontrollable terror made his knees wobble. He headed towards the crowd. Someone had just removed Titia from the well. At the sight of her discolored face and her staring, motionless eyes, he let out a cry of horror and fell flat on his back, unconscious.

"Damned coward," Sémiramis muttered.

To bring him back to his senses, she ordered a slave to throw a bucket of wellwater on his face.

Chapter 28

A Coward's Remorse

Titia's death was classified as an accident. Everyone was inclined to believe it—because in the not too distant past, a slave, leaning too far over the well to hoist up some water, fell into it.

Mamrie, with Lagniape's help, prepared Titia for burial. While removing her wet clothing, they noticed that her shirt was sewn together between her legs. This made them wonder. They realized Titia was taking precautions out of a sense of modesty, and from then on, it became evident to them that Titia had deliberately taken her life.

Mamrie naively explained this act of desperation.

"Titia té tro blanche," she said, "pou ain nesclave. Ça té fé li si tan onte que li préféré mouri."[i]

Lagniape did not accept this explanation, but she said nothing of it to Mamrie. For the moment, she felt unable to seek the real cause of such an unexpected misfortune. She was shocked. She racked her brain in vain. Titia's death took away from her the only being who loved her with a wholehearted tenderness—her, a deformed and wretched woman. She felt so alone in the world that she would have gladly welcomed death if she had not thought of Blanchette. She had to live in order to watch over the little girl. She wanted to see her grow up. She would tell her about her father, and one day he would come and make himself known to his daughter.

[i] "Titia was too white for a slave. She was so ashamed of it that she preferred to die."

Titia had spoken to Lagniape from time to time about Monsieur de Lauzun's passionate declarations of love. After the young woman's death, the old woman thought about what she had said. Monsieur le Duc's blackout at the sight of Titia's corpse often came to Lagniape's mind as a still unexplained event. Monsieur de Lauzun's behavior after the tragic drowning gave even more weight to Lagniape's emerging suspicions. Since he was naturally superstitious and cowardly, the death of his victim threw him into a constant panic. He believed in ghosts: any utterance of the words *graveyard* or *phantom* made him break out in a cold sweat. Now he refused be alone, especially at night, and he made a young slave named Windsor accompany him everywhere. He even made him sleep in his bedroom. The sight of water brought about sudden terrors—Titia's head rising to the surface and looking at him with her large eyes, clear and cold. She haunted him in his dreams. He woke up with a start, sweating and ice-cold. He called Windsor and asked him if he had seen or heard anything. He no longer went hunting, fearful of encountering Titia's ghost in the partial darkness of the woods.

One day, Monsieur de Lauzun had to pass through the living room in order to answer Saint-Ybars' call. The broad doors were half-open, the curtains drawn, and the room was full of shadows. Monsieur le Duc had a hallucination. He stopped suddenly, shaking all over. The pedestal table that occupied the center of the room moved and expanded. A black hole deepened in the middle. It was no longer a table that Monsieur de Lauzun saw in front of him—it was a well. He heard the water rippling. Titia, pale and stiff, rose straight out of the bottom of the well, holding Blanchette in her arms, and remained suspended in the air above the gaping circle.

Monsieur de Lauzun fell on his knees and cried out, choking as he gasped:

"Take pity on me, Titia! I give you my most sacred word of honor that I'll say nothing."

Titia bowed her head, and in a dead voice, she whispered:

"That's good. On that single condition, I'll leave you alone. If you ever break your word, you'll pay!"

She sank slowly into the darkness of the well.

When Monsieur de Lauzun left the living room, he looked more like a dead person than a living one. However, since he had promised in good faith that he would be silent, his terror subsided, and he returned to his natural state. But after this terrible apparition, he was obsessed by a compelling need to walk. Windsor followed him everywhere. When he stopped, he heard voices speaking from the earth, under his feet. He needed several months to return completely to his former self.

Chapter 29

Peaceful Years

The series of unfortunate events that had descended upon the Saint-Ybars plantation like a succession of thunderbolts appeared to end with Titia's death. The years followed one another peacefully, practically identical.

Pélasge abided by Nogolka's wise advice: not rushing to ask Madame and Monsieur Saint-Ybars for their daughter's hand in marriage. In love with Chant d'Oisel and sure that she loved him, he waited confidently. She continued to study under him, and nothing ever quenched her thirst for learning. For her, continually learning was a way to grow in the esteem of her professor, who had become her friend. As for him, he constantly broadened the horizons of his knowledge by studying with her, going deeper into the issues that concern the history of man and society. She admired him and was proud of him. She found him vastly superior to others in heart and mind! She immersed herself in his warm and beautiful soul and glowed with joy when she expressed thoughts he approved of, verbally or in writing. Like him, she had faith in the future. She did not worry about what her father would say if he discovered that she had become engaged to Pélasge. The idea that someone might consider him unworthy of her never crossed her mind. His character was developed, and he had not lost an ounce of his gentleness. He had grown more sure of himself and more confident in his decisions. He had become more like Démon. Chant d'Oisel had a high opinion of human character, and in all things she intended to reserve her free will as an inalienable right. She was openly opposed to the institution of slavery. By convention, she did not talk about it in front of the servants, but in the living room, she spoke her mind. She never abandoned her principles. She did not have opinions but convictions. If she had ever wavered in her beliefs, she would have felt she had committed in her conscience an act of cowardice and treason on the grounds of truth and justice. But she was a woman. When she heard the cries of a slave who was being punished, she wept. In these fortunately rare moments of anguish, Pélasge was her great comfort. He made her see the improvements that the force of events and the spirit of the time would certainly bring to the fate of slaves not yet born. He reminded her how much their condition had improved in the past fifty years. He was convinced that if the South's press proved to be worthy of its mission and had the courage to recommend the gradual abolition of slavery, the path to universal emancipation would take place without violence. If that ever happened, everyone who thought like Chant d'Oisel and Pélasge would continue to preach the progressive emancipation of the slaves without ever departing from calm and reasonable language. Chant d'Oisel, loved and respected by all, could do this better than anyone. Women had always played a fine role in social transformations based on justice. There was no more time to lose. The institution of slavery, condemned in theory for a long time, was in the nineteenth century an anachronism that outraged the public sentiment of the civilized world. Abolition was making tremendous strides. It had moved more quickly than the abolitionists themselves could believe. At the present time, Pélasge would not advise anyone to invest his fortune in slaves. Slaves were from now on the most precarious of all property.[1]

Chant d'Oisel, consoled by these arguments, wiped away her tears.

"You're right! I won't shed another tear," she said. "It's dishonorable. I'll speak out and act. I have the right to say whatever I think. Let them lynch me. I don't mind. I'm not so attached to life that to preserve it I'll keep silent about things my conscience condemns."

Blanchette was a living link between Pélasge and Chant d'Oisel. In the house, in the garden, on a walk in the field or on the bank of the river, she was always with them. They educated her and thought about her future. They always spoke to her using the language of reason and refrained from filling her mind with tales and legends. Blanchette had a cheerful nature, an easy intelligence, and a tender and loving heart. She was now a beautiful little girl with shiny, golden brown hair, fine and soft to touch. All her thoughts and emotions could be read in the transparent azure of her eyes. Under her white and rosy skin, it seemed as though life itself pulsed within her tiny, graciously sinuous veins. Although she was in good health, her constitution was extremely delicate. Louisiana's climate was too hot for her. She resembled one of those frail and pallid plants that grow in the twilight of narrow northern valleys that even one ray of sun could devastate. Because of this, Chant d'Oisel never let Blanchette go out in the middle of the day, except in winter.

Blanchette loved everyone, but for her, Chant d'Oisel was a special case. Démon's sister was her godmother, her natural protector, and her providence, and the child offered her the greatest part of her love, respect, and obedience.

A mysterious instinct told Blanchette that among all the men of the house, Pélasge was the one she naturally loved the most. He was her godmother's friend, and besides, he took the effort to teach her. He was so good to her. Never did he scold her. He played with her, and he always brought her such pretty things each time he made a trip to New Orleans!

There was a third person for whom Blanchette had a distinct preference: Lagniape. Without noticing the old woman's infirmity, she saw very well that there was something within her that made her an incomplete being fated to suffering and sadness. She awakened Blanchette's compassion, and the child defended her when other children teased her. As for Lagniape, she was besotted with Blanchette. She could not find any expressions tender enough to make the child understand how much she loved her. She was proud of her. She called Blanchette her little princess, her diamond. Seeing her so white, so rosy, so pretty, so intelligent, and so kind, she dreamt of a magnificent future for her, a destiny that one only sees in *Les Mille et Une Nuits.*[2] Her imagination's golden dreams were not mere dreams for Lagniape; she took them very seriously, and she considered them reasonable and legitimate expectations. A sort of poetic grandeur had always fascinated Lagniape. It was her weakness. She already saw a twenty-year-old Blanchette, shining like a star in the whites' society, admired and sought out by the sons of the richest families. She pictured her wedding—what a celebration! What luxury! What magnificent gifts lavished upon the bride!

Lagniape sincerely believed that she possessed the gift of prophecy, and she often predicted the future with an imperturbable certainty. Some people took her at her word while others only smiled and listened. Her authority increased considerably among those who believed in her powers when one of her prophecies came true. She had once announced in the presence of Saint-Ybars, Chant d'Oisel, Pélasge, Titia, and Fergus the blacksmith that Stoval, the slave merchant, would die on the scaffold. And sure enough, one morning, while skimming through the pages of a New Orleans newspaper, Saint-Ybars read that the same Stoval, ex-protestant minister and ex-slave trader, condemned to death for having slit his mistress' throat, had just been hanged in the courtyard of the parish prison. When this news spread throughout the plantations, Lagniape assumed a sacred nature in the eyes of the slaves. They greeted her with increasing respect, and the old slave women took more care than ever to express their testimonials of devotion to her.

Stoval had died repentant and in a state of religious exaltation. At the initiative of Dr. Deléry, the town's doctor, a petition had been addressed to the governor to ask for a commutation of punishment. The answer arrived the same day the execution was set. When the condemned learned that it had been denied, he began to sing hymns. His resounding and pitiful voice filled the prison, terrifying the other prisoners locked in their cells. Employed as a nurse during his custody, he had proven himself to be enthusiastic and devoted to the sick. Saint-Ybars' doctor, who at that time was standing in for the town's doctor, found himself in contact with Stoval every day. Thanks to this unfortunate man's secrets, he learned a great deal about the development of the condemned man's evil inclinations.

Stoval, dressed all in white, his arms bound behind him, walked towards the gallows with a steady step, singing one last hymn. There were nearly two hundred spectators in the courtyard. He sat down on a stool in the middle of the gallows platform. There, he was quiet and engaged in silent prayer. After a short silence, he said several words to acknowledge that he deserved the punishment that the law had prescribed for him. He spoke about his father and mother. He sang their praises and exonerated them from all responsibility regarding him, saying that since he alone was guilty, the infamy of his death must fall on him alone.

When he stopped talking, one of the prison's occupants, fulfilling the functions of the executioner, stepped forward dressed in a black robe, his face hidden under a mask. He slipped the rope around Stoval's neck, pulled the prisoner's white hood all the way to his chin to cover his eyes, and entered a cell adjacent to the gallows. The spectators heard the whack of a hatchet cutting the rope that held up the platform. The platform disappeared with a crash from under the condemned man's feet. Stoval's large, lifeless body spun in the air, twenty feet above the coffin that was waiting for him.

Hearing these details, Lagniape raised her eyes to the sky and said:

"The poor man! As for me, I forgive him."

Chapter 30

Vieumaite Predicts the Civil War

Vieumaite also tried to predict the future, but with him, there was no claim to the gift of prophecy. He carefully studied current events to logically infer what would happen in the future. As early as the spring of 1860, he foresaw a civil war in the United States because it seemed impossible to him, considering the views of the states in the North and South, that war would not break out shortly. Sensing the approaching storm, he took precautions. He first encouraged Pélasge not to change his citizenship, and he put the property that he had reserved for himself in Pélasge's name. In case things took a turn for the worse, he said, there would be something for Démon and Chant d'Oisel. Pélasge had savings. With Vieumaite's advice, he purchased the farm that he had built with Démon as well as a squad of slave children.

Towards the end of summer, Vieumaite visibly declined. After nearly a hundred years, he was fading away like a fire running out of fuel. In his last hour, his mind burned with an extraordinary brilliance. After having said his goodbyes to the whole family, he sent for Pélasge and said to him:

"You're the only one on this plantation who can retain his composure. You're the only person who understands reason. A torrent of passion is sweeping away my son and my grandsons. Southern fanatics and northern maniacs are going to destroy this great Republic. John Brown's hanging[1] is an act of defiance that the South is throwing at the North. The churchbells of New England are tolling for the poor victim in response. Here, everyone's drunk with pride—in the North, it's hatred and fanaticism. Here, we invoke state sovereignty, but what we want is to keep our slaves. In the North, they demand human rights, but what they want is to degrade the South. Fools! They're tired of the status quo that guarantees them peace. The giddiness of military glory clouds their brains. Military glory! The madness of blood, an old monomania that has given humanity so much pain to overcome.

"My young friend, civil war is approaching! Civil war, the most hideous of all evils.

"Poor South, what a sad fate awaits you! Victorious or defeated, your misfortune is certain. If victorious, you'll drag around a ball and chain attached to your foot—slavery. Your enemy will still be able to pursue you mercilessly on the grounds of morality. If defeated, your factories will be destroyed. Your property will be snatched away from you by unforgiving claws, torn down and devoured like Prometheus,[2] what a long time it will take to rebuild your health and strength! Perhaps a half-century.

"Monsieur Pélasge, I'm dying at the right time. My eyes will not see things that would make them weep. I beg you, cover me with my old travelling coat. It'll serve as my shroud.

"I want to be buried under the sachem without any ceremony. My father and mother wanted to be placed in a tomb, and I respected their will. Mine is to be set down in a simple ditch and for everyone to respect it. You're more than a friend to the family. You're part of it, in a way. I beg you, see that I'm buried as I desire.

"When you write to Démon, embrace him very affectionately for me.

"My life has been a long journey. I feel a great need for rest. Sleep is overcoming me. Death is sweet. Goodbye, Monsieur Pélasge."

Chapter 31

The War

Hardly had the yellow leaves of the sachem, blown down by winter winds, covered Vieumaite's grave when Fort Sumter's cannon marked the start of a fratricidal conflict that would last four years. Monsieur Héhé and Mademoiselle Pulchérie distinguished themselves among the most ardent Confederates. For them, the outcome of the war was certain. They believed that a Southerner, accustomed since childhood to the use of arms, was worth ten Northerners, and thus the matter would be settled in a matter of months. All Saint-Ybars' sons and sons-in-law enlisted. Of these nine courageous men, of whom six were married, only three would return.

When the Northerners took over Louisiana, Saint-Ybars was summoned to declare himself for or against the United States. He proudly responded that he was opposed to a Union imposed by force. Under the pretext that he corresponded with the Confederates, he was arrested. Brought before General Butler,[1] he was subjected to a string of questions, each more ridiculous than the last. After his trial, he was sent to Fort Lafayette, where he died exhausted from his physical and moral suffering. His princely home was transformed into a military barracks. Mademoiselle Pulchérie, having declared under oath that she had always been a Unionist, had the privilege of keeping her lodgings. Pélasge housed Madame Saint-Ybars, Chant d'Oisel, and Blanchette under Vieumaite's roof with Mamrie and Lagniape. Madame Saint-Ybars' daughters-in-law took refuge with their families. Pélasge settled on his farm.

Monsieur Héhé hastened to establish friendly relations with the federal officers. He ate, drank and smoked with them at the same table where he had shared so many meals with the former masters of the house. He watched the systematic plundering of the grand plantation with a callous eye. Feeling no outrage, he saw the familiar faces of the family that decorated the living room pierced by the blades of Yankee swords and bayonets.

The Federal troops tried in vain to use the plantation for their own profit, but the slaves had scattered like soldiers in disarray. To survive, some of them fished or hunted while others pillaged. Some reported for duty in the United States' army, and others had jobs in town. The young freewomen rushed to New Orleans, where a life of pleasure awaited them. Ditches filled in and grass grew everywhere. Horses belonging to a squadron of cavalry ravaged the gardens and devoured the bark of the most beautiful trees. Their withered and silent skeletons served as perches for the buzzards.

When the troops occupying the plantation moved on, the destruction increased in an astoundingly horrific way. In a single night, all of the fences disappeared. One morning, the roofs of all the huts were missing. Nearly every day, fresh remains lay in the field or in the courtyard: oxen, cows, mules, and horses had their throats slit and were cut up during the night. The domestics' lodgings, the kitchen, the ballroom, the hospital, the stables, the overseer's house, the slaves' huts, the poultry house, the dovecotes—everything, even the dog kennels, was demolished. The former slaves were accused of this nocturnal pillaging, but they threw the accusation back at certain white men who, in their opinion, were no better than them.

Despite Mademoiselle Pulchérie's presence, the master's house was attacked by thieves. The sun, the wind, the dust, and the rain started to enter the house freely as the doors and windows were removed. Mademoiselle Pulchérie was forced to leave, and she quickly imposed herself upon Madame Saint-Ybars' sister. The flooring of the old house vanished, followed by the beams, the joists, the panels, and the stairs. Soon, nothing more remained other than the brick frame, which resembled an abandoned fortress after a siege. Eventually, even the bricks themselves disappeared. Of Saint-Ybars' magnificent residence, nothing was left but a few sections of the ground floor wall, whose shadows provided a resting place for old wandering cows.

The sugar mill with all of its outbuildings was not treated any better. The Northerners, seeing that instead of sugar they had manufactured a kind of tar, abandoned the machines. Before leaving it, they sold the supplies that had been packed into the stockrooms. After their departure, the wood and bricks of the factory, the stalls, the warehouses, and the stables disappeared. The steam machines and the iron pieces, too heavy to be removed in one night, were left in place, exposed to the air. They became covered with rust, and the following spring, their crumbling bodies were buried in the middle of a desert of tall weeds.

Chapter 32

Démon Wants to Come Home

At the beginning of the conflict, Démon wanted to return to his country. Pélasge dissuaded him from doing so. "Why come back?" He wrote to him. "Probably because you think it's your duty and it's a question of honor. Like your brothers, you desire to pay your debt in blood to your native country. But the education you've received in Europe has given you other ideas, other feelings from those of your brothers. I have here, under my eyes, your letter from the nineteenth of November, 1860. I read this passage, which shows such insight that anyone would believe it to be written by a grown man: 'The Union, is it really in danger? I do not think that the South would benefit from breaking it up. The conscience of the nineteenth century condemns slavery. It's a dead belief in the minds of slave masters; it is no more than a brutal fact, a matter of money, and the question will definitely be decided against the South. If the South takes up arms, it will be frowned upon by the enlightened and liberal part of every nation-state. The emancipation of slaves is one of the demands of our time. It appears to me a lot closer than you would believe in the South. Do not call me a dreamer anymore. Look, barely several months ago, Italian unity was considered a utopia by Messieurs De Metternich, Guizot and Thiers,[1] and all of a sudden it has become a reality.'"

"Démon, believe me, do not come back. Consider this truth: the generous minds who are fighting for the principle of state sovereignty are few. People are fighting to keep their slaves, refusing to hand them over to the generals who want them to fight in the trenches."

The blockade posed an insurmountable obstacle to Démon's wishes. Correspondence between the professor and his former student became difficult. They were only able to write each other with the help of the French naval officers stationed in New Orleans.

Madame Saint-Ybars and Chant d'Oisel were very worried, thinking that Démon was short of money. For two years, he had settled into a routine. He lived in a small apartment in the Latin Quarter and took classes at Collège de France, at the Observatory and Jardin des Plantes.[2] How could they send money to him? They did not have enough for themselves. They were living off their small farm. They hardly had enough to buy flour to make bread. Mamrie had an idea. Démon needed fifty dollars a month in order to live in Paris. She promised to provide it as long as those ladies could do without her. Then she explained her plan, and it was approved. Chant d'Oisel bravely undertook the task of cooking, Madame Saint-Ybars of washing, Lagniape of ironing, and Blanchette of cleaning. At night, they sewed.

Pélasge worked in the garden, chopped wood, and kindled the fires.

Each person rummaged through his pockets. They collected several dollars, and Mamrie left for New Orleans. Two days after her arrival, she was set up on Canal Street, selling her homemade cakes and candy. Her pleasant appearance, her gracious manner of serving, and the excellent quality of her merchandise attracted regular customers, mostly the officers of the Federal Army, who were avid, infamous lovers of pastries and sweets. She earned roughly two dollars a day. She had an agreement with *la maison Lafitte & Dufilho*[3] that their correspondent in Paris would provide Démon with two hundred and fifty francs every month. She kept ten dollars for food. She stayed with an old Negro woman, a friend of Lagniape's, for free.

Mamrie, knowing that Démon was free from want, was as happy as she could be after such great disasters, even though she was so far away from Madame Saint-Ybars, Chant d'Oisel, Blanchette, Pélasge, and Lagniape. She wrote as often as circumstances allowed her, and her letters were answered regularly.

This way of life lasted until the end of the war.

Chapter 33

After the War

Once the war was over, Pélasge analyzed the situation. A new social order was starting, with new possibilities opening on every side. Pélasge built a shop near the road that ran alongside the river. At first, he sold vegetables, eggs, dairy products, and fruits from the farm. After a short time, he was able to offer fabrics and shoes to buyers. In less than six months, he had to expand his store. Finally, his business expanded so much he had to hire assistants. At that point, he was able to tell Démon, who greatly desired to see his family again, that he was sending him funds to make the trip. Blanchette jumped for joy, imagining that she would see her godfather at the beginning of autumn. She had heard so much about him! He had sent her so many pretty little gifts! He must be so kind! His portrait, saved from the damage, hung in Chant d'Oisel's bedroom, and Blanchette looked at it often. She found him very handsome. "Only," she said, sighing, "why does he look so sad?"

Mamrie had come back, and Pélasge had hired a cook and a laundry woman, former slaves of the plantation. A young freewoman did the cleaning in return for her food and a small daily allowance.

As far as business was concerned, everything was going well. But Pélasge had a serious concern: the desolation, the deprivations, and the chores too taxing for a young girl accustomed to the pleasures of luxury had endangered Chant d'Oisel's health. She had been coughing and losing weight for several months. Despite her efforts to appear cheerful,

Pélasge found her anxious and sad. It had been agreed between them that they would wait for Démon's return before they married, but as the desired moment drew near, Chant d'Oisel's health deteriorated more. One morning, as she stood up after an intense coughing fit, she spit up an abundant amount of blood.

Pélasge, alarmed and brokenhearted, called three doctors for consultations. They gave him some hope, but he was not fooled by their optimistic words. After accompanying them to their carriages, he came back to Chant d'Oisel's bedside; he thought he had regained his usual composure, but with her penetrating and gentle eyes, she read on his face what he was trying to hide. She motioned for him to sit down on the edge of her bed. She wrapped her arms around his neck and said to him, "Dear Pélasge, there's no hope for me. I've known for a long time what the expected outcome will be. I've remained silent because of you all; I didn't want to distress you too soon. Death is a villain, a covetous thing. The prospect of our marriage aroused its jealousy. It didn't want us to be happy. But it won't have what it hoped for. Before leaving this world, I want you to give me your name. I would love nothing more than for people to call me Madame Pélasge after I leave this world. You won't refuse me, will you, dear friend? It's a thought that I've been entertaining ever since I felt the threat of death. It's been my consolation during sleepless nights. My dear Pélasge, will you put your hand in mine and announce, in front of the judge, that you're giving me your name? After being your fiancée for so many years, I'll be so happy to be able to leave this world with my wedding ring! Do you promise?"

Pélasge embraced Chant d'Oisel, consoled her, and promised.

From that moment on, Chant d'Oisel's condition worsened without the least respite. Soon she was no more than a ghost of herself, still beautiful with her large, black, velvety eyes and her magnificent hair. She was sad but accepting, and there was never a sign of impatience, never the least complaint. Every time Pélasge entered her room, she had a smile for him. Her eyes, penetrating and thoughtful, filled with tenderness as they met his. Her voice, which was not more than a whisper, affectionately murmured his name. One night, when a storm was brewing, she felt worse than ever. She was breathing with increasing difficulty. Around six o'clock in the morning, she felt a little relief. The weather had cleared up, and she had someone open the window that was near her bed. It was March, and the scent of the blooming orange trees filled the air. The birds were singing, and the dragonflies were bathing in the early morning sun. Chant d'Oisel cast her eyes longingly on the countryside dripping with light and the sky speckled with small rose-colored clouds. She smiled and little by little lost herself in a long reverie. She returned to reality, sighed, and said to Mamrie:

"Mamrie, vou connin, cé pou jordi."[i]

"Ça to di?"[ii] Mamrie asked.

"Mo di vou," continued Chant-d'Oisel, "cé jordi mapé mouri."[iii]

"Pé don! Pa parlé comme ça,"[iv] the good woman interrupted, making an effort to hide her emotion.

"Si fé," resumed Chant-d'Oisel. "Fo bien mo parlé. Mo gagnin tou plin kichoge pou di vou. Dabor, mo pa oulé ain ote que vou touché mo pove piti cor, vou tendé? Asteur, pranne moin é metté moin su sofa-là."[v]

Mamrie took her into her arms and laid her on the sofa, thinking to herself:

"Chère fie, to pa pésé lour, non!"[vi]

And out loud:

"Di moin ça to oulé mo fé. Ma fé tou to volonté."[vii]

"Couté moin bien," Chant d'Oisel responded. "Metté dra prope dan mo litte. Apré, couri cherché dolo tchiède dan ain gran bakié. Va vidé ladan ain flacon plin dolo cologne, épi va lavé vou piti Chant-d'Oisel, comme vou té fé dan tan lé zote foi, eau Démon avé moin nou té tou lé dé tou piti. Apré ça, ma di vou ça vou gagnin pou fé."[viii]

[i] "Mamrie, you know, today is the day."

[ii] "What did you say?"

[iii] "I told you that today is the day I'm going to die."

[iv] "Be quiet! Don't talk like that."

[v] "Well, I have to talk. I have all kinds of things to say to you. First, I don't want anyone other than you to touch my poor fragile body, do you understand? Now, pick me up and lay me on the sofa over there."

[vi] "Dear child, you don't weigh much at all!"

[vii] "Tell me what you want me to do. I'll do anything you desire."

[viii] "Listen to me closely. Put clean sheets on my bed. Then, go fetch some hot

"Oui, chère fie," Mamrie said. "Ma contanté toi."[i]

And she walked out. In less than ten minutes, she came back balancing a large red cedar tub lined with brass on her head. She put it down near the sofa, closed the doors, and returned with a thick, delicate sponge and a decanter of eau de cologne.

"Comme li changé! Comme li maigre! Mo senti mo tchor tou séré, mé fo pa mo pleuré. Ça sré fé li tro la peine."[ii]

When she had finished washing and drying Chant d'Oisel, she slipped a batiste nightdress on her, one of the last remains from the days of splendor, and placed her back in her bed. The ill girl lay down on her right side, saying:

"Mo lasse. Ma repose ain brin."[iii]

After several minutes, Mamrie helped her sit up, leaning her against some pillows.

"Thank you, Mamrie," Chant d'Oisel said. "Asteur couri di moman li vini. Nou pas gagnin tro tan. Mo bien gene pou respiré. Mo faible, faible."[iv]

Mamrie went to find Madame Saint-Ybars.

"Mother," Chant d'Oisel said, "the time has come. This morning, your daughter's getting married and leaving you. You promised me, you know, dear mother… You're going to dress me in my bridal clothing, which will also be my preparation for death. My clothes are there, in the armoire. They have been waiting for me for three weeks."

"My daughter," said Madame Saint-Ybars, "so you absolutely wish…"

"Yes, mother, I insist, I insist on being loved by you until the end. Be brave now. You've shown so much courage during all our misfortunes! Do what I'm asking, dear mother. Help me pass with a

water in a large tub. Empty a decanter of eau de cologne into it and then bathe your little Chant d'Oisel, as you did in the past, when Démon and I were both small. After that, I'll tell you what you have to do."

[i] "Yes, dear child. I'll do what you want."

[ii] "How she's changed! How she's lost weight! I feel my heart aching, but I must not cry. That would cause her too much pain."

[iii] "I'm getting tired. I need to rest a bit."

[iv] "Now go tell my mother to come over. We don't have much time; I'm having difficulty breathing. I'm weak, really weak."

happy heart. Pélasge knows. I had Mamrie tell him to go and bring back the judge."

Madame Saint-Ybars and Mamrie dressed Chant d'Oisel in her wedding clothes. She even wanted them to put her white satin shoes and gloves on her.

"My hair," she said, "is the most beautiful thing I have left. Let it fall on my shoulders and neck. It'll hide my gauntness."

When her wedding veil was attached and her gown spread out, she had someone tell Blanchette to bring a basket full of roses and violets. Blanchette came in, her eyes full of tears.

"Blanchette," said Chant d'Oisel, "you've always obeyed your godmother. Obey her one last time: don't cry. Scatter these flowers on my bed all around me. How fresh they are! Such fragrance! It looks like they are trying their best to please me. Roses and violets have always been my favorite. They're blooming just in time to receive my farewell."

They heard noise in the living room. Chant d'Oisel recognized Pélasge's footsteps, and he was told to come in.

The judge who accompanied Pélasge was an old friend of the Saint-Ybars family, a venerable old man who had suffered a long sequence of tragedies like the Saint-Ybars.

To please Chant d'Oisel, Pélasge had dressed in his best clothes, though his face was pale and tense. It was apparent that he was making a tremendous effort to control his grief.

The witnesses had signed the marriage certificate ahead of time and remained discreetly in the adjoining room.

The judge read the marriage certificate and made a short, fatherly speech. His voice was full of emotion. He was thinking of his own daughter, dead only a month, at the same age as Chant d'Oisel.

Madame Saint-Ybars held the wedding rings in a small engraved silver tray, a family heirloom that had fortunately escaped the war's calamities.

Chant d'Oisel removed the glove on her left hand. Pélasge slipped a ring onto her finger. Chant d'Oisel, in turn, placed the ring that was destined for Pélasge onto his finger.

After the ceremony, Chant d'Oisel appeared happy, despite her extreme fatigue. Her breath was short and frequent, and her lips had turned blue. A cold dew had formed upon her forehead. She told Mamrie to climb up on her bed to hold her head up. Mamrie sat down beside her, and Chant d'Oisel rested her head on her nurse's bosom. She held Pélasge's right hand, saying, "Thank you." Madame Saint-Ybars, leaning on her elbows on the opposite side, held her other hand.

Chant d'Oisel, gasping more and more for air, told Blanchette to open all the windows.

Lagniape was in a corner, repeating softly, "To die so young!"

Chant d'Oisel looked at everyone and said:

"You all want to please me, don't you? Try to hold back your tears. Death is as natural as life; whether it's a little too early or a little too late, it always comes. I only regret that it didn't leave me enough time to see Démon, my dear brother! How sad he'll be when he sees the results of this dreadful war. Kiss him for me.

"Goodbye, dear mother. I was as good of a daughter as I knew how to be, loving and respectful towards you.

"Farewell, Mamrie. Vou connin, mo conté su vou pou couché moin dan mo cercueil. Il là dan lote lachambre, diboutte dan larmoir."[i]

Indeed, Chant d'Oisel had anticipated everything. She had even ordered a casket from Donaldsonville.[1] She took another breath and continued:

"I want to be placed in the the tomb with grandmother Saint-Ybars."

She squeezed Pélasge's hand.

"Will you come from time to time to visit me under the old sachem?" she asked.

"From time to time?" Pélasge responded. "No! Every day."

"Thank you, thank you!" she said, squeezing his hand again. Looking at the judge, she added:

"Monsieur Dugué, I'm not selfish. I love Pélasge too much to want to shackle his future. One day, as must happen, he'll fall in love with another woman, as he deserves. More fortunate than me, she'll live to share his joy and pain."

Pélasge shook his head sadly.

[I] "You know, I'm counting on you to lay me out in my casket. It's there in the other room, upright in the armoire."

"My dear little wife," he said, "my days of love on this earth are over. My heart follows you. Keep it forever."

One last remnant of warmth stained the cheeks of the dying woman. Her eyes burned brightly, and a sweet smile hung on her lips, a return of her former beauty. Looking at Pélasge, she repeated several times in a soft and affectionate murmur:

"My dear little wife! Yes, your dear wife who loves you with all her soul."

She motioned to Blanchette to come over and told her:

"Blanchette, you love your godmother. Please her all the way to the end. Sit yourself down at the piano and play Schubert's *Adieu* very slowly. But first, I want to shake Lagniape's hand. Where is she?"

Mamrie, looking in Lagniape's direction, said to her:

"Vini, lapé pélé vou."[i]

Lagniape crawled up to the edge of the bed. Chant d'Oisel extended her right hand towards her, trembling from weakness.

"Lagniape," she said, "I've always been good to you, haven't I? I never hurt you, to my knowledge."

"No, never!" exclaimed the old woman, covering Chant d'Oisel's hand with kisses.

Blanchette, stifling her sobs, sat down and played Schubert's *Adieu.* They listened in reverent silence. Hardly had she finished when a mockingbird came to settle on the window near the piano. He often came there. He was so tame he ate out of Chant d'Oisel's hand. She had even given him a name: Ali.

Ali gracefully extended his body and head as birds do when they see something that surprises them. Having recognized Chant d'Oisel, he started to sing in soft voice. It was rather a twittering, as if the bird had feared to be lacking in tact by being too boisterous.

"Ah! There you are, you too," Chant d'Oisel said to him. "You want to be part of my last thoughts. That's fair. You kept me company more than once in my hours of loneliness and sadness. Goodbye, Ali. Farewell."

Although Chant d'Oisel's voice was only a breath, Ali heard his name. He took off, crossing the room, and passed over the bed before

[i] "Come, she's asking for you."

flying out the window facing the rising sun. Chant d'Oisel's gaze followed him in the rosy light of the morning; her eyes, aimed towards the sky, remained fixed. The passage from life to death happened so gently that it was imperceptible. Mamrie, no longer seeing her breathe or hearing her heart beat, said to her:

"Adieu, mo piti fie! Cé chagrin é tro travail ki tué toi."[i]

"Yes," the judge said, "Mamrie's right. Chant d'Oisel is one more victim among so many others that this cursed war swept away in its course. And when I think that with a bit of reason and a simple monetary sacrifice, we could've saved ourselves from this four-year war and its terrible consequences! Ah! Truly, men are mad, mad and fundamentally vicious."

---

[i] "Farewell, my dear child! Too much grief and struggle have killed you."

Chapter 34

The Funeral

Mamrie placed Chant d'Oisel in her casket as she had placed her in her cradle as an infant. According to custom, the casket was placed on a table covered with white sheets falling down to the floor and decorated with petals of orange blossoms pinned onto the drape.

Pélasge sent messengers on horseback to several neighboring plantations, formally inviting a number of families to the burial. Madame Saint-Ybars' sister came in the morning with her sons and daughters.

At five thirty in the evening, the house was filled with guests. A little before sunset, the procession began. Four young men, Madame Saint-Ybars' nephews, carried the casket on their shoulders. Pélasge walked directly behind them, alone. Behind him, Madame Saint-Ybars, Mamrie, and Blanchette, side-by-side. Then came Chant d'Oisel's aunt and female cousins. Between the family and friends, an old black man pulled a cart that carried Lagniape.

That morning, a squadron of former slaves, paid by Pélasge, had gone down to the fields to chop down the large weeds obstructing the path.

The crowd, silent and meditative, hats in hand, crossed the vast plain. Formerly a lush, green sugar cane field busy with workers, the plain now stood deserted and overrun by wild plants.

Some people were absent. Chant d'Oisel's sisters had followed their husbands, one of whom had gone to seek his fortune in San

Francisco, whereas the others had all left together for Texas in hopes of establishing a small colony there. Her two brothers, returning mutilated from the battlefield, had died after the end of the war. So, of this large family, only Madame Saint-Ybars remained to accompany Chant d'Oisel's coffin.

The sun had set when the procession arrived under the old sachem. Two black masons had opened the tomb. Pélasge helped the pallbearers place Chant d'Oisel beside her grandmother's remains.

After the masons replaced the marble top that sealed the sepulchre, Pélasge dismissed them.

The crowd silently left. Some people noticed that Mademoiselle Pulchérie was not present. They learned that that she had had a falling out with Madame Saint-Ybars' sister and that she now managed a middle-class boarding house that mainly hosted officers of the Federal Army. They also learned that Monsieur Héhé was her permanent tenant and that he presided over the table and served the food to the guests.

An old mulatto woman, Saint-Ybars' former slave, had travelled from very far to attend the funeral of Chant d'Oisel, whom she had always called her little mistress. Invited by Lagniape to sit in her cart, she asked about Man Miramis and Monsieur Salvador. Lagniape informed her that they were in Mexico, where they were living the good life. However, she added, Man Miramis would have preferred to settle in Havana in order to have slaves to train, but Monsieur Salvador, being the good man that he was, had preferred Mexico because it was a country where everyone was free.

Pélasge remained under the sachem, immersed in grief and sullen thoughts. The evening's breeze, wailing within the leaves, attracted his attention. He raised his head and noticed that many of the oak tree's branches were withered and that Spanish moss had taken them over.

"And you too, old giant, you are going away," he said. "Death has you in its claws. It's already made great holes in your leafy branches. It will never loosen its grip on you. It'll devour you branch-by-branch. It will penetrate your enormous trunk and go down all the way to your roots. A shroud of moss will cover your body. Well, what do you expect? Everything takes its turn. Everything dies, and everything disappears.

That's the rule. The ground itself, the cradle and tomb of so many beings, will have its end. A night will come, a mournful and chilly night, where mankind, reduced to a small number of families, will wait in vain for the return of the sun and will be buried under a shower of snow. But what does it matter? You'll die content because you'll have lived as long as your species can live. But who will tell me why this lovely young woman whom I just placed there died in the prime of life, even at the very threshold of happiness? Who will prove to me that this is fair, that this is good? I have no choice but to recognize that the force of the things that burden me is more powerful than I am, and in fact, I must resign myself to its inexplicable blows. But what I do not understand is that the event that buries me in despair might be divinely right—but must I conclude that it is necessarily fair? No. I know only one justice. If there are two of them, where is the other? Who saw it? Who knows it? This other justice, arbitrarily called divine, mankind dreamt it in order to explain his miserable destiny, and his sad dream doesn't explain anything."

He looked at the tomb once again, sighed, and slowly walked away.

Chapter 35

Echoes of Tragedy

For six months, the house where Chant d'Oisel had died was so silent it seemed uninhabited. Madame Saint-Ybars hardly spoke anymore and had entirely lost her ability to converse. She spun around endlessly in the black circle of her memories. An outsider to the world of the living, she dwelled among the dead. She saw only them, and she heard only their voices. For her, they were reality. Pélasge, Mamrie, Blanchette, and Lagniape were ghosts that passed her again and again in a fog. One could attract her attention only by shaking her by the arm and talking very loudly. She frightened Blanchette, especially when she stared at her: she resembled a person sleeping with her eyes open.

Blanchette was sixteen years old. Naturally cheerful, she would have shone like a beautiful spring morning without the presence of this miserable old woman, who sometimes aroused her compassion yet sometimes made her tremble.

When Madame Saint-Ybars was asked a question, she only responded with monosyllables. But there were two words that she repeated spontaneously in a lifeless voice, night and day, with the regularity of a clock. Whether she was awake or asleep, one was sure, every hour, to hear these two words come out of her mouth: "Silence! Rest!" The words resonated like a bell tolling in the stillness of the house. Madame Saint-Ybars resembled a cadaver who walked the earth, seeking a solace she could never find. Consequently, when Blanchette saw her plunge into her long silences, the young girl would tiptoe through the house. She put down and picked up objects as quietly as possible. She hardly dared to breathe.

Pélasge seldom left his room, except for meals. However, taking pity on Blanchette, he made her go out as often as possible. Outside, she was a different person. As her cheerful nature took over, she ran, she danced, and she jumped, intoxicated with light and liberty. In the presence of this dynamic girl, glittering flashes of joy cut through Pélasge's melancholy. Blanchette was seized by uncontrollable laughter. She laughed at her own foolery, teasing Pélasge and putting him to the challenge of running and trying to catch her. Then, she apologized to him for her insolence, threw her arms around his neck, and called him her dear father.

For some time, as a result of her violent headaches, Mamrie's vision had been declining in a disturbing way. No remedy was overlooked to stop the paralysis that took hold of her eyes, yet the disease continued its march at an inexorable pace. Towards the end of September, Mamrie was blind. She accepted her misfortune with resignation. Only once did she happen to say that the good Lord was very hard on her, that he should have at least left her time to see Démon again. She continued to work. She cleaned the silverware, ground the coffee, pounded the maize, and grated the potatoes, producing a multitude of small services that kept her so busy that she did not lose a single hour in her entire day. Sometimes at sunset, when she wanted to breathe in the outdoors, she called for Blanchette's help. Blanchette was good-hearted. More often than not, she anticipated Mamrie's request, suggesting a walk. Mamrie put one hand on Blanchette's shoulder, and Blanchette moved forward first with a slow, regulated step. They chatted. Blanchette delighted in talking with Mamrie. She questioned her about the past—the good old days, as she said—when Blanchette was an infant. Démon and Chant d'Oisel inevitably occupied a considerable place in everything that Mamrie spoke about. Mamrie and Blanchette's conversations always ended with Démon. He was to arrive soon, the first days of November at the latest. Naturally, they were not able to contain their joy. But Blanchette always came back to the question she had asked herself so many times while looking at the portrait of her godfather. "Why does he look so sad?" She asked

Mamrie about it, adding, "Godfather always looks like he is frowning." Mamrie sighed deeply and said that that was due to a wound he had inflicted upon himself around the age of thirteen. Blanchette wanted to know how the accident had happened. Mamrie, out of respect for the memory of her former master, evaded the question.

Chapter 36

Démon's Return

On October 31st, at six o'clock in the morning, there was an unusual excitement in Vieumaite's former house. Everyone was waiting for Démon. He sent word that he had arrived in New Orleans. They expected him at eight o'clock. Blanchette had gotten up first to make coffee. Mamrie came and went, fumbling about and knocking over chairs. Lagniape worked with prodigious energy. She glided from one room to another like a fleeing grass snake. Madame Saint-Ybars, dazed and alarmed, was making a superhuman effort to understand what they were trying to explain to her. "Yes," she said, "I understand all right. Démon is my son. Where is he?"

They repeated:

"He's arriving today, this morning, at eight o'clock."

"Ah! It's eight o'clock already," she murmured, "It can't be. It's not today yet. It's still yesterday."

And she went back to her plaintive refrain: "Silence! Rest!"

After having coffee, Pélasge left. He went first to check on his shop and then to go meet Démon.

The boat always stopped at the plantation's former dock.

Without wasting a minute, Mamrie and Blanchette set off as well. Lagniape took charge of Madame Saint-Ybars. Blanchette walked across the plain and arrived at the main road that once crossed the sugar cane field parallel to the river. She and Mamrie wore mourning clothes in memory of Chant d'Oisel. The color of Blanchette's ensemble highlighted her white, rosy skin. Her black dress trimmed with transparent crepe, light as a breath, complimented her delicate, supple body. Seeing Blanchette, one could say that nature had used the most delicate components possible to create her. She resembled those little dragonflies that are so light they float in the air without effort. Glimmers of light reminiscent of precious stones emanated from her shimmering golden hair, from her sky-blue eyes, from her dainty mouth, and from her smile. She had a sweet and silvery voice. Like all young Louisiana women, especially those from the countryside, her accent was musical.

Ever since Mamrie went blind, her appearance had changed. A gentle sadness had replaced her former cheerfulness. When she looked up, as if to look for the light, she felt good if the weather was nice. Her darkness changed into a reddish night in which large objects vaguely became blurred like elusive shadows.

As she crossed the plain, Mamrie rolled her large, still expressive eyes in the air and said:

"Pa gagnin nuage bon matin."[i]

"Cé vrai," Blanchette responded. "Fé ain tan superbe pou parrain rivé."[ii]

"Ataune," Mamrie resumed, "kichoge apé pacé dans ciel comme ain gran riban noir. Ki ci ça?"[iii]

"Çé ain band zozo sauvage,"[iv] Blanchette replied.

"Çé signe liver pa loin," Mamrie remarked. "Mo contan pou Démon. Li linmin tan frette plice pacé tan cho."[v]

They passed in front of the ruins of the old plantation and turned onto the main avenue that led to the river. One could hear the faraway purr of the boat. At times, Mamrie and Blanchette pushed forward

[i] "There are no clouds this fine morning."

[ii] "That's true. It's superb weather for the arrival of Parrain." ("Parrain," meaning "godfather," is often used as a name in Louisiana culture, much like "Papa" or "Grandfather").

[iii] "Wait, something passed through the sky like a long black ribbon. What's that?"

[iv] "It's a flock of wild birds."

[v] "That's a sign that winter's not far. I'm pleased for Démon. He likes cold weather more than hot weather."

with difficulty. The path was cluttered with dead wood, and in certain places, uprooted oak trees blocked the passageway, and they had to retrace their steps.

When the boat docked, Pélasge immediately recognized Démon among the ten or twelve passengers who disembarked. Seeing a tall, handsome young man approach, who carried his head high like all Saint-Ybars men, Pélasge went straight to him. As for Démon, he recognized his former professor despite the changes that time and grief had brought about in his body. They hugged each other like two brothers.

Two passengers descending at the same time as Démon said hello to Pélasge as they passed. He returned their greeting so coldly that Démon looked surprised.

"I see you don't recognize them," Pélasge said. "The older man, the larger one, is your previous tutor, Monsieur Héhé. The other is the young quadroon your father spoiled so much and called Monsieur le Duc de Lauzun. I think I told you in one of my letters that their first act, when the Northerners arrived, was to throw themselves at their feet. They were suspected of having denounced your father. They didn't recognize you. Otherwise, they would've approached you, believing to do you great honor, for at the moment, they're high political figures. When they realize who you are, they'll certainly come to see you just to flaunt their importance to you. Those are two dangerous men, especially Monsieur de Lauzun. He's hateful and vindictive. As a result of his superstitious nature, he's become skeptical and quarrelsome. He even brags about the faults and flaws in his integrity. As you see, he has prospered. He wears three lapel pins on his shirt, has a gold watch and chain, sports three or four rings on each hand, and uses a cane with a handle made of gold. And watch how casually he smokes his Havana cigar. He's come here on a political tour. He speaks with ease, and everything that comes out of his mouth is an article of faith to the former slaves. He, like all politicians, has only one thing in mind—making money. He's neither respected nor liked, even by the people of his class, but they seek him out because he gives jobs to his sycophants.

"As for Monsieur Héhé, he's still the fat, selfish, greedy pedant you knew. He's involved in shady dealings with the Federal officers and with Monsieur de Lauzun. He's rich and talks about retiring. It's certain he's going to settle down in Paris, where he hopes to do well in the American community."

While talking, Pélasge and Démon had arrived at the main avenue. The wagon in which Démon's trunks had been placed took the public road.

Démon felt a pang seeing the traces of neglect and disorder all around him and thinking that the land on which he walked was occupied. Fortunately, Blanchette and Mamrie came over to change the course of his thoughts. As soon as Blanchette saw him, she began to run without hearing Mamrie's shouts not to leave her. Démon opened his arms to welcome her. She threw herself onto him, shouting, "Parrain! Parrain!"[i] and she covered his lips with kisses.

Mamrie was moving forward and waving her arms like someone searching for something in the dark.

"Démon, mo cher piti," she proclaimed, "coté to yé?"[ii]

She suddenly felt two powerful arms surround her and hug her. Recovering from her shock, she let her hands wander over Demon's head and over his shoulder and arms.

"To ain bel homme asteur," she said.[iii]

Coming back to his face, she touched his beard, his temples, and his forehead. Between his eyebrows, her fingers came across a protuberance tougher than the rest of his skin. It was the scar. It rose up and disappeared in the middle of his forehead. She remembered a very sad day. Mamrie sighed. Démon said:

"Mamrie, why think about that? Let it go. There are memories that need not ever be evoked. They're like the dead: one must let them sleep in peace."

"Ça cé bien vrai," Mamrie replied. "Tan pacé gardé so chagrin. Tan prézan gagnin acé comme ça avé so kenne. Mo fi, ta trouvé tou bien changé. Mé mo pa changé, moin. Ta trouvé même Mamrie to té linmin dans tan lé zote foi. To linmin li toujour, èce pa?"[iv]

---

[i] See second footnote on previous page.

[ii] "Démon, my dear child, where are you?"

[iii] "You're a handsome man now!"

[iv] "That's very true. The past preserves its sorrows. The present has enough of

"Yes, I still love you!" said Démon, clasping her to his chest again. "More than ever, good Mamrie. You nourished us with your milk, Chant d'Oisel and me. You watched over our childhood with a mother's tenderness. You remained a slave when you could've been free so that you could remain close to us. When tragedy and ruin came to ravage my family, you didn't run away from them. After the abolition of slavery, you were able to earn your living working wherever you liked and would've had time to rest. You preferred to share the poverty and sufferings of my mother and Chant d'Oisel. The only reason you left them was to help me. You gave me your time and your energy. You made sacrifices to send me money in Paris. Mamrie, you're a saint. Not only do I still love you, I have as much respect for you as I do gratitude."

"Pé donc! Pa parlé comme ça," Mamrie said. "Mo fé ça mo té doi fé. To blié parlé créol. Mo oua ça. Tapé parlé gran bo langage de France. Épi asteur, effronté, to tutéié to Mamrie. Mo palé grondé toi pou ça. An contraire, ça fé moin plésir to tutéié moin. To acé gran pou ça."[i]

Pélasge and Démon led the way. Passing by the ruins of his father's house and its outbuildings, Démon stopped for a bit. His eyes filled with tears. Pélasge squeezed his hand.

"Friend," Démon said, "be assured that I'm not sad about the house but rather about the people whom I loved there and who are

---

them on its own. My son, you'll find everything changed. However, I haven't changed. You'll rediscover the same Mamrie you loved in the past. You still love me, don't you?"

[i] "Hush! Don't talk to me like that. I did what I had to do. I see you've forgotten your Creole. You speak the grand, fine language of France, and now, rascal, you dare address me using the "tu" form.* I won't scold you for it. On the contrary, it gives me pleasure for you to address me like that. You're old enough for that."

*(Note: In French, the subject "you" has two forms: *tu* is used when a person is speaking to someone familiar, like a friend or sibling. But *vous* is used when addressing someone of superiority to show respect, like an elder or a new acquaintance. Mercier uses the verb "tutoyer" in this sentence, meaning to address someone in the familiar "tu" form. In this case, Mamrie is not offended, for it is socially acceptable that Démon address her more familiarly as he is an adult now instead of a child.

no longer here. The social conditions from which I was born were based on a flagrant violation of human rights. They were doomed to disappear, and they did, dragging my father's heritage into the abyss. I take consolation in it. I'm even happy about it. I blushed with shame more than once thinking about the source of the money I spent. I welcome my poverty and owe the calm in my conscience and my self-respect to it. And to you I owe, friend, the revelation of a truth that makes a man strong and proud. You taught me that work is the fundamental law of humanity and that without it, there is no real happiness."

Chapter 37

Mother and Son

The route was quite long, but Démon did not notice, absorbed as he was in a discussion that revealed something interesting at each step. When they arrived, Pélasge said to him:

"Let me enter first. I'll announce your arrival. Restrain yourself as best you can. Grief has greatly weakened your mother's mind. A too-sudden emotion could make her worse."

They entered. Démon remained in the dining room. Madame Saint-Ybars was in the living room, seated on an arm chair, her hands on her knees. Lagniape, her thick silver glasses on her nose, was sewing by the light of the window. Démon shuddered when he heard his mother's voice. She was repeating, in a pleading and pitiful tone, her melancholic ritornello: "Silence! Rest!"

Pélasge announced the arrival of her son.

"He's here, my dear child," she said. "So, have him come in."

Démon walked in. His mother had aged horribly. Her face was marked by a distressing sadness. He was so shocked that he stopped halfway. Pélasge walked up and said to him softly:

"Let's go in, Démon; be brave!"

Démon knelt down in front of his mother and said to her:

"It's me, dear mother, Démon, your youngest son, your Benjamin, Chant d'Oisel's twin."

"Démon?" Madame Saint-Ybars sighed. "Démon and Chant d'Oisel? But she's gone, Chant d'Oisel."

"And I came back to comfort you, to love you," Démon replied. "Look at me, dear mother. I'm Démon. Take a good look at me."

Madame Saint-Ybars placed her hands on her son's shoulders and looked at him for a long time. By intensely stretching the small bit of willpower that remained inside her, she recalled her son from memory. Understanding gradually reappeared on her face like a distant light that became larger and larger in the darkness as it drew near.

"Yes," she said, "you really are a Saint-Ybars. You're the spitting image of your father. You take after me, too. You have the same eyes that I had long ago when I was young and beautiful, and you have my family's brow."

She stopped, frowning. She was looking at the scar. Then, she made a gesture as if to chase away an unpleasant memory.

"My son," she began again, "your father had fine qualities that many men did not have. We should cherish his memory."

"Yes, mother, I do. I respect him."

"That's good, Démon. Give your old mother a hug."

Démon hugged his mother and, clasping her against his chest, said:

"I know what you need. You want peace and quiet. You'll find comfort here in grandfather's house. He built it so those in old age could have the peace they so desire. Don't worry about anything. I like work, and I'll make this humble property produce everything you need to live well. Blanchette will watch over you like a dutiful daughter, and good Lagniape, who I imagine hasn't lost her penchant for chattering, will keep you company."

He stood up to go shake Lagniape's hand.

"So you didn't forget me?" the old woman said. "Ah! I recognize you now, still kind, still compassionate. Thank you, Démon. May happiness return here with you. We greatly need it."

With Démon, life seemed to come back into Vieumaite's house. He wanted to see everything. He went upstairs, came down, and went up again, asking questions and seeking explanations. When Blanchette returned, her cheerfulness added to Démon's excitement, and the whole place took on a festive atmosphere. A new spirit was touching everyone. Pélasge felt ten years younger. Mamrie and Lagniape came and went, tottering and laughing at their own awkwardness and chattering incessantly. Madame Saint-Ybars seemed to have come out of a long lethargy. She wanted to be a part of everything that was happening to celebrate her son's return. At dinner that night, she spoke as she had not done since Chant d'Oisel's death. She was even excited. Her dull eyes flared up again, and warmth colored her withered cheeks. That evening, she asked Démon questions and made several clever remarks, although she retired fairly early because she was feeling tired. As she lay down, she told Blanchette that her head was burning but that it would pass if she slept.

Chapter 38

Démon Inquires About the State of the Country

Since the night was cool and sparkling, Pélasge and Démon went for a walk. Démon took the opportunity to ask his old mentor about current conditions in rural Louisiana.

"We're going through a difficult time," Pélasge responded. "The war has left us with many problems to solve, all the more difficult because it caught us unexpectedly. I'm talking about the reorganization of labor. Perhaps we could settle the matter were it not for political complications. Opportunistic invading hordes from the North declared themselves the guardians of emancipated slaves and formed an alliance with the free people of color. You haven't forgotten, I imagine, what it means to be a person of color here. The Creoles formed a natural buffer between whites and blacks; many were free and enlightened before the war, well-off financially and accounting for a considerable number of honorable families. According to their beliefs, they formed an aristocracy compared to the blacks. They weren't wrong in doing that if aristocracy means being wealthier and more educated than the masses and having a more consistent and refined life than the poor. They instinctively strive to get along with the whites. With a few easily-made concessions, we could gain their sympathy and their support for the reconstitution of the work force in Louisiana. After all, what are they asking for? Simply what might be called public equality—that is, their place next to whites in theaters, at concerts, at restaurants, in steamboats, etc. As for social equality itself, or in other terms, that which pertains to the affairs of private life, they are the first to acknowledge that it's a matter of personal conscience and taste, and that everyone on both sides must religiously respect the free will of each individual.

"The white population wants to recapture its former supremacy over state affairs. Creoles of color and blacks, advised by their Northern allies, compete with whites for power, resulting in violent animosities, bloody brawls, and battles where the majority of casualties are black. To sum it all up, we're threatened with a new civil war complicated by a social war.

"One of the most deplorable effects of the current situation is the renewed outbreak of racial prejudice and hatred. You'll notice that even the idea of caste is more pronounced than it was in the time of slavery.

"The war was only a prelude to the social and political revolution that'll change the way we've lived. This revolution is happening now. And yet, you know, nothing more resembles death than change. Anyone witnessing current events would believe that Louisiana's going to be engulfed in an abyss of blood and ruin. The Republican Party declares that it's necessary to wipe out the former white aristocracy. They claim that the former slave owners are looking to do away with the blacks and to replace them with Chinese laborers. You'd be astonished by the casual manner with which people in this democratic nation talk about exterminating entire classes of citizens. You'd think you were in Turkey or in Russia.

"How do we solve this problem? I'll tell you what I honestly think.

"Time and experience have proven that the blacks were, at least up until now, the most efficient workers in a climate like Louisiana's. Instead of rejoicing in their dimishing numbers, as certain people are doing, we should want their number to grow. For this to happen, the state must educate the former slaves. Help him develop a strong sense of family. If he continues to drink himself to death, or be systematically murdered at every election, if young black women continue to reject the responsibilities of motherhood and to flock to cities to support themselves through prostitution, blacks in Louisiana will share the same fate as the Indians.

"There's talk of replenishing our workforce through European immigration. I don't see this happening. Foreigners know that yellow fever is currently spreading throughout the countryside. For an immigrant to brave that peril, he would need to be guaranteed considerable income.

"Right now, blacks are the real working class of Louisiana. We've lived with them as slaves, so why not live with them as freemen? They aren't spiteful—as could be seen during the war. They could've done enormous harm to their former masters without fear of punishment. Not only did they not do it, but they didn't listen to the malicious advisors who urged them to do so.

"For me, the black race has more easily adapted to our civilization than Native Americans. In addition to the fact that they aren't lazy and show a great desire to learn, they're gentle, affectionate, and compassionate. But I forget you're Creole. You know better than me all the good there is in the race to which Mamrie belongs. As for the Creoles of color, you would never persecute them. In fact, the majority of Louisianans feel and think like you and me, but they lack the courage to say so, like some of our valiant young men who faced death for four years on the battlefield, who are stricken by a superstitious fear in front of the ghosts of ignorance and pride."

Pélasge and Démon's conversation lasted well into the night. At last, they parted ways. Pélasge went to the farm, and Démon went to claim Vieumaite's bed.

Like the followers of Pythagoras, Démon was in the habit of reminiscing about the events of the day before going to bed and briefly jotting down the thoughts that came to him. This is exactly what he did as he sat down at that large table illuminated by the same lamp that had been used so many times during his grandfather's working evenings.

"So," he said at the end, "this house is all that remains of our brilliant fortune, and I am the last Saint-Ybars."

As he lay on that bed where Vieumaite had rested in the past, his childhood memories came back in multitudes. Who could have predicted that upon his return to the plantation, he would find only his mother! His thoughts kept him from falling asleep. Fortunately, Blanchette's pretty smiling face appeared like a light amidst the dark background of his thoughts. He saw only her, and when sleep finally took him away, he continued to see her in a dream.

Saint-Ybars

Part IV

Chapter 39

The Next Day

At seven o'clock the next morning, Démon was still sleeping. Arriving from the farm, Pélasge decided not to wake him, even if it meant postponing breakfast.

Blanchette, as usual, entered Madame Saint-Ybars' bedroom. Surprised at not seeing Demon's mother up and already dressed, she looked toward the bed. Madame Saint-Ybars seemed to be sleeping, but Blanchette thought she was very pale. She drew closer and listened. She did not hear the sound of her breathing. Then, trembling all over, she touched Madame Saint-Ybars' cheek. She stepped back, unsteady.

Pélasge was on the front balcony, enjoying the fresh air from the river and reading a newspaper. A hand grabbed him by the arm. He raised his eyes. Seeing Blanchette's distressed face, he immediately knew something had happened.

"What is it?" he asked. "What's wrong with you, Blanchette?"

Incapable of uttering a word, she pulled him towards her and led him into the bedroom. Pélasge touched Madame Saint-Ybars' body. She was stiff and cold. Death must have taken her as soon as the night began. What a shock it would be for Démon when he woke! At the very thought of it, Pélasge felt broken, as if the house had collapsed on him.

Démon accepted this new misfortune with stoic strength. Not one complaint escaped his lips, not one cry of anger against the fate that seemed to pursue him with an implacable relentlessness. He was left with only a somber sadness. Pélasge would have liked to comfort him, but since Démon never talked about his mother's death, no one ever brought it up in front of him. Démon's attitude worried Pélasge. All of the Saint-Ybars had shown, more or less, a tendency to superstition. Vieumaite alone had been the exception to that rule. Pélasge feared that this family flaw also existed within Démon. He suspected that his young friend believed that he was under the spell of an inexorable destiny. Unfortunately, Pélasge was right—Démon did indeed have lugubrious premonitions. He never spoke about them out of pride. He would not have wanted, not for anything in the world, to face hearing that he had any weaknesses or lack of will. In the depths of his mind, he knew he was born for misfortune. He braced himself internally against the wickedness of fate and waited, in stoic silence, for its additional blows.

Chapter 40

Blanchette Consoles Démon

Only Blanchette dared to confront Démon's melancholy. She proceeded to do so indirectly and devised a clever plan. She had often heard of the extraordinary power of music on the men of the Saint-Ybars family, particularly on Démon. To console her godfather, she decided to play her piano whenever she could without disturbing anyone. She consulted Pélasge. Judging by what he told her, she thought that she could indeed begin playing again. Actually, the piano for her was not a simple matter of pleasure. Chant d'Oisel had taught Blanchette to consider the instrument a source of revenue in case of necessity. Blanchette, despite her childish cheerfulness and her mad whims, was in reality a hard-working young woman who was as practical and serious as anyone her age could be. She always had an astonishing ability to learn and a truly marvelous memory. She played everything by heart, even the most difficult and lengthy sonatas. She graciously asked her godfather for permission to take up her studies again. Six weeks had gone by since Madame Saint-Ybars had died, so Démon consented to Blanchette's request. The first time he heard her, he was both charmed and surprised. He expressed his amazement to Pélasge:

"Did you know that Blanchette is an extraordinary young person? Such skill and such precision! She draws an astonishing volume of sound from her piano and has as much expression as a thirty-year-old woman. Can you believe it? She plays Weber and

Beethoven as if she had composed their music. I didn't hear anything as good in Paris, even though I attended a lot of concerts."

Every time Blanchette sat down at her piano, she knew Démon would soon enter the living room. Then, pretending to play German, Hungarian, or Russian works that he was unfamiliar with, she performed pieces according to his state of mind. Little by little, Démon's sadness became a sweet reverie, and he began to pour out his heart. Blanchette would go to him, take his arm, and say:

"Parrain, would you take a walk with me? I really feel like getting some fresh air."

They would leave, walking at random, absorbed in the exchange of intimate thoughts that made them more and more dear to each other. For Blanchette, to see Démon and to love him had always been one and the same. She loved him even before his arrival. She had so often heard of his excellent heart, and she had had many occasions to get to know him through his letters. He was just as she had imagined him, even the same sweet and exquisite face, the same voice, the same smile, the same distinguished air, and the same manner of walking. To love Démon in person as she had loved him from afar was an altogether simple thing for her, so natural that she constantly told him how much she cared about him and that she would give her life to make him happy.

Démon had completely withdrawn from the world; only with Blanchette did he feel suspended in a sort of waking dream, where he felt himself living a life of neverending delight. For him, it was real life, the life of his heart and mind. The past, with its sufferings and miseries, seemed to him like a distant night, a night crossed by sinister ghosts receding and fading in front of a light that shone around him and Blanchette. He had forgotten the pain. He remembered it only when Blanchette was not near him. At such times, he felt an uneasiness that could be compared to the unrest of a person searching, as in a dream, for his disembodied spirit.

Démon had become attached once again to his native land. His grandfather's house seemed to him the best place in the world to live happily with Blanchette. She would become his wife as soon as the end of his mourning dispelled the last shadow placed between them and happiness. In the meantime, they worked together to improve the house and the garden. They drew up wonderful plans together. In the middle of the day, when the sun's heat prevented them from going out, they sat on the balcony in the shade of the tall curtains and read out loud, taking turns. Later, they went downstairs to the living room to listen to music and relax. There, they told each other, in the divine language of sounds, those profound and mysterious things that only melody and harmony can express. In the evening, they contemplated the spreading vastness of the stars, the dark masses on the horizon, and the great river winding majestically in the silence, reflecting the opaline light of the sky, spreading a salutary freshness on the sleeping countryside. They soared away together into boundless space, on the wings of reverie and hope. They lost themselves in the infinity of love. They forgot that there is a chain that keeps us all attached to the earth; however high we may rise in our minds and hearts, tragedy is the immovable rock to which our lives are chained.

This life of enchantment lasted for six months. Nothing disturbed it except the visits that Démon and Blanchette received every now and then that they felt compelled to return. These calls were torture for Démon, but no sooner did he regain his freedom than he instantly forgot the people he had just seen; he hastened to plunge himself back into the world of ecstasy where Blanchette was everything to him and he was everything to her!

Pélasge, Mamrie, and Lagniape were happy for Démon and Blanchette. They shielded them as much as they could against the disturbances of idlers and inquisitors.

Démon had suffered cruelly during the two or three times when Monsieur Héhé and Monsieur le Duc de Lauzun had come to see him. The first seemed rather mocking to him, the second conceited and envious. A third character had also left an unpleasant impression on him. He was a very pretentious country gentleman named des Assins. This man had an exaggerated opinion of his personal worth. He ascribed such importance to himself that he did not leave any of it for others. He talked about nothing but himself, as if the whole world had been created to pay homage to him alone. After a long and tiresome visit that irritated Démon, Monsieur des Assins left peeved;

Démon's reserved and dignified bearing had displeased him. Démon had not even smiled at his jokes. It was an unforgivable crime. He had become an enemy of Monsieur des Assins, and Monsieur des Assins was not an inconsequential enemy. He had already killed two men in duels, a third in a rough and suspicious brawl at the end of a ball, and he had maimed a fourth man for the rest of his life. After his visit with the young Saint-Ybars, des Assins resolved to take his revenge. He went everywhere repeating that this pompous young man thought very highly of himself and that he needed a lesson.

Chapter 41

The Prejudice of Race—The Insult

If Monsieur des Assins sought an opportunity to pick a quarrel with Démon, circumstances served him well.

A strange rumor, a discovery—no one knew where it came from—spread from plantation to plantation, setting all tongues in motion.

"Can you believe it, my dear?"

"What?"

"Mademoiselle Blanchette is a woman of color."

"Impossible!"

"Yes, my dear. She has black blood in her veins. The honorable Mademoiselle Pulchérie has proof of it. She read a letter in which the whole affair is discussed. Do you know who the mother of this counterfeit white girl was? My dear, one of Saint-Ybars' slaves. As for the father, it was Monsieur X***. You know, the one who was killed at Shiloh."

A reconciliation had taken place between Démon's aunt and Mademoiselle Pulchérie. It was springtime. Mademoiselle Pulchérie had been very busy during the winter, and she had come to rest in the countryside at her old relative's house. Démon's aunt had also offered shelter to Monsieur Héhé, who was, as everyone in the area knew, a long-time acquaintance. About the same time, Monsieur le Duc de Lauzun was starting a new political tour in the countryside, haranguing the emancipated slaves and inciting them against their former masters, whom he insisted on calling *Bourbons.*[1] He only spoke English now. He claimed that he had forgotten French.

Démon's peaceful and happy life was abruptly disturbed. His aunt, his female cousins, and Mademoiselle Pulchérie invaded his house like a swarm of screeching starlings; under the pretext of friendship, they unpretentiously declared to him that they would spend a week at his home. Démon, despite all his efforts to be polite, could not prevent his bad mood from breaking through. Blanchette restrained herself better. She even strove to be more obliging and more pleasant than ever in order to conceal Démon's discontentment. So she was surprised that the guests treated her with a haughty indifference.

Mademoiselle Pulchérie and Démon's aunt went to the farm and asked Pélasge to speak with them privately. They insisted that he lock the doors. They took two hours to tell him what could have been said in five minutes—that Blanchette was Titia's daughter. They launched into considerations of honor and respect for the family, all of which required Démon to no longer treat Blanchette as an equal.

At the end of this conference, Pélasge was very worried. He foresaw the deplorable results of this recent revelation. He wracked his mind and heart for the best way to prevent a catastrophe. When he believed he had found it, he took Démon under the old sachem to disclose his plan. There, after disclosing the truth about Blanchette's birth, Pélasge revealed to him that Mademoiselle Pulchérie, Démon's aunt, and her cousin were united against him and his fiancée. Pélasge urged him to leave the country, generously offering his savings to the young couple so that they could lead an independent and happy life wherever they wanted. Démon shook his hand vigorously and replied:

"You have a noble heart. To strip yourself of your savings so that we can be happy! To reduce yourself to poverty to protect us from prejudice! No, that's too much, my friend. Even if I were willing to consider your own sacrifice, I would refrain from it out of respect for myself. Imagine leaving, running away like a criminal, exiling myself for fear of criticism! That would be a victory for injustice. It would give credence to tyranny and exclusion. I will not do it. I'll stay. I'll marry Blanchette. Too bad for those who don't like it."

Pélasge did not insist. Deep down, he thought like Démon. It was agreed between them to keep it from Blanchette, at least for the moment. There was no need to distress her unnecessarily.

A dreadful assault was waiting for Démon at home. His aunt, his female cousins, and Mademoiselle Pulchérie locked themselves in with him. Citing "family first" as a basis for their argument, they set about proving to him that he could not, out of respect for his blood relatives, marry a woman of color.

Démon had never impressed people with his patience. He interrupted the ladies' indictment and said sternly:

"You ladies are really amusing. You treat me as though I belong to you. You reject everything I want and try to force me to live by your outdated and ridiculous ideas. Tell me, please, when I was abroad without money, did you share with me the wealth you were enjoying here? When I returned, did you offer any assistance? Come on! Let's drop this imaginary solidarity. Everyone is responsible for his own actions. You make me laugh, pretending to throw in my face that Blanchette is a woman of color. She is whiter than any of you. You've envied her complexion and hair in my presence numerous times, dear little cousins. But you argue that she has black blood in her veins. What the hell! To see that, you must have very good eyes. The next time Blanchette pricks her finger while sewing, I'll take a drop of her blood and bring it to you. We'll look at it together and compare it to a drop of your blood. You'll explain the difference to me. But even if Blanchette were as black as ebony, I'd still love her, and you couldn't say a word. I'm the only survivor of the Saint-Ybars family. I'm the only one who carries the name, and I'm free to give it to Blanchette if it suits me.

"Don't interrupt me. I won't be long. What I have to say to you doesn't represent a tenth of what you've forced me to listen to.

"Believe me, dear aunt, dear cousins, let's not worry so much about the color of our ancestors. Let's be who we are, and let's see others for who they are. Blanchette is as white as a lily. She's kind, good, witty, very knowledgeable for her age, musically talented, and cheerful, never saying anything bad about anyone. So see her like she is, and don't say another word about the black skin of her foremothers.

"But you ladies, can you say with certainty what color your ancestors were? You know, I'm sure, that time has disproved all those haughty legends that established a blood connection between primitive men and angels. First, your angels are imaginary beings, but let's put that aside. Secondly, whether you like it or not, you know that some scholars today strongly suspect that you and me, that all of us who are so proud to call ourselves men, are the descendents of a race that was at least first cousins to the apes. This shocks you. Too bad. As for me, this doesn't affect me at all. I'm not less than what I am, a Saint-Ybars, a child of the nineteenth century, a free man born in Louisiana, where I'll live as I please.

"You blame Blanchette for having had a slave for a mother. You forget, dear friends, that our ancestors were also slaves. Yes, all of us who live under this blessed sky of America, descendants of the French, English, Spanish, Italians, Germans, Portuguese, Swiss, Swedes, etc., all of us are the grandchildren of poor men who made their way through long centuries, their backs hunched under the weight of servitude. It was a cursed time when brute force was the law. Then, people lived on war and plundering. The defeated ones were burdened with chains and condemned to work for the victors. As we were in turn victorious or conquered, slavery spread everywhere, similar to those ominous epidemics that spared one country only to strike another. The only consequence of all this is that there is no one who cannot count slaves among their ancestors.

"And don't think, dear cousins, that we need to go back very far in history to come across our ancestors wearing collars inscribed with their masters' names, like the collars we put on dogs. Decency prevents me from telling you how masters treated our foremothers when they were young and pretty. Are we less respectable or less free because of that? No, not at all. For me, Blanchette is as pure as the whitest of white women. I say that she received the education that is given to the young girls of the best families, and finally, I love her. Thus, I'll marry her. If you came here deliberately to dissuade me from doing so, you can consider your task finished."

Démon bowed politely and left. He went to find Blanchette and took a long walk with her. Démon was more outgoing and tender than ever. Blanchette was happy. She listened to Démon's words with delighted shivers. She gazed into his eyes, as if to say she lived entirely for him, and that if their walk could last indefinitely, the Golden Age would be realized on earth.

They came back by the levee, delighted to be alone in the silence at sunset, forgetting that there are hypocrites and envious people throughout the world for whom the happiness of others is torture, people who must be dealt with sooner or later.

As they were rounding a bend that followed the river, Démon and Blanchette saw a group of nearly a dozen people in the distance. Thinking that they had to pass by these strangers, Blanchette pouted like an upset child. As they moved closer, Démon recognized Monsieur des Assins. Démon saw him move forward and place himself at the edge of the path.

There were three ladies in the group, all whispering behind their fans.

"This is the first time," said one to the others, "that I've seen the young Saint-Ybars. He's quite a handsome young man. But he's wrong to go out in public with a colored girl."

"Poor little Blanchette!" said another. "It's a real shame. She's so kind!"

"She would've always passed for white if it hadn't been for Pulchérie's nasty tongue," the third lady remarked. "What a wasp. What a scorpion. What a rattlesnake, that old maid!"

Blanchette also noticed Monsieur des Assins. She knew him by reputation. She disliked him, but as she did not like to deal with vicious people, she had never spoken of him to Démon.

At the moment when Démon passed in front of the group, Monsieur des Assins said out loud:

"There he comes with his nigger wench."

Démon heard all too well. He turned around, and looking at des Assins with disdain, he hurled a single word in his face:

"Ass!"

This was precisely what Monsieur des Assins wanted. He made a gesture with his head that meant:

"We'll see each other again soon."

Démon motioned to indicate that he understood and was ready.

"Another duel!" exclaimed one of the three ladies.

"Des Assins is wrong," the oldest one pointed out. "You don't insult a white man like that. Des Assins has confidence in his reputation as a duelist. If he kills this young man, it'll be an abomination! I'll no longer speak to him."

Blanchette had heard only the word "nigger." She did not have the least idea of the significance des Assins had attached to it. But she foresaw something very serious. She started trembling all over and tearfully begged Démon for an explanation of what had just happened. He reassured her as best as he could. She was not satisfied. She remained alarmed, telling herself that a duelist like Monsieur des Assins would never allow himself to be insulted without retaliating. On their return, Démon kissed her several times and urged her not to torment herself. He had regained his composure. He spoke in such a natural voice that Blanchette was partially reassured. She retired to her bedroom, her heart a little less burdened.

Chapter 42

The Challenge

Monsieur Héhé and Pelasge were in the living room with Démon's aunt and cousins. Mademoiselle Pulchérie was telling them about the miraculous healing of an old paralytic woman who had drunk water from the Salette.[1] When she finished, Démon took Pélasge and Monsieur Héhé aside and asked them to spend the evening at his home, thinking that he would probably need their services. He told them that in reply to des Assins' crude comment, he had used an expression that would undoubtedly lead to a duel. Later, alone with Pélasge, he explained things to him exactly as they had happened. Pélasge knew Monsieur des Assins and was sure that Démon's opponent had premeditated his insult for a long time. "I'm sure," he thought, "that he's been practicing a great deal with the weapon of his choice. Wretch! Yes, Démon told the truth. Des Assins is an ass, a tremendously stupid ass. If something happens to Démon, the wretch will have to deal with me."

Mademoiselle Pulchérie came to tell Démon that someone was asking for him in the living room. He went immediately and found himself facing two friends of Monsieur des Assins.

"Gentlemen," he said, "are you here to set the terms?"

"Yes, Monsieur."

"Monsieur des Assins challenged first, gentlemen, so that he could choose the weapon. Although, since I was insulted first, I should have the right to send the challenge. No matter. I accept Monsieur des Assins' challenge. What weapon does he choose?"

"The double-barreled rifle."

"The rifle, gentlemen? That figures. Monsieur des Assins is one of the most skilled hunters in the country. Very well. What conditions does he propose?"

"You'll fight each other at forty paces with guns that have never been used. Only one of the barrels of each rifle will be loaded. Once the opponents are in place, one of the witnesses, the oldest one, designated to be in charge, will say, 'Gentlemen, are you ready?' If no reply is heard, he adds, 'Fire!' and he counts from *one* to *ten*. You'll be able to shoot from the word *fire* up to *ten.*"

"Gentlemen," Démon said, smiling ironically, "I see what Monsieur des Assins wants—a fight to the death. Allow me to tell you that he's going about it the wrong way. I refuse his conditions. Here are mine. Each opponent will bring his own rifle with gunpowder and several bullets. The *two* barrels of each rifle will be loaded. We'll fight each other not at forty paces but at twenty, and we'll be able to shoot from the word *fire* up to *twenty*. Gentlemen, I'll send two friends to you with ink, pens, and paper. They'll set the terms of the duel with you in writing."

Monsieur des Assins' friends, left alone, looked at each other.

"My goodness!" said one of them. "He's fearless."

"Ah! I'll say," said the other. "Do we accept such conditions? What will they say about us? It's a massacre."

"Well yes, too bad," the first one added. "We can't retreat."

Pélasge and Monsieur Héhé entered. Pélasge spoke:

"I regret, for you and for us, gentlemen, to have to write up such conditions of combat. Monsieur Saint-Ybars peremptorily refuses to change them unless it would be to make them more dangerous. Do you accept, gentlemen?"

"We accept."

"The duel will take place," Pélasge continued, "on the avenue of the former Saint-Ybars plantation, near the ruins of the house. We'll be there tomorrow morning at seven o'clock. The place and the hour suit you, I imagine."

"Perfectly, Monsieur."

"In that case, gentlemen, I'll dictate the terms, and Monsieur MacNara will write them down. If one of you could do the same… Ah! Excuse me, gentlemen. I'm forgetting one important clause. If one of the opponents is wounded but he can still shoot, Monsieur Saint-Ybars wishes the fight to continue."

"That's understood, Monsieur."

There was a two to three minute silence. Then, Pélasge's deep and strong voice dictated, item by item, the terms of the combat. Monsieur Héhé, proud of his role and frowning aggressively, wrote with dramatic flourishes that would have made a notary's clerk envious. Everyone present signed. Pélasge kept the sheet written by Monsieur des Assins' emissary and gave him the other one. They parted by bowing to each other courteously and saying:

"Tomorrow morning at seven o'clock."

It was agreed that Démon would sleep at the farm, as he sometimes did when he had to leave early with Pélasge. He spent the rest of the evening with Blanchette. She was horribly worried. The visit from Monsieur des Assins' friends was too significant for him to hide the motive from her. Démon found himself forced to admit the facts, though he said they were engaged only in negotiations and that the affair would be resolved the following day. But he did not know how to lie. Blanchette said to him:

"Parrain, you're deceiving me."

And she burst into tears.

Démon took her in his arms, covered her face with kisses, and said:

"All right! Yes, Blanchette, I'm fighting tomorrow morning. Be calm. I'm hopeful. If you want me to retain my courage and composure, you must not cry.

"I'll obey you, Parrain," Blanchette said, wiping her eyes. "I won't cry anymore."

"I'm telling you," Démon continued, putting his hand on her brow, "something tells me that I'll come back to you safe and sound."

He embraced her one more time and left.

Mamrie and Lagniape were leisurely talking in the kitchen. They knew nothing of the evening's incidents.

When Monsieur des Assins learned of Démon's conditions, he burst into laughter.

"The fool!" he exclaimed. "So he's afraid I'd miss him at forty paces? Well, since he wants to receive my bullet at twenty paces, let's use the distance that pleases him."

Monsieur des Assins was about forty years old. He had great experience on the field, not only for having fought often but also for having been either a witness or a spectator in all of the duels in his parish for twenty-two years. He had unbounded confidence in his adroitness and cunning tricks. While preparing his rifle for the next day, he said to his friends:

"Here's what'll happen. This tall, gangling fellow, like the novice that he is, will only have one thought—to shoot first. With the fear of death on his mind, he'll hurry so much to kill me that he'll miss. First, I'll start by throwing off his aim. He'll start to shake when I rock my rifle like this as soon as we're in position—like this, take a good look, up and down and down and up, just following the median line of his body. This is an excellent trick. It's already worked for me twice. I recommend it to you. This swaying has an astonishing effect. Your opponent becomes flustered. He shoots without aiming, and his bullet goes off to the devil. You, then, you aim as you wish and bam! You pierce his hide."

"That's all well and good," someone pointed out, "but all of this assumes that you're dealing with a man who loses his head easily. But if your opponent retains his composure, you take a terrible risk by letting him shoot first."

"That's precisely the point," des Assins resumed. "Will your opponent retain his composure or not? Of course, if I fought with an old quartermaster like you, I'd use another trick. This idle young Saint-Ybars boy has never been in a duel, and when any gentleman has a man of my reputation in front of him the first time he fights, he is scared as hell."

Monsieur des Assins' reasoning was specious. Démon was already well-versed in weapons, but he had only used them to practice his skill and to amuse himself. He had never picked a living being as a target. He made no secret of admitting that he loathed shooting at pigeons. He even disapproved of hunting as a form of entertainment, reasoning that it is only just when it is necessary as a means of existence.

"This des Assins," he said to Pélasge, "is a vile being. Instead of attacking me directly, he insulted me through a young woman who never gave him the least reason to hold any resentment against her. He decided to hate me, and I don't know why. He wants to kill me—that's obvious. You know me, my friend. You know that I'd never take a life, not even the life of an insect. But tomorrow, in the presence of this savage beast, it'll be a legitimate defense, which I believe to be a service to society as well as to myself. I'll do my best to kill this villain; he put a cold and implacable anger in my heart that may spell his own misfortune. If I succumb, my place waits for me under the old sachem beside my grandfather. I beg you, please get me a pen and paper. I want to leave what little I own to Blanchette. I entrust her to you. Protect her and make her as happy as she can be without me."

Pélasge shook Démon's hand affectionately and said:

"You're not anticipating your death, are you?"

"No, not at all," Démon replied. "On the contrary, I'm confident."

"Well done."

"But I could be mistaken. Fate is so treacherous!"

"Try to sleep well," Pélasge resumed, "so that tomorrow you are in good physical condition."

"Oh! As for sleep," Démon responded with a smile, "you know that nature blessed me greatly. Even knowing I was going to die when I got up wouldn't prevent me from sleeping. I'm counting on you to wake me at five o'clock."

While Démon was talking with Pélasge, Monsieur Héhé was with Mademoiselle Pulchérie. He did not hide any secrets from her. He told her all about Démon's crisis with Monsieur des Assins, advising her, however, to keep it all a secret.

"If anyone happened to find out," he remarked, "that the letter I gave you is the cause of what's happening, that would make a bad impression."

Hardly had Monsieur Héhé left to return to Pélasge and Démon when Mademoiselle Pulchérie, forgetting her friend's recommendation in order to satisfy her own nastiness, entered Blanchette's bedroom and berated her, saying that she was the cause of Démon's forthcoming and inevitable death. Mademoiselle Pulchérie even had the cruelty to reveal the secret of her birth to her. She went as far as to tell her that if slavery still existed, she would be put in her true place and that she would be whipped bloody as she deserved for having caused a duel between the last offspring of the Saint-Ybars family and a man who always killed his opponent.

Blanchette was overwhelmed with despair and terror. In less than a few minutes, she had just received two shocks, either one of which was enough to devastate her. Her reason wavered. She wondered if she was really Blanchette, or if little Blanchette was a dream or a thought that Chant d'Oisel had left behind and forgotten. Mademoiselle Pulchérie's sarcastic laugh brought her back to the sense of her own existence. She shrank back in horror. Clasping her hands together, she said:

"Please, Mademoiselle, please, that's enough for tonight! I'm crushed. You couldn't have hurt me more—to go on would be like striking a corpse. Leave me alone with my unhappiness."

Blanchette was young and pretty. Mademoiselle Pulchérie had long ago ceased to be young, and she had never been pretty. Blanchette was pleasant and loving, but Mademoiselle Pulchérie was only hateful and envious. Mademoiselle Pulchérie hated Blanchette bitterly, and Blanchette, born to love, did not understand hatred any more than a child understands algebra.

Mademoiselle Pulchérie returned to the living room. Still foaming with venom and anger, she told Démon's aunt about how she had just treated Blanchette. Great was her surprise and her mortification to see Madame Saint-Ybars' sister moved with pity.

"You've gone too far, my dear," the old lady said. "Making this unfortunate child responsible for Démon's death is too much. It's unfair."

She went to Blanchette and tried to console her. Blanchette threw herself trustingly into her arms.

"At least you are good, dear aunt," she said. "You have pity on me. Let me call you aunt again one last time. Let them tell me all they want that I'm black, that my mother was a slave, and that I was born to be one as well. But it's horrible to blame me for this duel when I'd give my life to save Démon. Ah! If my godmother were here, she'd stand up for me. No one would treat me like this."

Madame Saint-Ybars' sister could not hold back her tears. These tears consoled Blanchette more than anything else.

Around eleven o'clock, calm was restored in the house. Blanchette had thrown herself on her bed to cry. Sleep, ushered in by the exhaustion of body and mind, took over her, despite the sobs that continued to shake her body.

Pélasge had sent a message to his doctor to ensure his services. He waited for an answer before going to bed. The doctor let him know that he would be at the duel.

Chapter 43

The Duel

It was April. Awake before sunrise, Monsieur des Assins opened his window. The sky was clear, the air was fresh, and the birds were singing.

"This is the beginning of a beautiful day," Monsieur des Assins thought, "and young Saint-Ybars won't see the end of it. He's out of luck. Too bad for him. It's his own fault. Why did he act so haughty with me? Why didn't he agree with everyone else that no one in Louisiana is wittier than me? He's a conceited, insolent man who deserves punishment. He'll get it."

Monsieur des Assins took a long bath, as if he were going to a party, and drank a glass of sherry. He jumped into a two-horse carriage, accompanied by his witnesses and a servant. Two other carriages carrying several friends and spectators followed. Then came the doctor's cabriolet. They took the public road at the bottom of the levee.

A man on horseback had ridden ahead of the carriages, and he stood waiting at the entrance of the avenue. It was Monsieur le Duc de Lauzun. He had never witnessed a duel. Putting on a brave façade, he wore a rose in his buttonhole and smoked a cigar while humming a tune from *Fra Diavolo*.[1]

When Pélasge woke Démon, he said to him:

"It's fairly chilly. Dress yourself warmly, but be careful to put on comfortable clothes. It's important that you be able to move absolutely freely."

Démon dressed in black and buttoned his frock coat up to his neck.

"Now," said Pélasge, handing him his shotgun, "take aim three or four times."

Démon executed the maneuver.

"That's good," Pélasge remarked. "You aren't hindered by your sleeves. That'll do. Let's go have some coffee."

Monsieur Héhé was in the dining room. He had slept poorly. His thoughts forced him to consider all sorts of terrible possibilities. Démon might miraculously escape Monsieur des Assins' bullets. And what if he discovered that it was MacNara who had allowed Mademoiselle Pulchérie to read the letter that Monsieur de Lauzun had stolen from Lagniape's pocket! The young Saint-Ybars would be furious. His anger would make him challenge his former professor to a duel. What a prospect for Monsieur Héhé! He broke out in a cold sweat thinking about it.

When Démon and Pélasge entered the dining room, Monsieur Héhé was already there. He had asked someone to bring him a carafe of cognac.

"Gentlemen," he said, "let's have a small glass of Dutch courage."[2]

"Thank you, my dear former professor," Démon replied, "but I think you'd be better off abandoning such a manner of speaking. You see, the Dutch, just like us, don't need alcohol to be brave."

"Démon's right," Pélasge pointed out, "and since the occasion presents itself, I'll have you notice, dear friend, that you also have the habit of saying *like a Polish drunk, like a Parisian jokester, as devious as a Greek, as treacherous as an Italian,* etc. These expressions can be dangerous. One day, you'll end up meeting someone whom you'll offend, and he will challenge you to a duel."

Monsieur Héhé shivered and remained silent.

They prepared to leave. Démon and Monsieur Héhé climbed into Pélasge's carriage. As for Pélasge, he took a seat beside the coachman. He was carrying the shotgun.

When they reached the avenue, Pélasge could see three four-wheeled carriages and a cabriolet in the distance.

Monsieur des Assins had not arrived first unintentionally. As soon as he saw Démon descend from the carriage, he dramatically stood squarely in his way. Démon stepped forward at his ordinary pace, his hands in the pockets of his coat. He immediately understood that his opponent wanted to intimidate him. While passing by, he threw him a look in which there was as much contempt as there was courage. One of Monsieur des Assins' friends was strangely impressed. He said to his neighbor:

"Hum! That glance says a lot. This young man is going to fight with admirable composure."

At the chosen place for the fight, nearly all of the oak trees had died. Tufts of Spanish moss hung here and there; their withered branches let plenty of light shine through. Pélasge measured the distance between the combatants. The opponents were asked to take their places. They had drawn lots because one position was not as good as the other. Luck favored Démon. He had his back to the sun.

Monsieur des Assins took off his coat, his frock coat, and even his vest. He threw them nonchalantly to his servant. He kept his hat on. Monsieur de Lauzun could not admire him enough.

Démon removed his jacket, folded it with care, placed it at the foot of an oak tree, and put his hat over it.

While the witnesses loaded the rifles, one of Monsieur des Assins' friends approached him and said in a low voice:

"I believe, dear sir, that you'd do well to abandon your idea of letting your opponent shoot first. There's a confidence and precision in all of his movements that proves that he's in absolute control of himself. Believe me. Be on your guard."

"Bah! So what? Forget it," Monsieur des Assins replied. "I'm telling you again that he's going to shoot too fast. Like the novice he is, he'll miss me, and then I… be calm. I know what I'm doing."

Monsieur de Lauzun had tied his horse a little further away. He approached Monsieur Héhé, who did not look comfortable.

"So what's wrong with you?" he asked. "You look perturbed."

"I'm worried," Monsieur Héhé responded.

"The fact is," remarked Monsieur de Lauzun, "you *should* be worried about the last Saint-Ybars. When a man has des Assins opposite him in a duel, he's a dead man."

"It's not Démon I'm worried about," Monsieur Héhé responded. "It's for myself. He might escape safe and sound from this terrible episode, no matter what you say. We've seen more extraordinary things than that. If he discovers that I'm the one who showed the letter to Mademoiselle Pulchérie, I'll be in a terrible position. Heavens! I immensely regret that you had the unfortunate idea of giving me that letter."

"Don't fear anything," said Monsieur de Lauzun. "You're going to see des Assins pierce the chest of the last offspring of the illustrious Saint-Ybars family."

The witnesses had finished loading the guns. Monsieur Héhé hoped, from the depths of his heart, that Monsieur des Assins' rifle would fulfill Monsieur de Lauzun's prophecy.

As the oldest spectator, Pélasge was designated to give the command to fire.

One of Monsieur des Assins' witnesses carried his shotgun to him. Démon received his from the hands of Pélasge, who encouraged him:

"Démon, my son, make the most of your advantages. Your enemy's arrogance has made him commit a serious error. His shirt between his hat and his black pants is like a target that's waiting for your bullet. Move a little bit more to the right. Look over my shoulder without being seen. Do you see the leafless twig of that plant that's between you and him?"

"Yes."

"Aim at it. You understand, do you not?"

"Oh! Perfectly well. If I shoot first, des Assins will never kill another man."

"Goodbye, Démon."

"Goodbye Pélasge, my friend."

Pélasge shook Démon's hand and went to stand at his post at the edge of the avenue, an equal distance between the combatants.

"Gentlemen," he said to the assistants, "step aside."

They lined up on both sides about fifteen paces from the line between the two combatants.

Monsieur des Assins folded the edge of his hat down to protect his eyes from the sun, and he immediately began to swing his rifle as he had told his friends he would do. The two barrels that rose and fell opposite Démon, showing their black muzzles, had a dreadfully menacing appearance. But Démon was not concerned at all. His eyes were fixed on the small dead stalk. He waited, as motionless as a rock.

Pélasge began in a strong and clear voice:

"Gentlemen, are you ready?"

There was a silence. Only the sounds of the horses striking the earth with their hooves could be heard, tormented as they were by flies.

Pélasge continued:

"Fire! One, two, three…"

At the word *fire,* Démon took aim. Between *two* and *three,* he fired.

Monsieur des Assins shuddered from his head to his feet, as if he had been jolted by an electrical shock. Démon was sure he had hit him. He was surprised to see him still standing.

Monsieur des Assins had received Démon's bullet right in the middle of his chest. He made a tremendous effort to aim at his opponent, but his shotgun was not yet positioned horizontally when Pélasge, still counting, said:

"Four, five…"

At the word *five,* Démon's second shot left his gun. Monsieur des Assins fired nearly at the same time, or rather, his finger convulsively bore down on the trigger. His bullet struck the dirt ten paces from him and ricocheted, disappearing into the tall grass. His knees buckled. He dropped his gun and sat down, leaning on his right hand. His friends ran to him. One of them arrived just in time to support him. His head fell over, and his hat rolled down into the dust. Torrents of blood reddened his shirt. Demon's second bullet, like the first, had gone straight through his chest. Monsieur des Assins was still breathing but slowly and more and more weakly. His mouth was open wide, and his lips were pallid. His eyes, looking up, rolled from right to left and from left to right.

Monsieur de Lauzun, nearly as pale as Monsieur des Assins, nudged the doctor, saying to him:

"Well! Doctor, why aren't you doing anything? Do something! This man is wounded!"

"Idiot! He's dead," the doctor replied.

"Dead!" Monsieur de Lauzun repeated in a choked voice.

Monsieur des Assins was no longer breathing. His friends laid him on the ground. They gathered together a few steps away from him and spoke to each other quietly.

Pélasge, Démon, and Monsieur Héhé were forced to pass in front of the corpse to get to their carriage. Monsieur de Lauzun stopped Monsieur Héhé, and after looking at him for a good while with a terrified gaze, he repeated mechanically:

"Dead!"

"I very well see that, damn it!" Monsieur Héhé responded. "Go to hell, you and your cursed letter!"

Monsieur des Assins' friends had not come to the field to witness his defeat. Their friendships disappeared with his death. His body was put into a carriage, but no one hastened to accompany him. The doctor was forced to take responsibility for this sad job.

Chapter 44

Mamrie's and Lagniape's Discussion

Blanchette had gone up to the observatory. Worried to death, her eyes flooded with tears, she waited at a window on the east side. Finally, she recognized Pélasge's cabriolet from afar. This time, Démon was sitting next to the coachman. As soon as he saw Blanchette, who was leaning outside the window, he waved his handkerchief.

Lagniape and Mamrie were in the courtyard, still not suspecting a thing. They heard piercing screams and a rumbling noise immediately after. It was Blanchette, who was running down the stairs. She made her way through the house as quickly as a bird on the wing and ran to meet Démon. She lost her comb on the way, her hair bouncing in the sun.

Démon jumped onto the pathway and enfolded her in his arms. Blanchette took him to the river bank, to a place she loved because of its solitude. There, they had a long and delightful discussion accompanied by the steady sound of the small waves that rippled at their feet. There they enjoyed one of those moments of which there are so few in life, moments of perfect contentment where the past and the future are forgotten in the joy of the present, as if that present moment would last forever.

The news of Monsieur des Assins' death spread everywhere. Mothers rejoiced in it. His funeral oration did not take long. Everyone said, "That was well-deserved. It serves him right after everything he's done!"

When Démon returned with Blanchette, Mamrie grabbed him as he passed and reproached him for going behind her back and risking his life. Démon replied that it was better that way, that at least he had shielded her from the anguish of fear.

Démon's cousins congratulated him for having rid the country of a dreadful man like Monsieur des Assins. Mademoiselle Pulchérie coldly predicted that there might very well be other duels if he persisted in his idea of marrying Blanchette.

Mamrie wanted to know the cause of the duel. She questioned Démon's youngest cousin. Lagniape was beside Mamrie. She did not lose one word of what the young lady said. Mamrie was at first surprised to learn that Blanchette was Titia's daughter. After having thought about it, she began to laugh and said to Démon's cousin:

"Ah! Ouëtte, tou ça cé bétise. Si kékeune té pas montré lette-là à Mamzel Pulchérie, Blanchette sré toujour ain blanche. Malgré lette-là èceque so lapo pa pli blanche pacé vou kenne! Pour sûr si vou té capab changé vou lapo pou so kenne, vou sré pa di non."[i]

Lagniape added:

"Mademoiselle, believe me," she said, "don't blame Blanchette. Listen to your heart rather than your prejudices, Mademoiselle. I saw you weeping as you read that story about a young outcast. You thought it was unfair and cruel that the young man who loved the woman in the story wasn't allowed to marry her because they weren't from the same class. The pity that you have for that outcast, don't you have it for Blanchette? Trust what an old lady is telling you. The greatest beauty for a young woman is to be kind and generous."

Démon's cousin left, very contemplative. Her name was Georgine.

Mamrie and Lagniape talked for a long time. They revisited the past. Mamrie plied Lagniape with questions concerning the circumstances of the letter's theft. She was convinced, she said, that Mademoiselle Pulchérie had read this letter. She asked Lagniape if she had ever suspected anyone. Lagniape replied that she had

[i] "Ah! All of this is stupid. If someone had not shown that letter to Mademoiselle Pulchérie, Blanchette would still be a white woman. Despite what that letter says, her skin is whiter than yours! If you could exchange your skin for hers, you certainly wouldn't refuse."

thought several times that it was Monsieur de Lauzun who had done the nasty job. She remembered very clearly that at that time, he was in love with Titia and spied on her constantly, that he pursued her with propositions, but she did not want him. Mamrie remained silent and thoughtful. She asked herself this question: "Did Lauzun have anything to gain by stealing the letter?" She answered back, "Yes." She asked herself another question: "Was he a man who would blind Lagniape for that?" She replied again, "Yes."

The conclusion itself was obvious to Mamrie. All of the evil came from Lauzun.

"Ain jour ou ain ote la payé moin ça," she said, "malgré mo aveugle."[i]

Monsieur Héhé considered it wise to move away. Under the pretext that business called him back to New Orleans, he took the first boat that came along. Mademoiselle Pulchérie did not take long to meet up with him. She left without even giving notice to Démon, abandoning him, like she said, to his unfortunate fate, since he was foolish enough to persist in his idea of marrying Blanchette.

---

[i] "One day or another, I'll pay him back for that, even if I'm blind."

Chapter 45

"Prejudice is the King of Vulgar Souls" – Voltaire

Démon wished his aunt would cross the river and return home, but he refrained from saying anything to her because she had been good to him when he was a child. He loved her and respected her. She was not a malicious person, most certainly, but she dragged behind her a long past whose influence she could not escape. She retained the habits and beliefs of the middle class in which she had lived and grown old. She believed, in good faith, that the honor of the family gave her the duty—the sacred duty—to do everything she could to prevent Démon from committing an act that would reflect shame upon her and her children. So she showed no inclination to return home. This greatly irritated Démon. In order to hide his discontent, he spent very little time in the house. His aunt wanted to take advantage of his long absences to influence Blanchette, so she changed tactics. She no longer reproached the young woman in the least; instead, she charmed her with kindness. She fought against their plan for marriage and used Blanchette's affection for Démon to do so. "If he married you, he would constantly be expected to defend his honor. There would be people who would no longer greet him. He'd feel insulted and challenge them to a duel, and by repeatedly fighting, it would very likely end with his being killed. Without doubt, your sacrifice is enormous, but if you don't have the courage, then it's Démon whom you are sacrificing. You'd destroy his future; this would show a horrible ingratitude to all of the kindness that the Saint-Ybars family has shown you."

Démon's cousins spoke to Blanchette the same way. They flattered her. They promised her that in private, they would continue to treat her as an equal. They asked her to leave with them. It was not appropriate that she remain under the same roof as Démon anymore.

Of all that was said to Blanchette, she only retained one thing: in becoming Démon's wife, she was putting him in an untenable and dangerous position. She told herself that Pélasge thought that as well, since he had offered his fortune to Démon so that he could live abroad with her. This offer was very much a means of salvation, but Démon would never accept it. What to do?...Alas! She had to resign herself to fate and sacrifice herself out of love for Démon. After many tears, this was the only answer Blanchette saw.

When Démon noticed a change in Blanchette, he became violently angry against his aunt and cousins. He blamed them, in the most bitter terms, for having come to his home as hypocrites to ruin his happiness. He told them that he had always loathed gossiping and that if all the indiscreet people who pried into the affairs of others were put into a bag and thrown into the river, he would be delighted. He left choking with rage but hoping that after such a scene they would leave his house quickly. Nothing of the sort happened. These ladies deserved credit, in Blanchette's eyes, for enduring Démon's insults in order to save him from the abyss toward which his erratic behavior was pushing him.

Démon did not return until sunset. He barely touched the dinner that Blanchette served him. That evening, he took her aside and asked her once again if she truly had decided not to marry him. Her voice was soft. He affectionately pressed Blanchette's hands into his and then onto her heart. Blanchette barely had enough strength to answer him.

"Parrain, dear beloved Parrain," she said, "what I'm doing is out of love for you. I see very clearly now that being your wife would be a source of misfortune for you. You lived in Europe for a long time. You forgot that prejudice rules this country. You'll thank me later, my good Parrain. Ah! It hurts me to cause you pain. I wish that my mother had left me in the woods where I was born. I'd be less miserable among the beasts than within a civilized society that treats me with so much barbarity. Oh well, that's fate. We must accept it."

At the mention of the word *fate,* Démon's sense of reason rebelled. His tendency for superstition disappeared in a moment of clarity.

"Fate! Fate!" he exclaimed. "That sounds like a word my aunt and cousins use. You're wrong, Blanchette. What you call 'fate' is only the effect of human injustice. You can't say we're the victims of some sort of inevitability. Fate has nothing to do with it. The torment that would like to separate us is born of pride and ignorance. It doesn't exist in nature, and it doesn't have a name in the eternal order of things. It only has a name in the language of men: it's called prejudice. That's what stigmatized the young patrician who dared to love a plebeian. It's what delivered to the stake the young, Jewish woman who dared to love a Christian."

There was a long and painful silence. Blanchette bowed her head like a condemned woman. Anger and despair fought for Démon's soul. Despair was the winner.

"Parrain," said Blanchette, "I'm so unhappy. You're angry, and you've grown silent."

"Ah! You regret not having grown up in an uncivilized tribe," Démon replied. "You're right! There's more justice and kindness in the Indian's hut than in the cities of civilized men. Why not listen to those desolate words that have appeared since the dawn of civilization, as if they were the natural cry of developing cultures? Listen to them! They've been repeated from century to century, and I, just like so many other victims, am only repeating them for myself:

"Curse the day when I was born! Why did I not die in my mother's womb? Why was light given to a poor soul like me? Why was life given to those who are bitter in heart?... God grant that I had died and that no one had ever seen me because I would now sleep in silence, and I would find peace as I slept!"

After having said these mournful words, Démon ascended to his bedroom. Blanchette, altogether dismayed, withdrew to hers. Exhausted by the sacrificial efforts that she had just made, she fell nearly unconscious into an armchair.

Chapter 46

Despair Overwhelms Démon

Two days passed during which Blanchette drank in the bitter satisfaction of her painful duty. She believed that the hardest part of her ordeal was finished. But noticing that Démon's sadness was growing steadily, she felt her own grief increase. Démon no longer left his bedroom. He came down only at meal times, and the bell had to be rung two or three times before he decided to come. At the table, he barely spoke. In the middle of meals, he stood up and went upstairs. He seemed to find relief only in the company of his dark thoughts, hidden away in his grandfather's former bedroom on the second floor. This room adjoined the turret, at the top of which was the observatory. At one end was a chemistry laboratory, at the other a physics laboratory. A wide corridor passed in front of these rooms, separating them from the library that encompassed an entire side of the floor. To the south, the corridor led to a balcony that overlooked the river. To the north, it opened up onto an upper balcony whose view included the fields and to the right, the imposing and stern dome of the old sachem.

Like the second floor, the first floor was made up of two sets of rooms separated by a corridor. On one side was the living room, the dining room, and the office. On the other were the bedrooms; the one in the middle, where Blanchette slept, was located below Démon's.

From her bedroom, Blanchette heard Démon pacing in his. He stayed up late, pacing steadily as if pondering something. Sometimes, he would stop abruptly and remain motionless for a long time. He lay down and got up again several times, relit his lamp, and read or wrote. In the silence of the night, Blanchette heard the pages of his book turning or his quill racing across the paper. Sometimes, she even heard him sigh.

When it came time to eat and Blanchette saw Démon descend, his face pale and weary, her heart broke. She would have liked to console him, but she did not dare speak since he seemed so depressed and showed little inclination to open his heart. He resembled a wandering stranger lost in a country where nothing interests him, everything bores him, and the desire to leave constantly torments. An immense disgust of all things possessed him. Blanchette would have trembled—would have grown pale from terror—if she had been able to hear his inner monologue. Contempt for life had fiercely seized hold of him. "How," he said to himself with a bitter irony, "how can men persist in loving this absurd and painful existence? In order to find a reason to live, to justify the contradictions, to forgive the abundance of wrongs, what have men not invented? What poor and inane explanations they have extracted from their philosophical and religious dreams! And all of this effort and willingness to be wrong—to what will it lead? To arrange a way of life that makes you forget you are living. To numb yourself in pleasure, to exhaust yourself in work, to intoxicate yourself in war's rage, to waste your breath in the pursuit of money, to bury yourself in devotion, to swoon in anticipation of a happy afterlife—such are the ingenious resources to which man has turned in order to escape the feeling of his miserable destiny. Man's best state is when he is sleeping, when he is submerged in a life that most resembles death. Death! What is it? Without doubt, a sleep, but better than that: a nothingness. Why not? Why would it not be after my death as it was before my birth? Where were we one hundred years ago, all of us who at this very moment are passing over the earth like shadows only to soon make way for other shadows? A century ago, we were without a doubt in the same place we will be when we leave this life. Since there was a time when we were not, there will be a time when we will no longer be. They tell us that the hope of another life can bring us consolation; I reply that to hope is to dream something desired and possible, but there is nothing certain about it. If a dream is enough to console you, so much the better for you. I would never want to deprive you of it."

Démon sank further and further into his dark thoughts. Pélasge did not notice, despite his usual insight, that his young friend was rapidly heading towards suicide. There was a heroic calm within Pélasge; his logical mind accepted that life was a battle against physical and moral evil. Setting aside all metaphysical chimeras, he saw an unbridled strength in humanity that prepared it for the struggle ahead. He emphatically believed in free will. He was convinced that humanity would one day rid itself of the numerous false ideas that had given birth to so many wrongs and that it would, one day, sort things out to create the best possible world on this planet where we dwell. Since Chant d'Oisel's death, Pélasge had spent more and more time in study. In science, he searched for and found a way to silence his heart and bring serenity to his mind. Yet, in his own serenity, he neglected to watch out for warning signs within others. He saw very well that Démon was distressed, but he was far from suspecting that he was likely to give in to despair after having shown so much courage in a duel. He sincerely pitied him and counted on time to heal the wound in his heart. He knew very well that there are injuries that kill, but he did not suspect that Démon's wound was of that nature.

Chapter 47

Tragedy

Towards the end of the week, Démon's aunt informed him that she was leaving the following day and taking Blanchette with her.

"Very well, aunt," he replied.

And he did not utter another word.

That evening, as he was retiring to his bedroom, he said to Blanchette:

"Tomorrow, I won't have the courage to see you leave. It's better that we say our farewells now."

He took her in his arms. Choked by sobs, she felt his chest against hers. He said nothing. He feared, if he spoke, that he would dissolve into tears. He climbed the stairs slowly without once turning around. When he reached his bedroom, Blanchette was still in the same place at the bottom of the stairs. Démon's silence frightened her. Without knowing why, she had the feeling that an immense black abyss had suddenly been opened between them. Was this what usually happened when two lovers separated from each other? "It's likely," she thought. But then, there was something dreadfully deathlike about it. It was worse than death, for death at least frees you from suffering.

Blanchette walked away unsteadily, putting her hands over her eyes several times like someone awakening from a nightmare, struggling to believe that it was only a dream. She slept fitfully. When she heard Démon pacing, she sighed, saying to herself, "He can't sleep either." When she no longer heard him, it was as if she had already left and had been separated from him forever. At times, she dozed off, but then would wake up suddenly, only to find herself caught between the still-visible ghosts of her horrible dreams and the re-emergent anguish of reality. Then, she sat down on her bed and mumbled between her tears:

"This is too much suffering to bear. Death is better than such a life. I'd prefer to be with Godmother."

At last, daylight appeared. Blanchette got up at six o'clock. She was to leave at eight. She plunged herself as usual into her bathtub. The freshness of the water revived her and made her forget the fatigue of insomnia. She slipped into a gown and continued the preparations she had begun the day before.

Rising before Blanchette, Démon wrote to Pélasge. When he finished, he went into the laboratory and brought back a small decanter that he put down on the table. Etched in black on the flask's label were a skull and crossbones and these words: STRYCHNINE—POISON. He then took his loaded revolver and placed it on the table as well. He sat in his chair and leaned on his elbows. After thinking about it, he pushed the revolver aside, saying:

"No, no noise."

He picked up the decanter:

"This," he said, "acts nearly as quickly as a gun. Two or three spasms, and it's over. It's silent."

He knew the amount of strychnine needed to kill a man. He put some of it in a glass, a little more than the required amount, and poured a few drops of hydrocloric acid on top to expedite the dissolution. Then he added some sugar water. That done, he went to one of the windows facing the old house where he was born. As he cast a look of farewell over the countryside, his eyes came to rest on the old sachem.

"You're waiting for me," he said, "my good old sachem, whom I've loved so much! Here I am. I'm going to sleep in your peaceful shade, beside my ancestors, my mother, and Chant d'Oisel."

As he was turning away from the window, he noticed a small white cloud rising and fading quickly in the blue skies above the ruins of his father's house. He saw an image of his destiny in this early-rising mist, which, barely formed, was about to disappear.

As the cloud was vanishing, he waved at it and said:

"Goodbye."

He returned to his armchair, sat down, took the glass, and drank.

All was calm in the house and in the courtyard. Démon's aunt and his cousins were getting up. Mademoiselle Georgine was quietly singing Rosine's cavatina from the *Barber of Seville.* It was her routine. She always sang while getting up and getting dressed.

Mamrie, sitting outside the kitchen door in the open air, was cleaning the knives. While rubbing them on a plank covered in crushed brick, she talked with a young mulatto girl who had belonged to the Saint-Ybars family and who now sold notions. She was a pretty girl, hardworking and wise but too trusting. She had let herself be taken in by Monsieur de Lauzun's pretty promises. As a politician, he had sworn to marry her, but as a Don Juan, he was in no hurry to do so. Livia (the young mulatto woman) had learned from several other young girls that Monsieur le Duc had deceived them and made the same oath as he had to her. She had sworn to get even with him, but she never realized that by talking to Mamrie at this very instant, she was setting in motion a terrible punishment for Monsieur de Lauzun. He had been foolish enough, in his self-conceit, to boast in front of Livia about the ploy he had used to reveal Titia's secret. He went so far as to tell her that it was he who had arranged for Monsieur Héhé to allow Mademoiselle Pulcherie to read Lagniape's stolen letter. Hating Démon, he believed he had played a good trick on him by revealing Blanchette's origin to the world. Livia had always trusted Mamrie, and she told her everything.

Chance, as is often said, is the most powerful of playwrights. When it composes a tragedy, nothing is missing.

A little before seven o'clock, Monsieur de Lauzun had gone to the farm, needing to see Pélasge on business. He learned that Pélasge had gone to see Mademoiselle Blanchette, who was leaving with Démon's aunt, and that if he wanted to meet with him, he had to hurry.

Livia was still talking to Mamrie when she saw Monsieur de Lauzun arrive. He addressed them informally and asked them, without even removing his cigar from his mouth, if Pélasge was there. Mamrie responded that he was in the living room. Monsieur le Duc, crossing the courtyard, blew Livia a kiss from his fingertips, as if to make fun of her. As he entered the house, he threw away his cigar and put on a respectful expression. His hat in his hand, he stopped in the doorway of the living room and politely asked if he could enter. He was afraid of Pélasge. He was aware of his liberal opinions, but he knew not to be too familiar with him. Pélasge returned his greeting and told him to enter.

Passing by the bottom of the stairs that led to Démon's bedroom, Blanchette heard the sound of a chair shaking violently and soon after, a moan. Her heart leapt. Who was groaning like that? It could only be Démon. What was wrong with him? Surely, he was suffering. Blanchette did not hesitate. She ascended and ran to Démon's bedroom. He was pale and breathless, his features drawn and stiff. Blanchette rushed to him.

"Ah! Parrain," she said, seeing the decanter of strychnine, "did you take any of this?"

"Yes," Démon replied. "Please, Blanchette, no fuss. Let me die peacefully."

"Let you die!" Blanchette said. "To die like this, without having told me, to leave me all alone. Ah! Parrain, this isn't right. No, no, this can't be. I'll go with you."

Démon, seeing that she was going to take the flask, grabbed it. Immediately afterward, he felt another convulsion. His arms and legs stretched out, and his whole body began to quake and make the chair rattle. Then his head flung back, and his spine bowed into an arc. After a few seconds of immobility, he came down again, collapsing and hardly breathing, but his clenched hand still held the decanter.

Blanchette caught sight of the revolver. She grabbed it. Démon, unable to move, saw her aim the barrel against her chest, level with her heart. The shot fired. The bullet pierced the gown and her shirt, grazed her skin, and broke a windowpane. Blanchette fired another shot. This time, she felt a sharp pain. The detonation was followed by a shrill cry. Blanchette bent over Démon, her head on his chest as if it was on a pillow. They took their last breath at the same time.

The sound of footsteps, screams, and wailing filled the house. At the sight of two corpses, Mademoiselle Georgine, who had never seen a dead person, was gripped by uncontrollable terror. She went back downstairs shouting, barely dressed, disheveled, her eyes wild, and then went running into the courtyard. Livia stopped to ask what happened. From the young girl's incoherent words, Mamrie and Livia understood one deplorable fact: Démon and Blanchette were dead.

Livia, overcome with curiosity, entered the house. Mademoiselle Georgine fled again and escaped into the countryside.

Lagniape was in the kitchen. She was shouting, calling everyone here and there, raising her arms to the sky, and asking what misfortune had befallen the house.

Livia went to Mamrie. She described, while crying and wailing, what she had just seen. Mamrie did not utter a sound. She remained motionless, seated on the floor. Large tears rolled from her useless and fixed eyes. Suddenly, her tears stopped. She asked Livia where Monsieur de Lauzun was. Livia replied that he was in Démon's bedroom with Pélasge.

"Cé bon," said Mamrie. "Couri côté Lagniape ki apé crié comme ain possédé, san li connin cofair. Di li ain bonne foi ça ki rivé. Au moin la crié pou kichoge."[i]

While Livia spoke to Lagniape, Mamrie searched among her pile of knives. Finding the carving knife, she concealed it in her blouse and summoned Livia. She asked to be led to Démon's bedroom. A little before arriving at the door, she said to Livia:

"Largué moin."[ii]

Livia left her. She arrived at the doorway, fumbling about. There, she stopped and said:

"Lauzun, mo fi, to là?"[iii]

"Yes, Mamrie," Monsieur de Lauzun replied, "mo là. Ça vou oulé?"[iv]

---

[i] "That's good. Go with Lagniape, who's crying like a possessed woman, not knowing what to do. Tell her what happened. At least she'll cry for something."

[ii] "Leave me."

[iii] "Lauzun, my boy, are you there?"

[iv] "I'm here. What do you want?"

"Tan pri, Lauzun, pranne mo lamin pou condui moin côté mo cher piti Démon."[i]

Monsieur de Lauzun took Mamrie by the hand and led her to the chair nearby. With her right hand, she identified Démon's body. She caressed his face and hair lovingly. She stopped on his scar. She bent down and kissed Démon on the same place where he had been injured.

Pélasge no longer had the strength to endure this painful sight. He walked out.

Mamrie touched Blanchette's hair, kissed her still-warm cheeks, sighed deeply, and stood up. She removed her left hand from Monsieur de Lauzun's, put it on his shoulder, and said:

"Lauzun, mo fi, to pa connin ça moune di?....Eh bien! Yé di cé toi qui cause tou maleur laïé rivé. Cé toi ki souflé, avec ain cerbacane, di poive é piman dan zié Lagniape, pou volé ain lette dan so poche. Cé toi ki cause Titia néyé li même dan pi. To cause Démon pranne poison-là. To cause Blanchette mouri oucite. E to té eré tou ça sré pacé comme ça comme arien! To cré ta sorti mézon cilà pou trompé fie encor avé to bel promesse, épi apré ça pou fé to faro é to vanteur. Non, mo garçon. Tan pou réglé to conte vini."[ii]

Mamrie grabbed Monsieur de Lauzun by his tie and said:

"A genou, céléra!"[iii]

"Mamrie, pa tranglé moin comme ça," Monsieur de Lauzun exclaimed, "ou sinon ma cognin vou."[iv]

---

[i] "Lauzun, will you kindly take my hand and lead me to my dear little Démon."

[ii] "Lauzun, my boy, do you know what's being said about you? ...Well! It's said that you caused all of the misfortunes in this house. It's you who blew hot pepper into Lagniape's eyes with a blowgun to steal the letter in her pocket. It's you who made Titia drown herself in the well. You made Démon take poison, and you caused Blanchette's death. And you believe that all of this will take place without any consequences! You think that you will just leave this fine house to deceive girls again with your nice promises and continue to be pretentious and boastful. No, my boy. The time to settle your accounts has come."

[iii] "On your knees, villain!"

[iv] "Mamrie, don't choke me like that, or else I'll strike you."

"Cognin moin, toi!" Mamrie retorted. "Cé pa ain capon comme toi ka fé moin largué ça mo tchombo… A genou, mo di toi."[i]

Mamrie twisted his tie, and without giving Monsieur de Lauzun the time to orient himself, she made him fall down on his knees. Frantic and half suffocating, he tried to speak, but his voice could not overcome the twisted cloth that encircled his neck.

"Si to gagnin ain laprière pou fé, dit Mamrie, fé li vite."[ii]

And she pulled out her knife.

Monsieur de Lauzun made a horrible grimace in seeing the sharp, shiny, clear-cut blade. He waved his hands and feet and tried in vain to strike Mamrie. She let him struggle for a few seconds. Then, in a sudden movement, she tightened his tie again. Monsieur de Lauzun quickly raised his hands to his neck and tried, with one last effort, to pry away Mamrie's fingers. This was the precise moment she was waiting for. She used this instant to plunge her knife into his chest, exclaiming,"

"Cé pa la peine to résisté, céléra. Fo to mouri."[iii]

Feeling the weight of Monsieur de Lauzun's body, she knew he was lifeless, and she let him go. She approached Démon and Blanchette and kneeled so her back was leaning against their bodies. Mamrie's last words, delivered in a booming voice, reached the ears of Pélasge and Livia. They ran upstairs together. Mamrie had just wiped her knife on her dress. She tilted her head back, saying:

"Chant-d'Oisel, Démon, Blanchette, cher piti, zote apé attanne Mamrie. Alà li!"[iv]

She positioned the point of her knife between her collarbone and her neck.

Pélasge and Livia rushed towards her to stop her hand. They did not arrive in time. The blade disappeared up to the handle. Mamrie stretched out her arms, one on Démon, the other on Blanchette, and tilted her head slowly in Démon's direction, as if under the weight of a sweet sleep.

---

[i] "You, hit me! A coward like you can't make me lose my grip… On your knees, I tell you."

[ii] "If you have a prayer to say, do it quickly."

[iii] "There's no point in resisting, villain. You must die."

[iv] "Chant d'Oisel, Démon, Blanchette, dear children, you're waiting for Mamrie. Here she is."

Chapter 48

Isolation

The horrific tragedy was not over. What had become of Mademoiselle Georgine? A search party looked for her all day in vain. Her mother and her sisters spent a night in anguish, but at sunrise the following day, the runaway was brought back by several freedmen who were cutting wood in the cypress grove. She was in a deplorable condition and had completely lost her senses. She was naked and her body, hands, and face were torn and covered in blood and dirt. She howled with pain and fury and struggled like a wounded, savage beast. Her mother and sisters had a difficult job cleaning her up and getting her to bed.

Early in the morning, a few of Monsieur de Lauzun's friends had come to claim his body.

Pélasge had given the order to dig a large grave under the sachem, and he had let friends of the Saint-Ybars family know that the burial of Démon, Blanchette, and Mamrie would take place at eight o'clock in the morning. The caskets were placed in an open-topped, four-wheel carriage. About twenty people accompanied the group. Pélasge walked at the head of the procession.

Three freedmen seated at the edge of the grave waited, smoking and talking quietly. When the procession arrived, they stood up and respectfully removed their hats. Pélasge had Mamrie's casket placed first, then Demon's, and to the left of Demon's was Blanchette's. Then, heaps of earth piled up on the three caskets with a dull sound. A few people exchanged thoughts in low voices. The gravedigger's work was done, and the crowd left. Silence was restored under the old sachem. The birds accustomed to living under its branches calmed down from the fright of seeing all those people, and they confidently resumed their morning song.

Upon returning to the house, Pélasge learned that Mademoiselle Georgine had just died after a long convulsion. He was told that her body would be transported to the other side of the river since the young girl's mother and sisters wanted her to be buried in their parish's cemetery.

At sunset, a long skiff operated by four blacks crossed the river. It carried the young, dead girl away. She was lying on a mattress, covered with a white quilt, accompanied by her mother and sisters. The weather was calm, and the water was nearly as smooth as a lake on a breezeless day. The skiff glided easily on the golden surface and moved away rapidly.

Pélasge was alone on the balcony of the house where death had snatched away five people in less than thirty hours. His eyes followed the distant craft, listening in a sort of stupor to the rhythmic and increasingly faint sound of the oars. Leaning on a column, he remained motionless long after the small boat had disappeared into the shadows of the opposite bank. The evening breeze started to blow strongly. It moaned through the cracks in the doors, in unison with Pélasge's sadness. Hearing it, he awoke from his trance as if he had heard the compassionate voice of a friend. He went back inside. It was already nighttime. He went downstairs and was surprised to see light coming from Blanchette's bedroom. He gently pushed the door open. The lamp illuminated a sofa that held the last dress Blanchette had worn and her goatskin ankle-boots. Motionless before these objects, Lagniape was staring at them and weeping.

Pélasge felt a twinge of anguish. He moved towards her and affectionately held out his hand to the old woman.

"My good Lagniape," he said, "here we are all alone! Of this large and brilliant Saint-Ybars family, no one remains. Masters, children, servants, everyone is dead or scattered. Only you, a former slave, and I, a foreigner, can speak of them. Such is the way things go in this world. Why should we believe in happiness? Why count on tomorrow? Lagniape, what are your plans? Where do you want to go? Is there anything I can do for you?"

"Sadly, my dear Monsieur," Lagniape replied, "what can a sick old octogenarian like me do? Just give me a small plot on your farm where I can wait for death in peace. It won't be long now."

"You'll have whatever you wish, Lagniape. You won't lack for anything."

"Thank you, Monsieur Pélasge. You're a generous man. You remind me of my first master, Monsieur Moreau des Jardets."

The very next day, Lagniape settled on the farm. Livia came often to see her. Livia's common sense and orderly mind caught Pélasge's attention, and he employed her in his store, where she did such a good job that she soon became the manager. In fact, he was tired of a profession that consisted in buying and reselling just to make money. He had more money than he needed due to his simple tastes and his moderate habits, and Livia had replaced him so well that business continued to move along as if there had not been the least change. So Pélasge started a new life that consisted of reading his books and visiting the old sachem. Every day, when the sun was nearly set, he came out of his study and went on foot to the venerable tree. He spent two or three hours there, sometimes more, immersed in his memories and meditations. He found not happiness but at least serenity. He pictured in his mind all the people he had loved the most in Louisiana: Chant d'Oisel, Démon, Blanchette, Mamrie, and Vieumaite. He was no longer a man living in the present. He lived wholly in the past. He always walked away from the old oak tree with regret. When he left its silent shadows, the stars had been shining for a long time.

Sometimes, Pélasge talked with Lagniape, but it was only to speak of people and things that no longer were. He also came to miss Lagniape. Death at last remembered the poor old cripple and had the grace to carry her away. Then, Pélasge found himself absolutely alone. His meals were served to him by an old black woman of a sad and concentrated nature who never spoke unless a pressing necessity compelled her. From time to time, he wrote to Nogolka. He had never stopped corresponding with her. She was the only tie that he had to

Europe. He had lost his father and mother, and he was an only child. Distance and time had removed the faces and even the names of his oldest friends from his mind. Since death had created an emptiness around him, his letters to Nogolka became longer and more frequent. He gladly opened up to her. On her part, she spoke to him with an open heart. She had never stopped loving him, and she did not hide it. She was, however, married. She had also lost her parents. Finding herself alone in the world after their deaths, she had eventually given in to the pleas of an old Russian nobleman who passionately loved her. She had a thirteen-year-old son and a ten-year-old daughter.

Chapter 49

Count Casimir Dziliwieff

Nogolka's husband, Count Casimir Dziliwieff, was one of those handsome, sprightly, and active old men who would make even the most indifferent adore life so much that they take it to heart and take care to use it with dignity. He had a warm and enthusiastic nature, an open mind, and an iron will. Nogolka, having accepted his offer of marriage, had told him frankly that there was a man in America whom she loved, and she would love him as long as she lived. Dziliwieff admired her sincerity. It was one more reason why he was attracted to Nogolka. After their wedding, he did not oppose at all her continuing to correspond with Pélasge. Even more, when Nogolka was impeded by some reason from writing, he filled in for her. Little by little, a direct exchange of letters developed between Dziliwieff and his wife's friend. The more the old man saw into Pélasge's mind, the more his trust in him grew. He even started to want to see him in person.

Dziliwieff, despite his age, nurtured vast plans. He wanted to see his country free and functioning like the United States, or at least progressing like England. In his heroic naïveté, he had at first outlined his plans for reform to the young princes of the imperial family. They had called him an old fool and had even threatened to send him to the Siberian mines. So he had said to himself, "Since they don't agree with me, I'll act in a revolutionary way." And he had begun to plot. Determined to sacrifice his life, if necessary, for the triumph of his ideas, he had made careful provisions for the future well-being of Nogolka and his children. He had sent a large part of his fortune abroad, where one of his friends in Switzerland had allowed Dziliwieff to use his name to buy property near Lausanne. He wanted his son to be educated in a republic where notions of equality would be ingrained in his education. Two times a year, Dziliwieff vanished under some pretext. Everyone thought he was in Holland or Egypt, but he always returned to Russia incognito to sow the seeds of the revolution.

Dziliwieff had formed a very high opinion of Pélasge's personality and abilities. He had said to himself more than once that if his young friend lived in Europe, he would be a powerful assistant to help him achieve his plan. But Pélasge showed no interest in returning, and it was likely that after his wedding he would settle down permanently in Louisiana. When Dziliwieff learned of Chant d'Oisel's death, he went back to thinking that Pélasge would be a great help to him if he came to Switzerland. The simultaneous deaths of Démon and Blanchette convinced him: what had been only a hypothesis became a hope. When he saw the cold, hopeless sadness into which Pélasge was sinking further and further, he said to himself:

"It's going well. Soon, the pear will be ripe."

Dziliwieff was an expert on the human heart and mind. He knew all the good that can come from young men who have been absolutely devastated by sorrow. It was among them that he recruited his most reliable members. He called them his *dead ones.* He went everywhere looking, as he said, for dead people to bring back to life. He put new life into them and gave them a goal to pursue. He passed on his strength of will to them. He excited them with the grandeur of their fated mission. He reached them with that spirit of tireless perseverance that assures, sooner or later, the ultimate triumph of one's cause.

Chapter 50

The Old Sachem

Dziliwieff wrote more often to Pélasge after Démon's death. Prompting frequent responses, he studied, as he told himself, his *dying man* in America. With increasing anticipation, he watched closely for the throes of death.

Pélasge buried himself more and more in the silent profundities of his studies. Each day, the chasm that separated him from the normal interests of life widened. Only one tie held him to the earth. This link was the old sachem. It was his companion and his confidant. He had loved it for eighteen years. His heart was there; in the shadow of its branches, silence and serenity reached down to surround him and to protect the dreams in which he saw Chant d'Oisel, Démon, Blanchette, Mamrie, and Vieumaite run up to him, smiling and talking.

No one had ever seen Pélasge cry. Who knows? Maybe he cried more than once at the foot of the old sachem. That is a secret people always keep to themselves.

Pélasge lived this internal and isolated life for fourteen months. He left his solitude and silence only at rare intervals when Livia came to settle his accounts. He no longer believed in happiness. He yearned only for peace of mind. But life always retains its right to save surprises, good or bad, for whoever feels sheltered from its vicissitudes. One night, Pélasge was awakened by a violent storm. The rain fell in torrents, and the thunder rumbled without interruption. Finally, at the arrival of dawn, the claps of thunder relented. There were even a few minutes of silence. Pélasge thought the storm had ended when a sudden and brief detonation of tremendous strength occured. In a quick, involuntary movement, he sat up in his bed. He thought lightning had struck the farm. A heavy and prolonged noise immediately followed this unexpected explosion. The ground shook, and every section of the house cracked. Pélasge, dazed, wondered what this could be. A fireball? A meteorite? An earthquake? He stood up. This time, the storm was definitely finished. The countryside had regained its usual silence. The clouds parted to the east and let the sunlight pass through. Before going out, Pélasge opened the window that faced the sunrise, as he did each morning in order to greet his old friend the sachem with a nod. He recoiled at the sight, quivering and placing his hand on his heart as if he had received a fatal blow. The dome of the venerable oak tree had vanished. In the middle of the void, its colossal trunk stood like a funeral column, stripped of all of its limbs.

Pélasge, breathless, crossed the savannah with an unsteady step. A distressing spectacle awaited him. The whirling storm had uprooted all the trees in the oak grove. Lightning had scattered gigantic branches on every side of the old sachem. Saint-Ybars' tomb, crushed and pushed into the ground, had disappeared entirely under a pile of wood and leaves. Branches as thick as gigantic trees were thrown chaotically onto the graves of Vieumaite, Démon, Blanchette, and Mamrie. In other places, the ground was covered with small bits of stone and wood. The forest, literally reduced to dust, was piled up in scattered, yellowish mounds. No trace of the interior cypress trees could be seen. Piles of singed leaves stood out from afar against the plain's verdant background. Planks from the departed Indians' cabins had been stripped away like wisps of straw and thrown out of sight.

Pélasge returned to the house, his soul dead. He felt, in his moral being, a void similar to the one the vanished, old sachem had left. He lost his desire to study. An evil that he had never known—an evil horrible for a man like Pélasge—beat down on him. It was apathy. No longer interested in anything, he left and walked aimlessly and wearily in slow, uneven steps, as if he were carrying a mountain on his shoulders. He no longer wrote to his friends. Nogolka, concerned by his silence, sent several consecutive letters to him. With great effort, Pélasge gathered the last remnants of his energy, and he wrote a long letter to his friend.

Chapter 51

Death Can Occur More Than Once

One morning, Dziliwieff, returning from a stroll by the lake, entered his wife's bedroom as she was finishing reading Pélasge's last letter. He found her in tears. He anxiously inquired about the cause of her grief. She held out the letter to him and said, sadly shaking her head:

"Pélasge has sunk into despair. He'll die from it."

The count took the letter, read very carefully, and replied with the greatest composure:

"You're mistaken, dear friend. He won't die from it. He's already dead."

"Dead!" Nogolka exclaimed fearfully.

"Yes, dead, oh! Very dead this time," Dziliwieff continued, as if talking to himself. "Dead for good."

Then, enthused and waving the letter in the air like a victory flag:

"Dead in America," he exclaimed, "to come back to life in Europe. Dead to the dreams of happiness, he's going to be reborn for duty. He belongs to me now. I'm going to drag him out of the grave and make him a soldier in the service of liberty."

Nogolka looked at Dziliwieff with a combination of astonishment, pain, and admiration.

"At last, the pear is ripe," the old man said, rubbing his hands together. "We're going to gather it."

He started to walk at a fast pace, still rubbing his hands together.

As Nogolka fell back into her melancholy thoughts, Dziliwieff stopped suddenly and said:

"Ah! So you didn't realize, dear Nogolka, that you can die more than once, twice, even several times? Look at me. I would know; I've already died four times. I died after my first love betrayed me, I died after the tragedy I wrote failed miserably, and I died the day I realized my best friend had always envied and hated me. Lastly, I died after questioning my own philosophical and religious beliefs, bitterly exclaiming: 'Idiot! You've lived for forty years with the most insane of dreams.' After all of those deaths, I emerged more and more alive. It'll be the same with Pélasge, or else he's not worthy of being your friend, nor is he a man. I'm going to send him a telegram. Wait for me in my study. I have to speak to you. See that we're all alone."

Dziliwieff went to the telegraph office and sent Pélasge a telegram, purposely designed to arouse his curiosity. He came back shortly and locked himself in the room with Nogolka. The discussion lasted an hour. When Nogolka walked out, her face was glowing with joy and pride.

Dziliwieff's telegram intrigued Pélasge. He reread it several times without completely comprehending the meaning. What he clearly understood was that Dziliwieff was asking him to wait twenty days, whatever his plans might be. "In twenty days," the telegram said at the end, "someone will explain the matter to you in person."

During these twenty days, Pélasge mostly wondered what Dziliwieff wanted from him. All sorts of speculations came to his mind. He thought about how he would respond, and his replies were always negative. He considered his life to be over, that he had outlived himself. "I no longer have anything to do on this earth," he said to himself. "I'm like an actor who, after a performance, when everyone's left the theater, continues to wander solemnly on the stage, still wearing his character's costume."

Chapter 52

New Life

Pélasge's memories often drew him to the avenue that led to the former home of the Saint-Ybars. He loved to picture himself there entering with Chant d'Oisel for the first time. She had been such a charming little girl with a profoundly sweet and thoughtful face. He thought back to the best days he had spent on the plantation. They had been such an important part of his existence. Every day, for some time now, he left the farm at sunset and crossed the savannah, bleached here and there by the bones of animals killed during the war. He sat on an uprooted oak tree along the avenue, close to the river. From his vantage point, he saw carriages passing by on the public road and boats coming up or going down the river. He looked at them indifferently, or rather, he did not look at them. They were like blurred shadows gliding before his eyes.

One Saturday, Pélasge was sitting in his usual place, his head resting on his hand. He had removed his hat to feel the fresh, southerly breeze from the river. His black hair, amongst which snaked a few silver strands, swayed in the breeze. He was immersed in one of his meditations on the future of humanity, something that offered him refuge against boredom ever since he lost his taste for books. A carriage that stopped at the entrance of the avenue attracted his attention. A young man descended from it and after him, a lady dressed in elegant travelling attire. The strangers, after exchanging several words with the coachman, walked down the avenue. Pélasge stood up to walk away down a side path. But the lady, from a distance, opened her arms and held them towards him as if to say:

"Please, stay."

Pélasge stopped. The lady gestured, and the young man who accompanied her stayed behind. As the unknown woman approached, astonishment gradually spread across Pélasge's face. When she was a few steps away from him, he cried out and rushed to greet her, saying:

"Nogolka!"

Indeed, it was Nogolka. Pélasge enfolded her in his arms, and pressing her tightly to his chest, he asked:

"You're here?"

"Yes," Nogolka replied. "I've come to get you. My husband and I don't want you to wither away in this solitude. Oh! How sad everything is here. It's dreadful. Is this really the brilliant estate where we met each other? It looks like an abandoned graveyard. Pélasge, you no longer belong here. You've given enough of your soul to the past. The future is calling you. A man of your worth doesn't belong to himself. The needs of civilization and freedom impose duties upon him; he wouldn't know how to shirk them without incurring the condemnation of good people everywhere. Dziliwieff is waiting for you, and he sent me to find you. Pélasge, your mission calls you back to Europe. It is where the great battle is being fought: a battle between the determination of the past, which seeks to enslave us, and the modern ideals that seek to liberate us. America is master of its own fate and sets its own course. Europe is still struggling with injustices, especially the enemies of human rights, those same rights for which you spilled your blood in the prime of your youth on the barricades of Paris. There are still families there who believe, or rather who would like to make others believe, that they were created to lead people, just as shepherds lead the flocks whose very own wool clothes them and whose flesh nourishes them. They're wealthy and clever, and they rely on minorities to preserve their power. They have armies at their service who are ready to drown, in blood, peoples' attempts to free themselves from the yoke. Under the pretext of external dangers, they constantly increase the size of their armies. They kindle in their soldiers' hearts every passion that makes one nation the relentless enemy of another nation.

"It's the same old struggle, the eternal fight between light and darkness, between ignorance and progress, between freedom and servitude.

"Pélasge, come with me; fight with us for light, progress, and freedom! You must come. Dziliwieff is counting on you.

"Time is critical. Europe's armed hordes, led by merciless chiefs without scruples, threaten to plunge us back into the darkness that always follows barbarian invasions.

"You know very well that there's a weapon that can serve you as well as the rifle, more formidable than all the guns in the world. The pen, held in your hand, will strike the blows that humanity's enemies fear the most. Dziliwieff is founding a newspaper, and you will be its soul and voice. He gave it the name *New Life.* The hypocritical, violent, covetous, ambitious, proud, and all the others who exploit the ignorance and credulity of the masses would have an easy time if men like you remained silently in the shadows.

"I promised them you would come. Your friends are anxious to see you. Let's leave now!"

Pélasge took Nogolka's hands, squeezed them, and looked at her with an expression of gratitude and enthusiasm. She had grown younger, and fatigue and grief were no longer written on her face. Her fresh, rosy complexion and sparkling eyes formed a bizarre but not at all discordant contrast with her hair, now uniformly white like Alpine snow.

"Nogolka," Pélasge said, "You are goodness itself, beauty, and greatness! You represent a return of life to me. You're hope, faith, strength, and light. Noble friend, I'll be worthy of your belief in me. I'll be worthy of Dziliwieff. I'll rise to the heights of your heroic generosity. Nogolka, I owe you the world for coming so far to help me! Use me as you wish. I belong to you entirely."

"I'll give you only enough time to settle your business affairs," Nogolka replied. "Don't waste a single minute. The sight of this desolate countryside breaks my heart.

"Now, let me introduce you to my son."

Nogolka turned and gestured towards the young man, who came forward.

"Ivan," she said, "You know Monsieur Pélasge. You've heard so much about him! Embrace your mother's friend."

Ivan eagerly obeyed. Pélasge received him in his arms, embraced him, and said to Nogolka:

"He resembles you so much!"

Two days after this meeting, a steamboat stopped for a half hour in front of the former Saint-Ybars residence and sailed down the river. Standing on the deck in the back, a man had his eyes fixed upon the shore. His clenched left hand pressed strongly against his chest. A lady held his other hand. It was Pélasge and Nogolka. Pélasge was looking at the mutilated trunk of the old sachem tree for one last time.

When the boat passed the cape, the sight of the former Saint-Ybars residence was lost. Nogolka turned to her friend:

"Here we are, separated from the past. The past is dead. May it rest in peace! It had its joys and sorrows. The future is calling us. It holds other joys and sorrows. That's what life is. Let us welcome it."

FIN

Notes

Introduction

"The day when French ceases to be spoken in Louisiana, if this day must come – which we do not believe at all – there will no longer be any Creoles; the original and powerful group that they formed in the great national family of the United States will have vanished, just as wine poured into a running river loses its flavor and color." Quoted in *Les colonies françaises,* Volume 4. Editor Augustin Challamel. Paris, France: Librairie Maritime et Coloniale, 1900: 241.

[2] Reinecke, George. "Alfred Mercier, French Novelist of New Orleans." *Southern Quarterly,* vol. 20, no. 2 (1982): 145-176. Also: Dana Kress, "Alfred Mercier: Les évolutions biographiques," e-mail message to Beth Julian, September 2, 2014.

[3] Anglophone refers to anyone who is part of an English-speaking population. Francophone, used as an adjective, means "French-speaking." As a noun, it defines a person who is a native French speaker.

[4] Hero, Alfred Olivier, Jr. "Louisiana Francophones: Origins and Evolution Since 1673." *Quebec Studies,* vol. 3 (Spring/Summer 2002): 103-115.

[5] Fortier, Alcée. "The French Language in Louisiana and the Negro-French Dialect." *Transactions of the Modern Language Association of America,* vol. 1 (1884-85): 96-111.

[6] Hero, 103-115.

[7] Hero, 103-115.

[8] Spitzer, Nicholas. "Monde Créole: The Cultural World of French Louisiana Creoles and the Creolization of World Cultures." *The Journal of American Folklore*, vol. 116, no. 459 (Winter 2003): 57-72.

[9] Créole does, however, designate a language.

[10] Spitzer, 57-72. Also: Bello, Bret, Elizabeth Lyles, and Rebecca Skelton. "Les poètes créoles." *Anthologie de poésie louisianaise du XIXe siècle.* Ed. D.A. Kress and Margaret E. Mahoney. Shreveport, LA: Les Éditions Tintamarre at Centenary University, 2010: 69-70.

[11] Clint Bruce, as quoted in Bello, Lyles, and Skelton, 69-70. Also: Spitzer, 57-72. Also see: Dessens, Nathalie. "From Plurality to Singularity: Otherness and Creolization in Nineteenth-Century Louisiana." *European Contributions to American Studies*, vol.61 (2005): 29-38.

[12] *Miscellaneous estate papers of Jean Mercier, Louisiana State Museum Historical* Center, Folder 10: 1825, Aug. 1: Bill issued covering tuition for Armand and Alfred Mercier at the *College de la Louisiane* totaling $13.50.

[13] Berryer (1790-1868) was the defense lawyer of Lamennais in 1826 and Chateaubriand in 1834, among others. He also was involved with Ledru-Rollin's radical Republication newspaper *La Réforme.*

Chaix-d'Est-Ange (1800-1876) was Baudelaire's defense attorney during his trial for "offending the public moral order." Part of a committee to build a hospital in Paris for the mentally ill, the lawyer might have been of particular interest to Mercier, as madness is a theme that appears frequently in his texts.

Barrot (1791-1873) was Prime Minister under Charles-Louis Napoléon Bonaparte from 1848-1851. Barrot and Ledru-Rollin advocated for universal suffrage. See Dana Kress, "Alfred Mercier: Les évolutions biographiques," e-mail message to Beth Julian, September 2, 2014.

[14] Dana Kress, "Alfred Mercier: Les évolutions biographiques," e-mail message to Beth Julian, September 2, 2014.

[15] Dana Kress, "Alfred Mercier: Les évolutions biographiques," e-mail message to Beth Julian, September 2, 2014.

[16] Published as the novel *Hénoch Jédésias.*

[17] Reinecke, 145-148. Also: Dana Kress, "Alfred Mercier: Les évolutions biographiques," e-mail message to Beth Julian, September 2, 2014.

[18] Dana Kress, "Alfred Mercier: Les évolutions biographiques," e-mail message to Beth Julian, September 2, 2014.

[19] Dana Kress, "Alfred Mercier: Les évolutions biographiques," e-mail message to Beth Julian, September 2, 2014.

[20] Reinecke, 145-148. Also: Dana Kress, "Alfred Mercier: Les évolutions biographiques," e-mail message to Beth Julian, September 2, 2014.

[21] Reinecke, 149-159.

[22] Sugar plantations dominated the economy of southern Louisiana, especially in the nineteenth century. The success of these plantations resulted directly from the slave trade, specifically from the mass importation of blacks into Louisiana. By 1853, Louisiana produced a quarter of the world's sugar. See Richard Follett's article "Slavery and Plantation Capitalism in Louisiana's Sugar Country." *American Nineteenth Century History,* vol. 1, no. 3 (Autumn 2000): 1-27.

[23] The word *feuilleton* first referred to serialized novels. Today, *feuilleton* refers to a "soap opera." The French term *récit social* literally means a "social narrative."

[24] Reinecke, 160-170. Also: Rosenwald, 219-20.

[25] Harrison, J.A. "The Creole Patois of Louisiana." *The American Journal of Philology,* vol. 3, no. 11 (1882): 285-296. Also: Spitzer, 57-72.

[26] Characteristic language of a social group; in this case, the Creole dialect. See J.A. Harrison's article "The Creole Patois of Louisiana."

[27] Rosenwald, Lawrence. "Alfred Mercier's Polyglot Plantation Novel of Louisiana." *American Babel: Literatures of the United States from Abnaki to Zuni.* Ed. Marc Shell. Cambridge, Massachusetts: Harvard University Press, 2002. 219-237.

[28] Narratives and tales.

[29] Harrison, 23. Also: Rosenwald, 222-23.

[30] Locution; words, expressions, or details characteristic of a region, place, or group of people; picturesque.

[31] Harrison, 286. Also: Rosenwald, 229-30.

[32] Rosenwald, 221.

[33] Dessens, 34-37. Also: Rosenwald, 235.

[34] Rosenwald, 228-229.

[35] Rosenwald 220. Also: Fortier, "French Literature of Louisiana in 1887 and 1888 II," 232.

[36] Rosenwald 220-221, 230-235. Also: Fortier, "French Literature in Louisiana," 57.

[37] For full text, visit http://laporteouverte.me/2012/09/08/une-cage-de-betes-feroces/.

[38] This "abbé," meaning "abbot" or "father," could potentially be Zola himself.

[39] Dana Kress, "Alfred Mercier: Les évolutions biographiques," e-mail message to Beth Julian, September 2, 2014.

[40] Hearn, Lafcadio. "Dr. Mercier's Essay on the Creole Patois." New Orleans *Daily City Item*, July 10, 1880. Also: Dr. Dana Kress, e-mail to author, April 10, 2011.

[41] Rosenwald, 233.

[42] Reinecke, 161, 174-75.

Chapter 1 – In Those Times

[1] Now known as Tazoult-Lambèse, Algeria, Lambessa is known for its "great convict establishment." During the tumultuous French conquest of Algeria, which lasted from the capture of Algiers in 1830 to the fall of Kabylia in 1857, Lambessa served as a sort of penal colony where the French built a penitentiary in 1855. See *Algeria* written by Anthony Ham, Nana Luckham, and Anthony Sattin, Lonely Planet, 2007.

[2] Alexandre Auguste Ledru-Rollin (b. 1807), known as "the father of universal suffrage," was a liberal lawyer and Socialist candidate who pushed for democracy during the Second French Republic. Ledru-Rollin greatly criticized the monarchy of Louis Philippe and desired the sovereignty of all

people through universal suffrage. He took special interest in the working and poor classes and believed in the development of a domestic program that would improve conditions for the poor. Since Ledru-Rollin boldly attacked Louis Philippe's government which resulted in imprisonment and even exile, his work continued in underground meetings and circles. For more information, see Alvin Rosenblatt Calman's book *Ledru-Rollin and the Second French Republic*, Columbia University, 1922.

[3] *Abeille* means "bee" or "honeybee." Founded in September 1827, the French-language newspaper *L'Abeille* included an English section for forty-five years but returned to French only in 1872. Initially published three days a week, its popularity grew until it became a daily newspaper and eventually the longest-lived newspaper in New Orleans, stopping publication in 1925.

[4] Known in the Hebrew Bible as King Ahasuerus (also known by his Greek name, Xerxes), he reigned for twenty-one years (B.C. 486 - 465) over the kingdoms of Persia, Media, and Babylonia, from India to Ethiopia.

[5] A *piastre* is a thin metal plate or coin that represented a great miscellany of currencies used as early as the sixteenth century. The *piastre* was accepted by traders in many parts of the world. It is used in the French text of the Louisiana Purchase and was a term that the French used for the United States dollar. Eighteen-hundred *piastres* today is estimated to be worth between $45,000.00 and $50,000.00.

[6] This amount today would be slightly under $60,000.00.

[7] A *tignon* is a kerchief that binds the hair. In June 1786, New Orleans Governor Esteban Rodríguez Miró enacted the infamous "tignon law," which made "excessive attention to dress" by women of "pure or mixed African blood" a criminal offense. Along with having to cover their hair with a kerchief, these women could not wear fine clothes or jewelry nor feathers or jewels in their hair. Physical appearance, according to Miró, reflected social standing or status. In effect, these free women were forced to wear the same garment that slave women wore to signify their status as workers. However, perhaps in an act of defiance, as well as a signification of unity, many women chose brightly-colored kerchiefs that were artfully knotted or enhanced with a jewel. See Sybil Kein's book *Creole: The History and Legacy of Louisiana's Free People of Color*, Louisiana State University Press, 2000.

[8] Saint-Domingue (present-day Haiti and Dominican Republic, or the Caribbean island of Hispaniola) was a French colony from 1659 to 1804. By the mid-eighteenth century, Saint-Domingue had a booming economy,

producing sugar, cotton, coffee, tobacco, and indigo. The over half-million slaves on the island were excluded from political participation. The slave revolt that occurred in 1792 was an international event. Saint-Domingue was tangled up in the French Revolution, civil war, foreign occupation, the institution of slavery itself, and the attempt to establish a republic. Slave revolts in Saint-Domingue made Americans fearful of their own slaves revolting. A large number of Saint-Dominguans left the island. While many American cities prospered from this sudden influx of vast peoples, the American South reacted sternly and swiftly to the rebellion, fearing a slave revolt on their own soil. See Thomas Fiehrer's article "Saint-Domingue/ Haiti: Louisiana's Caribbean Connection." *Louisiana History: The Journal of the Louisiana Historical Association*, vol.30, Autumn 1989, pp. 419-437.

[9] The title translates to *Seneca's Thoughts*. Seneca (born c. 4 B.C.) was a Spanish-born writer, lawyer, and philosopher known for his influence on the configuration of Elizabethan tragedy. Many of his philosophical writings discuss finding happiness and pushing readers to expand spiritually and intellectually. Ironically, he committed suicide, much like a tragic character in his plays. Seneca, like Ledru-Rollin, criticized the politics and leaders of his day. He is perhaps best known for developing the theory of Stoicism, a philosophy that maintained several main principles: society is best governed by a rational providence; suffering is a necessary and positive aspect of life; happiness can be achieved through a simple life in accordance with nature; and it is necessary to confront mortality and accept the idea of death. His writings are often very practical, offering a "how-to" guide for solving life's problems. For more information, see Moses Hadas' book *The Stoic Philosophy of Seneca: Essays and Letters of Seneca*, W.W. Norton & Company, 1958.

[10] A small gift given a customer by a merchant at the time of a purchase; broadly: something given or obtained gratuitously or by way of good measure. *Lagniape* (also seen spelled as *lagniappe*) is composed of the French *la*, "the," and a French adaptation of Spanish *ñapa*, which is taken in turn from Kechuan *yapa*, "a present made to a customer." For more information, see the *Dictionary of American Regional English.*

[11] *L'École normale supérieure de Paris* is a very prestigious school for higher education in France that trains many future teachers and professors. Although its original aim was to provide France with highly-qualified teachers around the time of the French Revolution, it has since expanded greatly to include schools for sciences, humanities, economics, languages, and more. For more information, see A.J. Ladd's book *École Normale Supérieure: A Historical Sketch,* Herald Publishing Company, 1907.

[12] This amount today would be around $2,170.

Chapter 2: Antony Pélasge and Chant d'Oisel

[1] *Huguenot* is a term that describes a French Protestant of the 16th and 17th centuries.

[2] See Chapter 1 footnote.

[3] Chant d'Oisel translates into English as "Bird Song."

Chapter 3: The Plantation – Vieumaite

[1] The Doric style or "order" originated in Greece. Columns in this style are very simple, characterized by short, squat columns with plain, round tops and no base. The Corinthian order, however, is much more ornate. Also originating in Greece, Corinthian-style columns consist of slender, fluted columns with an ornate top decorated with rows of leaves and scrolls. For more information, see Sir John Summerson's book *The Classical Language of Architecture*, MIT Press, 1963.

[2] The workshop of a cooper, a person whose work is making and repairing barrels and casks.

[3] *Vieux* meaning "old," *maître* meaning "master."

Chapter 4: The Family Dining Room

[1] A person of one-quarter black ancestry.

[2] Meaning "arid field" – M. Héhé repeats it here to show off his knowledge of Latin to Pélasge and to compare Démon's capacity of intelligence to a field difficult to grow or plow any "seeds of knowledge."

[3] Thucydides is a Greek historian (born c. 460 B.C.) known as "the father of scientific history." Tacitus, a Senator and historian of the Roman Empire (born c. 56 A.D.), is best known for his *Annals* and *Histories*, both of which examine the Roman emperors Tiberius, Nero, and Claudius.

Chapter 6: Mamrie

[1] The Bambara are the largest ethnic group in Mali, originating in the thirteenth century. Today their population exceeds three million.

[2] The term *petits blancs* refers to lower-class whites, including merchants, artisans, slave dealers, overseers, and day laborers. This system of racial hierarchy during the19th century was complex: between slaves, free people of color, mulattos, quadroons, petits blancs, and the white aristocracy, society was extremely divided by economic status as well as ancestry. For more information, see Thomas Fiehrer's article "Saint-Domingue/Haiti: Louisiana's Caribbean Connection," *Louisiana History: The Journal of the Louisiana Historical Association*, vol.30, autumn 1989, pp. 419-437.

[3] A language that developed from the constant contact between francophones and blacks during the eighteenth century, Creole patois sprung up entirely by ear and is thus based purely on phonetics, or what syllables are heard. Aside from patois being its own language, it also has several social implications. Patois was generally spoken among citizens of the lower class, but it was also usually the first language that children learned before they spoke Standard French. For more information, see introduction. Also see J.A. Harrison's article "The Creole Patois of Louisiana," *The American Journal of Philology*, vol. 3, no. 11, 1882.

[4] Pierre-Jean de Béranger (1780-1857) was a French songwriter. His writings were mostly satirical, and he was even imprisoned several times for the controversial political nature of his works. Auguste-Marseille Barthélemy (1796-1867) was a French poet known for writing political satires. From 1831 to 1832, he published a weekly series of verse satires called *The Némésis*, which attacked the government and criticized the ministers of King Louis Philippe. Alphonse de Lamartine (1790-1869) was a French writer, politician, and romantic poet. Like Béranger and Barthélemy, Lamartine was heavily involved in politics and was one of the leaders in the founding of the Second Republic.

Chapter 7: Man Sophie and Her Two Small Daughters

[1] Lisette has left the plains,
I have lost my happiness;
My eyes seem like fountains
Since I have not seen you.
During the day when I cut sugar cane,
I think of my love;
At night when I am in my bed,
In my dreams I hold you.

Though the author and origins are unknown, this well-known Creole song conveys the experience of captivity and starvation of slave life on the plantation as well as the psychology of love. The plight of the shackled lover is used as a metaphor for the brutal reality of slavery. See Deborah Jenson's article "Mimetic Mastery and Colonial Mimicry in the First Franco-Antillean Creole Anthology," *The Yale Journal of Criticism*, vol. 17, no. 11, 2004, pp. 83-106.

Chapter 8: The Camp

1 An early form of the banjo. Though the origin of the banjo is not definitively agreed upon, Africans in the mid-seventeenth century called the instrument the *banjar*. Along with several types of handmade drums, banzas continued to be constructed by slaves, thus first introducing the banjo to North America. The banjo then became the precursor to the guitar. For more information, see Michael Morgan's article "Rock and Roll Unplugged: African-American Music in Eighteenth-Century America," *Eighteenth-Century Studies*, vol. 27, no. 4, summer 1994, pp. 649-662.

2 "*Bien fol est qui s'y fie.*" François I (1494-1547) ruled as King of France from 1515 to 1547.

Chapter 9: Man Miramis and Monsieur Salvador

1 Toussaint Louverture was the valiant black military leader who brought Republicanism to Haiti and led the Haitian Revolution. Born in Saint-Domingue, Louverture was actually a slave for forty-seven years. Outraged about the conditions of slavery, Louverture led blacks in a fight for independence from the French colonizers, which resulted in the abolition of slavery and in native control over the colony. He also freed the slaves in Saint-Domingue. Even though Louverture signed a treaty with Napoleon and the French that there would be no more slavery, Napoleon still sent his brother-in-law General Charles Leclerc to seize Louverture and imprison him. While in prison, he died of pneumonia in 1803. Unfortunately, the colonies' relative freedom did not last long after his death. For more information, see Ralph Korngold's book *Citizen Toussaint*, Greenwood Press, 1979.

2 A *madras* is a piece of brightly-colored cotton or silk worn as a turban.

[3] Similar to the "cat o' nine tails," a *baleine* is a type of shortened whip made of multiple strips of leather and used for lashing in close quarters.

Chapter 10: The Indians – The Old Sachem

[1] *Sachem* refers to an Indian chief, specifically the chief of a confederation of the Algonquian tribes of the North Atlantic coast. In this case, the tree is known as "the chief of the field."

Chapter 11: Monsieur le Duc de Lauzun

[1] The title "Duc de Lauzun" was initially created for French courtier and soldier Antoine Nompar de Caumont (1632-1723). This prestigious title was then passed on to several renowned generals and marshals of France: Charles Armand de Gontaut (1663-1756), Louis Antoine de Gontaut (1700-1788), and Armand Louis de Gontaut (1747-1793).

Chapter 12: A Simple Change in Method

[1] Translates to "good joy."

[2] Written in the early 18th century, "Malbrouck s'en va-t-en guerre" is a French folk song named after Duke John Churchill of Malbrouck (a distant relative of Winston Churchill), who battled France to his death in 1705. (Some theorize that it is a satirical song written after the Duke's death.) This lament was very popular during the French Revolution. The title translates to "Malbrouck Has Gone to War." It is the same tune as the songs "For He's a Jolly Good Fellow" and "The Bear Went Over the Mountain."

Chapter 13: Li Mouri

[1] The original word is *sauvagesse*, but Indian would be more appropriate here.

[2] Coins of a small amount. The word still exists in Louisiana as *picayune.*

[3] "Father of the waters," a reference to the Mississippi River.

[4] The Choctaw Indian Nation is a Muskogean tribe tracing its roots to Mississippi, Alabama, Louisiana, and Alabama. Years before Europeans

arrived in America and forcibly removed them from their land and relocated the tribe to Oklahoma, the Choctaws were mainly farmers. Today, they are the nation's third largest tribe.

[5] Lacombe is located in St. Tammany Parish, on the southeast coast of Louisiana.

Chapter 14: The Twentieth and Twenty-First of September

[1] This phrase translates to "in this black light that falls from the stars." French playwright Pierre Corneille (1606-1684), known for his tragic plays, wrote this line in his most famous play *Le Cid*, a tragicomedy based on the legend of El Cid, an exiled military leader who ends up conquering and governing the city of Valencia, Spain.

Chapter 18: The Hurricane

[1] A fish soup.

Chapter 19: The Escape

[1] In Greek mythology, Castor and Pollux are twins, the sons of Leda and the Swan and brothers to Helen of Troy. The two brothers fought in the Argonautic expedition and then became engaged in a war with Idas and Lynceus, in which Castor was killed. Pollux was devastated by his brother's death and asked Jupiter if he could give his own life as a ransom for Castor. Jupiter instead allowed the brothers to spend alternate days on earth and in the heavens. In another version of the story, Jupiter placed them among the stars as Gemini, the Twins.

[2] A tilbury is a light, open, two-wheeled carriage that can be used with or without a top, popular in the 19th century.

Chapter 24: Calm Returns

[1] Adolphe Garnier (1801-1864) was a French philosopher and disciple of Théodore Simon Jouffrey, a proponent of the Scottish school of philosophy that emphasized the distinction between psychology and physiology.

Garnier succeeded Jouffroy as chair of the philosophy department at the Sorbonne in 1845. His most prominent work, *Traité des facultés de l'âme* (1852), discusses aesthetic questions, particularly the interpretation of art and beauty as a sign of intellectual or moral power.

Chapter 25: How Monsieur de Lauzun Took Possession of a Secret

1 Also known as Charles-Victor Prévot (1788-1856), le vicomte d'Arlincourt was a French novelist who wrote the highly successful *Le Solitaire* (1821), *Le Renégat* (1822), *Ipsiboé* (1823), and *L'Étrangère* (1825). Though his novels were translated into eleven different languages, Prévot was greatly criticized by his peers, mostly for his highly romanticized writing style. His novels are so full of figurative writing that his prose reads like poetry.

Chapter 26: A Villainous Plot

1 François VI, duke de La Rochefoucauld (1613-1680) was a French classical author known for his work *Réflexions ou sentences et maximes morales*, a collection of maxims and epigrams. La Rochefoucauld actively participated in the *Fronde*, a series of revolts between 1648 and 1653 that aimed to protest the tyrannical authority of Louis XIV as well as Cardinals Mazarin and Richelieu. After being wounded several times, La Rochefoucauld shifted his efforts to literature. Believing that all human behavior derives from selfishness, he published five editions of Maximes during his lifetime. The one referred to here is "*Nous avons plus de force que de volonté ; et c'est souvent pour nous excuser à nous-mêmes que nous nous imaginons que les choses sont impossibles.*" (We have more strength than will; and it is often merely to excuse ourselves that we say things are impossible.)

Chapter 27: How to Escape Dishonor?

1 Written by Jean-Baptiste Louvet de Couvray, *Les Amours du chevalier de Faublas* followed the romantic adventures of a young knight. The story was published in three parts, from 1787 to 1790. Most of the stories are comical, but the third part is darker and leans more towards *le roman noir*. One interesting aspect of the novel is that the male hero has a somewhat feminine physical appearance and is often dressed like a woman.

Chapter 29: Peaceful Years

[1] Omitted quotations from original text.

[2] *Les Mille et Une Nuits* translates to *A Thousand and One Nights*, known in English as *The Arabian Nights*, a collection of Arabic stories and folktales. Stories include "Aladdin and his Wonderful Lamp," "The Voyages of Sinbad," and "Ali-Baba and the Forty Thieves." The first translation was made in the early 18th century by Frenchman Antoine Galland.

Chapter 30: Vieumaite Predicts the Civil War

[1] John Brown (1800-1859) was born into a staunchly anti-slavery family in Connecticut. In 1850, he recruited forty-four men into the United States League of Gileadites, an organization founded to resist slave-catchers. With the support of several prominent abolitionists, he established a refuge for runaway slaves in Virginia. After leading twenty-one men in a successful attack against the federal armory at Harper's Ferry in 1859, in the hopes of forming an emancipation army, Brown was seriously wounded after being attacked by Robert E. Lee and his army. Brown was tried and convicted of murder, treason, and insurrection and was executed on December 2, 1859.

[2] In Greek mythology, Prometheus stole fire from Zeus and gave it to the mortals. As a punishment, Zeus had him bound to a rock while an eagle ate his liver every day, only to have it grow back at night.

Chapter 32: Démon Wants to Come Home

[1] Prince Klemens Wenzel von Metternich (1773-1859) was a German-Austrian politician and statesman who helped implement an alliance among the European powers after Napoleon's defeat, with the aim of undoing some of the political damage caused by the French Revolution. François Guizot (1787-1874) was a French historian and politician who served Louis Philippe as minister of public instruction and expanded the public education system. His support for restricted suffrage, however, acted as a catalyst for the revolution against Louis Philippe and thus the establishment of the French Second Republic. Adolphe Thiers (1797-1877) was a French journalist, politician, and historian who was the President of the Third French Republic (1871-73).

[2] The *Collège de France*, founded in 1530 by Francis I, is a state-supported research institution and center for adult education that does not grant degrees or certificates. The *Observatoire de Paris* is one of the largest astronomical centers in the world and is under the direction of the Academy of Sciences, The *Jardin des Plantes* is a botanical garden in France that houses a botanical school. In addition to the gardens, there is also a zoo.

[3] The house of Lafitte & Dufilho, commission merchants and real estate, was on Saint Louis Street in 1860 until its liquidation in 1886.

Chapter 33: After the War

[1] Donaldsonville, located between Baton Rouge and New Orleans, was an important town during this time, even briefly serving as the state capitol. In 1863, Confederate forces vainly attempted to gain control of the town, only to meet Union resistance.

Chapter 41: The Prejudice of Race—The Insult

[1] The Bourbon kings ruled in France until the overthrow of the monarchy during the French Revolution. Public outrage at an unfair system of taxation as well as the tyrannical abuse of royal power led to the storming of the Bastille on July 14, 1789, which marked the beginning of the French Revolution.

Lauzun is thus comparing himself to the French revolutionaries, implying that he desired to incite the slaves to overthrow their masters so he could impose his own "reign of terror" on the Saint-Ybars family.

Chapter 42: The Challenge

[1] La Salette is a small village on a mountaintop near Grenoble, France (the South). In 1846, two shepherd children named Mélanie and Maximin claimed to have had a conversation with the Virgin Mary, in which she revealed one secret to each of the children, which were then sent to Pope Pius IX in 1851. The Catholic Church investigated the apparitions and deemed the story credible. La Salette remains a popular place of pilgrimage where statues have been erected to depict the encounter between Mary and the two children. Many miracles were reported during the nineteenth

century, including numerous ones where individuals were healed by holy water from the La Salette spring. For more information, see J. Spencer Northcote's book *A Pilgrimage to La Salette*, printed by Levet, Robson and Franklyn, 1852.

Chapter 43: The Duel

1 *Fra Diavolo, ou L'hôtellerie de Terracine* (*Brother Devil, or The Inn of Terracina*), is an 1830 comedic opera by French composer Daniel Auber.

2 The expression in English "Dutch courage" refers to cognac, a variety of brandy.